D0514981

The
GOLF
Marketing
BIBLE

Andrew Wood

Select Press

Legendary Marketing
www.LegendaryMarketing.com
800-827-1663

Published by Select Press
Novato, California

ISBN 1-890777-15-3

Printed in Korea

*This book is dedicated to the PGA & LPGA
professionals, the unsung heroes of the golf industry. I
am glad to count hundreds of them among
my friends. I want to say a heartfelt thank you
to them for enhancing my enjoyment of the
game in every way. From my initial
introduction to golf, to my early lessons on swing,
etiquette, and history, a PGA professional was always
close at hand and still is today!*

Contents

INTRODUCTION

Perhaps the most potent quote I have ever read in my life is Albert Einstein's definition of insanity. He defined insane people as: *People who do the same thing over and over again and yet expect different results!*

Nowhere is that quote truer than in the world of golf course marketing.

I never cease to be amazed by the seemingly ostrich-like mentality of some people in this business. Clubs desperately cling to the hope that even though 200 of their closest competitors run ads almost identical to theirs in the *Golfers Guide* (or similar publications) that, this time, it will somehow bring them more business!

Clubs are putting up boring web sites and running weekly coupons in the newspaper, competing against each other by offering deeper and deeper discounts, losing five bucks or more a player and hoping to "make it up in volume!"

My company, Legendary Marketing, is an ad agency, but is very different from a traditional agency. We are a PR company but are also very different from a traditional PR company. We are a web site company, a telemarketing company, and a sales training company. Most important of all, we are a marketing company. That means that unlike a traditional agency that is only a cog in a wheel,

Legendary Marketing can help you do everything from generating prospects to selling prospects, to building a brand and building long-term customer relationships. We do golf, real estate, and destination marketing ONLY and we do it better than anyone.

The golf business is changing— and changing fast!

There are new rules for golf marketing. In fact, rather than rules, they are more like laws. If you break them, you will not succeed. There are plenty of courses that won't make the 36-hole cut in a tough market, which means they won't be playing at all on the weekend! That may not be you, but I urge you to read this book carefully. It is based on real marketing results from the hundreds of clubs and resorts Legendary Marketing has helped with their marketing. Whether or not you choose to do business with my company or pass this information on to someone else for immediate action, this book contains proven strategies for golf marketing success. Ignore them at your peril!

— Andrew Wood
Crystal River, Florida

Chapter One

The Legendary Point of View

HOW I DISCOVERED THE SECRET TO EXPONENTIAL GROWTH FOR YOUR GOLF CLUB IN—OF ALL PLACES— A KARATE SCHOOL!

I want to share a little history with you and explain how I developed a golf marketing system that NEVER FAILS. I am also going to show how you can grow your club's bottom line by at least $50,000–$250,000 this year (significantly more if you are a large operation).

Before you tell me how poor or saturated your market is, let me say this: I don't care where your club is located, what the economy is like, or how much competition you have. The principles I will share with you for explosive growth work anywhere, anyplace, anytime!

In *The Golf Marketing Bible*, you will discover numerous strategies for success in three potent areas:

✔ How to generate substantially more leads,

✔ How to gain more money from each sale you make, and

✔ How to get golfers coming back to you again and again!

Armed with this information, you can *instantly* improve your results and quickly DOMINATE your market!

Perhaps the biggest problem you will have in applying our Legendary system is that most people in the golf business don't believe in exponential growth because they have never experienced it. They have put their hearts and souls into running their clubs and have not seen growth for the last few years, so they cannot imagine generating a 200 or 300 percent increase in profits in a single year. Therefore, they don't even try.

I have been fortunate enough to enjoy such massive growth in three different ventures—actually four counting Legendary Marketing. Each time the growth was generated the same way: by finding the most effective marketing methods, not just copying what everyone else was doing, and then testing, tweaking, and changing every small detail of the sales and marketing operation until every single area produced maximum results. Before I disclose the secrets to achieving this kind of success at your club, let me share with you my life-changing experience in the karate business and how it propelled me into a career in marketing. I will also reveal the exciting discovery I made, and how it can catapult YOUR course, resort, real estate development, or teaching facility to the very top while your competition stumbles in the dark.

ALL I EVER WANTED TO BE WAS A GOLF PRO!

All I ever wanted to be was a golf pro, but one small detail held me back from a career on the Tour: lack of talent! Don't get me wrong,

I'm usually a scratch player and I worked at it for years, but I just didn't have that extra edge that a pro player needs.

As fate would have it, I gave a golf lesson to a karate instructor and soon after was accidentally thrust into a new career in the martial arts world.

Two years later, in the late 1980s, I experienced the thrill of exponential growth for the first time. I bought a small karate school in Irvine, California, with no money down. The first month, the business lost $1,000; the second month, it lost $1,000. At that point I was running my school the same way most people run their golf courses. I ran ads in the local paper which looked exactly like the ads all my competitors were running. What I didn't know then was that *all* those ads were terrible to begin with. When I copied them and made alterations, I only made them worse. I never really questioned if there was a better way. I was, as Henry David Thoreau so aptly put it, "Living a life of quiet desperation!" Sure, the phone rang occasionally or someone walked in with a coupon, but the weeks came and went with little real progress and zero profits.

Finally I sat down with a yellow pad and began some serious soul searching. First, I asked myself what I was doing wrong. Second, and perhaps most important, I wondered what I was going to do about it. The simple act of writing questions down on paper can bring amazing clarity. I quickly realized (surprise, surprise) that the first thing I needed was paying customers. I also realized that since the phone wasn't ringing, my ads were not working.

Please understand what kind of Quantum Leap thinking was going on at this point. Most business owners or managers don't ever think like that. Instead, they are more likely to subscribe to the Professor Slutsky theory.

THE PROFESSOR SLUTSKY THEORY

For those of you not familiar with the good Professor Slutsky's work, allow me to digress a moment. The noted professor did pioneer work with frogs. He started his experiments with a perfectly healthy frog. He yelled "Jump" until the frog moved. He then measured the leap. Then, under anesthesia (in the most humane way possible), he amputated one of the frog's front legs and repeated the "jump" experiment. After measuring again, he amputated the frog's other front leg, yelled "Jump" and measured the leaps, which, as you can guess, were decreasing in length. The frog's back left leg was cut off and again the professor yelled "Jump." The frog's wobbly attempt was duly measured, whereupon the final leg was removed. The professor yelled "Jump" once more but the frog did not respond. Professor Slutsky concluded that, "after amputation of all four legs…the frog became deaf."

I mention this story because whenever marketing doesn't work, most business owners immediately point to the medium rather than the marketing itself. The newspaper doesn't work, TV doesn't work, radio doesn't work, and the web is just worthless hype! Rarely if ever do they consider the simple fact that *their* marketing is at fault!

EUREKA!

I came to that exact realization one December morning in late 1987. What followed was a decision that changed my life forever. After acknowledging that I didn't *really* know the first thing about marketing, I rushed to the local book store and bought all eight of their marketing books. The first was David Ogilvy's classic *Ogilvy on Advertising*. I was amazed to learn how changing a simple headline could produce a 500 percent increase in response…how adding a picture of scissors next to a coupon could increase redemption by up to 35 percent…how reverse type (white letters on black) sharply decreases readership, and so on. Before I finished the second book, I ordered *twenty more books!* I was like a man possessed...highlighting, underlining, and taking notes for 30 straight days. All through the Christmas holiday I soaked up marketing information like a sponge.

Up until then all the ads that I had seen for karate schools were pictures of people flying through the air and kicking somebody in the face. What I didn't realize was that 80 percent of the world gravitates towards the negative. So when most people looked at these ads they saw themselves as the one getting kicked! Instead of running in to sign up for karate, most ran the other way!

After reading the books I designed some new ads. I began putting pictures of smiling women and children in the ads. I listed the benefits and changed the headlines to *Build Your Child's Confidence* and *Build Your Self-Esteem.* I changed the whole focus of my advertising to let people know that the martial arts were fun!

BINGO!

The phone rang off the hook. I signed up 30 new students in a single month as opposed to the five I typically signed up! I was ecstatic, but realized there was still work to be done. If I could get such a massive increase in response just by studying the gurus of marketing, perhaps I could capitalize on these leads even more by improving my sales skills. I purchased tapes from the likes of Dale Carnegie, Tom Hopkins, Joe Girard, and Zig Ziglar. Suddenly, instead of closing two out of ten leads, I was closing eight out of ten and it didn't cost me a dime more to do it!

Next, I turned my attention to customer retention, newsletters, thank-you cards, and follow up. I adopted the tactics I found in books like Carl Sewall's *Customers for Life.* By the end of the year customers were staying an average of six months instead of three!

*Imagine what it could do for your income if all
of your players played your course
twice as often as they do now!*

NATIONWIDE FRANCHISE FROM SCRATCH IN JUST SIX YEARS!

At 27 years of age, in my second year in business, I walked out of a 1,250 square foot karate school in a suburban strip mall with $128,000 in my pocket—a net gain of $121,000 over my previous year's income. And this was in the 1980s when you could buy a new TaylorMade Tour Burner driver for $115!

Six years later, I had 125 franchise schools, plus 275 affiliates nationwide and was making millions.

Lots of people built martial arts empires based on teaching styles and reputation. I did it solely on the RESULTS of my *marketing system*. I did it by creating a system that could be duplicated. Regardless of teaching style or location, a school owner could connect the dots and be guaranteed a predictable result for his time, money, and effort.

Here's what specific, proven, tested systems look like for karate schools:

- ✔ Do this specific promotion (Kids' Ninja Birthday) and you will get 15–20 leads.

- ✔ Run this ad (He Never Cleaned His Room Until I Took Him to Karate) in the local paper's family section and you will get 18–20 calls.

- ✔ Follow this script (Phone Script 101) when the prospects call and 16 of them will agree to visit for a trial lesson.

- ✔ Follow this exact process when the prospect shows up (from greeting to sign up and everything in between) and 12 of the 16 people will sign up for lessons.

✔ Of the 12 people that sign up, follow this procedure (Upgrade 101) and eight of them will upgrade to a $3,000 program in the first six weeks.

Bottom line? If you followed the program, there was very little chance of failure. Each component had been tried, tested, and measured so the results were within a tight range, completely predictable across the country regardless of city, state, facility, or style. Because it worked and because it was structured in a step-by-step manner that anyone could follow with little effort, it was hugely successful! You can do the same thing with your golf marketing.

LEVERAGE, SYSTEMIZE, SUCCEED!

The success I enjoyed in the karate business and am enjoying in the golf business all goes back to that one simple premise. Test to find the marketing techniques that work best. You can then leverage each individual aspect of your marketing plan by just a few percent and turn it into a system that can be repeated again and again. This process can have a cumulative result of *hundreds of thousands of dollars in a single season*. That means leveraging the power of every single ad, every single promotion, coupon, postcard, sales letter, and phone script. Follow this strategy and you can leverage your income exponentially anywhere, anytime, under any market conditions.

Think about it...

The newspaper and magazine ads that generate leads for your club cost the same to run whether they pull five responses or 500. Your Yellow Pages ad costs the same each month whether it brings in three calls or 300! The billboard on the highway is the same cost to rent each month whether people drive past it without a glance or hang an instant U-turn and head straight for your parking lot!

It costs you the same salary whether your outing or membership director converts two leads out of 10 or seven leads out of 10.

And it costs the same for the employees at the counter whether you sell a player a $45 green fee or a $2,800 membership, so you might as well MAXIMIZE every single aspect of your marketing!

TACTICS VS. STRATEGY

Most golf clubs, resorts, and real estate developments are run on a tactical basis, not a strategic one. Budgets are made and ads are run, but strategy and tactics rarely change from year to year. Clubs run the same type of ads, mail the same type of coupons, and resolve to do a better job of collecting e-mails and using the Internet. Whoosh… another mediocre year goes by.

But it doesn't have to be this way! In a very short time, YOU CAN DOMINATE YOUR MARKET. What it takes is a commitment to change and the use of proven systems.

Consider this...

Let's say that you have 1,000 e-mail addresses of golfers in your area and every time you send a blast it drives 10 rounds to your club at an average fee of $50. What would happen if you simply doubled the size of your e-mail list? This isn't exactly rocket science.

If you double the size of your e-mail database you will double your results, meaning every blast will now bring in 20 rounds. Now imagine what would happen to your bottom line if you tripled or quadrupled the size of your e-mail database. What could you get in a single month if you started using tools like the ones that Legendary Marketing provides? Exponential growth, that's what! Five thousand e-mails would drive 50 rounds or $2,500 as opposed to the $500 in revenue you presently generate from 1,000 names! And that's not just once—it's each and every time you do a blast!

Let me give you a real-world example...

One client recently built an e-mail list of over 8,000 names in less than a month when there was a foot of snow on the ground. (He also got them to answer 20 questions about their playing habits!) How many names did your web e-mail list grow this month? While most clubs would have been ecstatic capturing that much player data in a year, let alone a month, Kelly Marrow went a step better.

He called Legendary Marketing and entered his data in our data alliance, increasing his reach twofold. (The alliance lets you use twice as many of our names as you put in.) Now he will start the new season with access to 24,000 names, addresses, and e-mails of golfers in his market...up significantly from last year's total of almost none.

Let's assume he only gets 100 players to respond to each e-mail and he mails offers just twice a month. That's 200 players times $50 which is $10,000 a month, times seven months for a total of $70,000. And let's say each player spends an average of $20 on cart fees, beer, and balls. That adds another $28,000 worth of income for a grand total of $98,000 in income from just his e-mail marketing alone. Best of all, the promotion cost him nothing! That's an ROI (return on investment) so great that my meager math skills simply can't calculate it!

But exponential growth is not just about your e-mail marketing. It's about major improvement in your print ads, sales letters, brochures, web site, follow-up, and even the way you answer the phone.

Let's take another example...

Most courses spend X amount of their budget on print ads. (Ninety-nine percent of them are worthless, but I digress.) Suppose the ad demanded a response and that the club tracked the results. Let's even say that the response was good and 50 players brought in the ad. What most clubs do at that point is think, "Great, that worked, let's file it away for next year." What they should do is go back and TEST. Try a stronger headline, a different offer, or different approach. A simple change in the wording can increase response by 500 percent! Think about it...instead of 50 players, an ad could generate 250 players. And that applies to every ad, every mailer, every postcard! If you could increase response just 10 percent from each one, imagine what it would add to your bottom line!

A direct mail piece can produce staggeringly different results based on the call to action alone. For example, a golf real estate company produced a $200,000, 40-page direct mail brochure. Though it had lots of pretty pictures, it had no subheads to draw the reader into the copy and no captions under the pictures. So it had already broken two of the most basic laws of direct mail marketing. But it got worse. The only call to action was a bounce-back card. You know, one of those postage-paid deals that worked great in the 1980s before the advent of the Internet. What did the bounce-back card offer the reader? A DVD tour of the property? An invitation for an on-site visit? An invitation for the sales staff to call the prospect to answer some questions? NO. It offered the prospect another 40-page puff piece left over from the previous year's unsuccessful campaign. Exciting, huh?

A direct call to action on the last page could have turned this loser into a winner, increasing response exponentially. But the brochure looked nice so everyone okayed it without any thought as to what they wanted the prospect to do next! Amazing? Not really. Most golf marketing is awful when it comes to obeying the basic rules of response-driven marketing. A few simple changes to the offer could have made the difference between a meager 0.3 percent response and a 2.5 percent response...between 300 leads and 7,000 leads!

Don't stop me now, I'm on a roll...

Take those bland "Dear John Doe" follow-up letters that golf operations send to real estate leads, former resort guests, and potential event clients. They cost the same in printing and postage whether they generate 0.1 percent or 3 percent response. And that goes for however many of these things are sent out from your club! We're talking tens of thousands of dollars here.

APPLY THESE STRATEGIES TO THE GOLF OUTING BUSINESS

Why send out 100 corporate-speak letters to past tournament directors (some of whom might be dead) hoping that 20 of them book again this year? How about trying a completely NEW STRATEGY that none of your competitors will even dream of? Start with a telemarketing campaign to expand your database. Follow it up with an aggressive direct mail campaign once a month. You could bring in 15 more events this year at an average of $10,000 an event! There's another $150,000 to fatten your bottom line.

Imagine for a moment that your tournament database was 500 current names instead of 100 dusty names that haven't been checked in five years. If you contacted an additional 400 prospects in the next 30 days—I mean actually talked to the people who are going to hold a tournament in your market this year—how much more business would it mean for you? Double, triple, perhaps ten times more business!

Using just such a telemarketing approach, we generated 467 leads in Orlando; 375 in Denver; 480 in Westchester County, New York; and plenty more in other areas. Our in-house telemarketing staff makes over 4,000 calls and builds a database of prospects in your area including charities, large corporations, and fraternal organizations. How many courses have the time or personnel to do that in-house? Probably none! But how many outings would you have to book from a list of 400 prospects to make this type or service worth its weight in gold?

Let's just say you book 20 more outings this year. What percentage of growth would that mean for your outing business— 20 percent, 50 percent, or perhaps even 100 percent? That's my whole point. A simple change in strategy and a simple reallocation of funds could exponentially increase your outing business!

I haven't even touched on the different ways you can package your outings *without discounting* to bring in droves of additional business. For example, several of our clients out-marketed all their competitors last year by offering a $25 tee gift to every player who played in an outing. Instead of discounting their green fees to match others in the area, they changed the rules by offering more value. The tournament organizer looked like a hero by giving every player a gift. The course wins, too, because the gifts were closeouts that cost only $2 each. A classic win-win situation and a dramatic increase in outing business! That's the power of exponential marketing. By adding 400 more prospects to your database, contacting them more regularly, and making slight changes in the outing package, the results could easily increase outing revenues by $100,000 or more!

HOW TO CREATE A STRONG MARKETING SYSTEM

1 **Establish your desired results.** Each system should have a clear, concise statement of the result the system is intended to accomplish.

2 **Diagram the system.** The system should be presented in a diagram showing the sequence of events and how they relate to each other.

3   **Describe clear benchmarks.** Each action should be identified in sequence so that benchmarks or intermediate goals are created and that the process is clear and unmistakable to anyone who will perform the work.

4   **Assign accountabilities.** Accountability must be assigned for each system and for the overall system. Accountability should be identified by position, not by person. People come and go...accountability does not!

5   **Determine the timing.** Set specific timelines for each benchmark and document them.

6   **Identify required resources.** Every system requires resources such as staffing, postage, supplies, and information. A detailed list of the specific resources and quantities must be provided.

7   **Quantify the system.** How will you know you are getting the results you want? You need quantification to give you that objective view.

8   **Establish standards.** A good system sets the standards for performance and behavior of the staff operating it. Standards are most easily stated in terms of quantity, quality, and behavior.

9   **Document the system.** It's not a system until it's documented! You cannot expect people to follow a system that is not documented.

10   **Train in system usage.** Both management and staff must be trained in the proper use of the systems *so that EVERY lead is handled in a seamless, consistent, and systematic manner.*

The rest of this book will explain all you need to know to implement such a marketing system, from measurement to benchmarking to marketing methods.

CONCLUSION

Superior results come only from better marketing and better follow up. You can achieve better marketing by testing and improving each aspect of your approach. By improving many aspects of your marketing 1–10 percent, you will create MUCH better results overall. Don't expect to do what everyone else does and get better results! Remember that Einstein roughly said that you're crazy to expect new results when you do the same thing over and over!

The best way to ensure that follow up on your new, improved marketing is done consistently and professionally is to systemize it. If you make sure that every person is contacted the same way, the same number of times, and is sent the same follow-up materials, nothing will slip through the cracks. Sales will increase and so will your income.

Make no mistake, following a system in the short term takes more work. There are more steps to follow and more reporting is necessary. Ultimately, however, systems create *less work* as you become *more efficient* and make *more money*. You'll soon wonder how you ever got by without them! Using systems is actually easier than just doing what strikes you as right at the time.

Chapter Two

Don't Fall for These Marketing Myths

One of the major reasons that most clubs don't market effectively is that they are under the influence of marketing myths. Who knows how these misleading ideas got started, but many of them have been around for decades. So, before you start any marketing program, you first need to "clear the decks" of these marketing misconceptions.

In this chapter, you will discover:

✔ The secrets of successful golf marketing (an overview; later chapters will provide the details)

✔ What the biggest myths in marketing really are

✔ Why long copy works better than short copy

✔ Why if everyone likes your ad it is probably worthless

✔ How to avoid being seduced by the law of large numbers

✔ Why copying your competitors is a bad idea

To introduce you to the concepts in this critically important chapter I'd like you to read the following letter I sent to my clients.

How a man drowning in debt can change your entire perspective about golf marketing...And dramatically increase <u>Your Club's</u> PROFITS!

Dear Reader:

If spelling, proper punctuation and grammer mattered at all in the REAL world of marketing, I'd be pushing a shopping cart up 5th Avenue with a sign around my neck saying,

"Will Work For food!"

Instead, despite my lack of formal English skills, I have written 14 books, made millions for myself in three different industries and generated many millions more for my clients! (Some of my clients are already up 33% this year! The ones who listen and act!)

> So why then are people in the golf business so caught up in "proper" punctuation, typestyles, logos and image in their clubs' marketing efforts, rather than RESULTS?

> Why do they want short copy that ends neatly at the bottom of every page even though long ragged copy like what you are reading now is proven to be more effective in generating response?

> Why do they want, glossy ads, lavishly expensive brochures and National Geographic-like photography?

> Why do they insist on politically correct copy that polarizes no one and at the same time MOTIVATES no one to ACTION?

I'll tell you why...because the people making the marketing decisions at most clubs don't have to meet

---

payroll out of _their_ own wallets, that's why! (_Add to this the fact that most of them don't know much about marketing and you're really in trouble!_)

They have never had a 2nd and 3rd mortgage on their family's home at the same time! They have never had an additional 121,527 dollars and 58 cents, spread over five different credit cards to keep the kids in private school and to stop the payroll checks from bouncing!

<u>If they had they would quickly throw out the BS that passes for conventional marketing wisdom in the golf industry! And they would stop 95% of their existing marketing DEAD IN ITS TRACKS</u>! Especially if designed by a traditional ad agency!

Instead they would target ONLY those people they KNOW for a FACT are their true target market.

Then they would start trying to squeeze every single ounce of response from every single penny they spent reaching ONLY that market!

And they would measure it so meticulously that they would know to the penny what every single promotion produced in terms of leads, conversions and profits!

They would trash the $20,000 image brochures, and $10,000 print ads packed full of beautiful pictures and unreadable reverse type that SIMPLY DON'T INCREASE YOUR BUSINESS!

Instead they would go back to the REAL basics of GREAT MARKETING. Sound Marketing that will make you Millions!

I learned the REAL BASICS OF MARKETING SUCCESS a long time ago because the very food that my family was going to eat depended on my next direct marketing campaign! The lists I choose, the words I crafted, the offers I devised, the calls to actions, the testimonials and P.S. I wrote brought checks in the mail. Checks that were rushed to the bank in a never ending game of beating the bounce charges!

As I got better at targeting my TRUE market and writing headlines and copy, the checks increased until finally I hit pay dirt with a single 8-page letter. That letter, mailed many times brought in over 4 million dollars in three years with a profit margin so huge, even I am embarrassed to tell you!

So how does that information help your club make more money?

It helps you if you PAY ATTENTION to RESULTS not personal preference, image or what others (your manager, boss, owner, ad agency, spouse, etc.) expect you to do because that's what everyone else is doing in the Golf Industry.

It helps you if you stop wasting your money on worthless print ads, expensive brochures and instead turn your attention to finding targeted prospects and making paper sales pitches to the people who are most likely to respond to your offer. **Let me repeat that, a paper sales presentation** (or web presentation). That means they have a beginning, a middle, an end, a call to action, testimonials and an irresistible offer or Unique Selling Proposition. (See Chapter 8 for more on your USP.)

Here's The Formula for REAL Golf Marketing Success in a Nutshell:

1. Pick a target list of people who you think are REAL prospects. That means they play a lot of golf right now! Then use your web site or telemarketing to ACTUALLY qualify them as REAL prospects.

2. Market DIRECTLY to no one but them! NO ONE!

3. Mail them a sales pitch! Anything else is a TOTAL waste of Money! A real sales pitch on why they should show up at your club's door!

4. Get them to respond to something, anything that gets them to put their hands up and say "YES I'm interested!"

5. Follow up on the sale pitch with multiple invites to visit. Get them in front of you! (See the chapter on a Thunderbolt Campaign.)

6. Sell them a tee time, a lesson, a room or a lot with a carefully scripted presentation.

7. Ask for referrals and upsell!

By the way, I spelled *grammar* incorrectly at the beginning of this letter to make my point about spelling and grammar and just so someone could complain about it! (If you're worried about my spelling, you're not focusing on your marketing enough!)

Andrew Wood
Marketing Legend
(At least in his own mind!)

P.S. If you think your clientele is too rich, too smart, or too sophisticated for this type of direct approach you are wrong! Very wrong and you are losing millions in the process!!!

P.P.S. By the way I am not saying you should not have a brochure, it just shouldn't look anything like the one you have! And yes print ads can be a part of your marketing but not the 99.9% you see in the golf magazine on your desk! They are KILlING trees without getting a big response.

UNDERSTANDING WHY MOST GOLF MARKETING FAILS

Before I get into the "meat" of how to massively improve the effectiveness of your marketing, it's important to take time to debunk some of the common myths about marketing. This is a VERY IMPORANT step because on your journey to marketing success, mangers, owners, spouses, board members, golf pros, and cooks WILL QUESTION YOU AT EVERY TURN. They will question your strategy. They'll tell you that you must do this and that because that is what your competitors are doing. They'll beg you to discount, disagree with your long copy, and advise you on graphics, colors, and media at every opportunity.

There is no place for myth or
personal prejudice in a comprehensive,
results-driven, marketing system.

Most opinions are WRONG!

Everyone has an opinion about marketing. Rarely, however, are those opinions based on facts. Instead they are almost always based on personal preferences for colors or styles, or based on myths that have been handed down for decades from others and repeated so many times that they are now WRONGLY considered to be FACT by 99 percent of people. Most important, since the people judging your marketing are rarely the same people as the people you are actually trying to attract, their opinions on anything are basically worthless! Worthless because their opinions are based not on marketing science but are based on their own social, economic, and psychological preferences, NOT those of the people you are trying to attract!

Unless you are willing to drop your personal preferences and debunk years of marketing misinformation in favor of proven marketing science, you cannot accomplish your goals of achieving Legendary Marketing at your course.

The following pages include the biggest myths and inhibitors to marketing success. READ THEM, understand them, believe them and take them as gospel. Share them with your owner, boss, manager, spouse, or whomever else is most likely to sabotage your efforts. Get them to understand the science of EFFECTIVE marketing before you attempt to market, so that everyone is on the same page, moving in the same direction.

AN ESSENTIAL CRASH COURSE IN MARKETING MYTHS

1 **People don't read any more.** MYTH! The biggest myth in marketing is that *people don't read any more* or at least they won't read lots of copy. The truth is, in fact, the opposite. In almost every case, long copy will out-pull short copy. The key factor is INTEREST. If people don't care about golf, they won't read anything, long or short. If prospects are interested in what you have to offer, and if you provide information in a compelling fashion, they will read it. The more you tell them, the more they'll trust you and the more interested they'll get in your offer.

Send me a magazine on horses and I'll pass it to my wife without glancing at a single page. Send me a magazine on cars and I'll give it a quick flip through. Send me a magazine on sports cars and it will get a little more of my attention as I flip through every page, scanning for something that catches my eye. But send me a magazine on Ferraris and I will take it to bed with me and read it cover to cover, word by word, every article and every relevant ad. The difference in how I read these different magazines is my level of interest in the subject matter. If I am interested in a topic, I want to know as much as possible. If I am not interested, I don't want to know anything. Your customers are no different. They will pay attention to what interests them and will ignore what does not! They want more of what interests them and less of what does not!

2 **The more people who like your ad, the better your ad!** MYTH! Design your marketing to create response, not to please your owner, your members, or your wife!

Graphic designers are not marketers! In fact, in many cases they have the opposite effect!

Web designers are not marketers!

And, if the truth be told, most ad agencies are not marketers! A nice way of explaining this is that most ad agencies are bored with simple approaches that work. Or, they are so busy that they tend to produce generic ads. A more cynical way of explaining the failure of many ads produced by ad agencies is that the agencies are more interested in competing for awards and inflating their egos with their clever designs than they are in making money for their clients.

Recently I gave three important presentations to large potential accounts. In each case, several of the people in the room did not play golf and most had minimal "real" marketing experience! If you want to estimate what marketing will appeal to your audience—golfers—you should have your prospects judge it. That's what focus groups and market research are about. (Research with small numbers has problems, too, but at least it's a start.)

No matter what people say about being "open minded," they (as we all do) judge you on their preconceived notions about marketing and with their personal preferences for design, text, and style. They may know something; they may know nothing—but make no mistake about it, 99 percent of the time they judge your work based on what they like, or think they know about marketing, not on what will actually work!

The key to great marketing is not to design
ads, web sites, and mail campaigns that people like.
It is to design marketing that motivates
targeted prospects to take the action you want.

Your target market is a very tiny percentage of the entire population. Your ideal prospects are a certain age, have certain hobbies, wants, needs, and passions. If the people who make marketing decisions are not avid golfers they cannot possibly understand the emotional connection that a good ad will have with an avid golfer any more than I can possibly understand why my wife enjoys mucking out horse stables and riding the beasts. (I was once given some very sound advice which I will share now. Never take up a hobby in which the main party eats while you sleep!) Nor unless they have exceptional marketing experience are they qualified to provide any useful input on the ads in question—*but they will anyway!*

Some of the best golf marketing my company has ever produced has never seen the light of day because it does not meet the criteria of the person paying the bills. I call it the Everyone-Loves-My-Ad Syndrome!

Just because everyone loves your ad doesn't mean that the phone will ring or that people will buy your lessons or come to your course.

You should design ads specifically for the people who you think will buy.

You should test different ads and headlines based on *response*. It doesn't matter whether you like the ad, your wife likes the ad, or anyone on your staff likes the ad. What matters is whether or not the people you want to buy respond to the ad.

I once designed an ad for a well-known manufacturer of graphite shafts. At the time it was quite simply the best ad I had ever designed. With all due modesty, first let me tell you that I understand golf advertising better than just about anyone on the planet. Second, I backed up my knowledge with abundant and irrefutable research on what people look for when they buy a golf club. Third, I designed an eye-catching ad that showed the product in use, had a sub-box that highlighted the product, and copy that would have golfers foaming at the mouth in anticipation of owning such a club. The VP of marketing who had been in the golf business for many years loved it. So did a host of golfers with whom I had tested the ad! The new CEO, a recent Harvard graduate who *didn't* play golf, wasn't sure. He said he wasn't getting a "warm, fuzzy feeling" about it. He left the conference room, which adjoined the manufacturing plant, and entered the factory. There I watched in complete disbelief as he wandered from worker to worker, of whom 50 percent spoke no English and the other 50 percent were suffering from the effects of too much glue sniffing, and showed them the ad.

Five minutes later he returned and announced, "The boys don't get it!" **The boys didn't get it because the boys didn't play golf.** *He* didn't get it. He wanted the workers to feel good about the ad; he didn't want an ad that would work! Unfortunately this general scenario occurs in many, many businesses. Owners, CEOs, and marketing executives who don't know the first thing about advertising, and who don't truly understand their end users, make terrible decisions based on what they like, not what the customers and prospects are looking for or will respond to!

Shoppers buy only two things: benefits and solutions. They do not buy features. They do not buy because of your logo, because your picture happens to be in the ad, or because you have been in business for 20 years. They only care about what your business or product can do for them. Is it cheaper or more reliable? Will they feel more important being a member of your club? Will they hit the ball farther, straighter, and more consistently with your golf clubs?

After my first ad for the shaft-maker was rejected, I came back with another that offered information to people in the club-fitting business who were among the prime buyers of their shafts. This time the CEO turned down the idea because he feared it might generate too much interest—and clog up the company's phone system! I resigned after that one.

The shaft-maker's new ad agency designed a two-page color ad containing a picture of a large tree with a hole in it, the hole supposedly made by a golf ball on its way toward a distant green. One of their golf shafts lay across the bottom of the page. There was a weak headline, which I can't recall, but it had nothing to do with the product. That was it. No reason to buy, no benefits, no testimonials! Although they had a good market and a great product, they allowed themselves to be bought out by a larger company with deeper pockets because with marketing like that you can go broke quickly!

Before you hire anyone to design an ad campaign, educate yourself. Read a good marketing book. Discover the real principles of marketing from a true leader in the field, not from someone who happens to run a small design company down the street and thinks they know something about marketing. Read *Ogilvy on Advertising*—Ogilvy built the biggest ad agency in the world from scratch. In its pages you will discover many things you never knew, like why long copy ALWAYS sells better than short copy. Or get the classic book *Scientific Advertising* by Claude Hopkins, or Al Reis and Jack Trout's classic book on *Positioning*. Or one of Dr. Rick Crandall's newer books on marketing services. In books like this you will discover that the real secrets of marketing are not what most people think they are—in fact, very often they are the opposite!

The number one goal of a good ad, letter, or brochure is to connect with a specific targeted reader and motivate that reader to action.

In the case of an ad for a golf club, that means not just any reader. Not your wife who doesn't play golf, or son who is 14 and into rap music, but a targeted reader, a golfer.

Even better, you probably want a very specific type of golfer, a player of a certain age and income. Your ad should be written and designed only for him, not anyone else. What anyone but that targeted reader thinks of your copy or design does not matter one iota! In fact, if lots of unqualified people look at the ad and like it, it's an almost sure sign that the ad is not speaking to your target audience in an emotional and personal enough way to be effective. It's almost like "they" should be the only ones who get it!

③ Reaching 100,000 people in the local paper is typically more effective in generating revenue than mailing to 500 people whom you know for a fact play golf and live in your market area. MYTH! Thousands of ad salesmen make a living on seducing golf courses with large numbers.

It boggles my mind when I talk to golf courses looking for 100 new members. They're running ads statewide, even nationwide, in numerous glossy magazines that total 3 million readers when they are in fact looking for 100 people willing to spend, say, $75,000 on a membership and perhaps a half a million on a home. The theory is that a certain percentage of people who read your ad will respond. That, my friend, is simply not true!

In a 100-page magazine, only a tiny fraction of the readers will ever see your full-page ad with the picture of the signature hole in a section that has 12–16 pages of similar ads featuring a fairway as green as a shamrock flanked by water so blue that an Aegean postcard would go green with envy! Maybe only 1 percent will read your smaller ad.

The same is true of people who blanket market to new homeowners—a group where, statistically, 90 percent don't play golf!

Successful marketing is, and always will be,
about reaching targeted prospects.

A targeted mailing list of 5,000 prospects would be 70 percent cheaper and about 1000 percent more effective than mass advertising in the newspaper to 100,000 people. But that small number throws people off. They think BIGGER is better. In fact, TARGETED is better! That means targeted mailings, targeted e-mails, targeted web sites, and doubling or tripling the play of the people you already have as players.

WWW.PalmBeachgolf.com might only have had 11,214 unique visitors last month, but they were all there because they wanted to be. They all play golf and a large percentage of them gave us their name, address and phone number, plus an e-mail. *Each name is a golden lead for future marketing at a cost of zero.* Now, how much sense does that make?

If you ran an ad on that site and got 150 names, addresses, and e-mails, you would be so far ahead of the game compared to a local newspaper ad that it's not even funny. But most people just don't get it! They think the numbers are too small. Instead they are seduced by huge circulation numbers when they should be focused on the *quality* of the leads they get, not the *quantity!*

4   **You don't want to exclude or offend anyone with your marketing.** MYTH! Actually that's exactly what you want to do—exclude all those people who aren't good prospects so you don't waste any more time or money chasing them. When I say offend, I don't mean you stand up and insult them. Think of it more in terms of how a Republican might react to a Democrat's comments.

For example, say you are the proud owner of an 8,000-yard, Pete Dye masterpiece with water on every hole. Your market is clearly better players.

LADIES, SISSIES, WIMPS, AND 30 HANDICAPS NEED NOT APPLY!

This might be a nice provocative headline to appeal to macho single digits like me! Sure, some ladies or higher handicappers might take offense but the number of macho guys you excite by this headline will more than make up for the furor of a few people who are obviously NOT your true target market. In fact, if people make a fuss about your ad, you will get free publicity with the target market that matters to you!

You have to take a stand, and the more targeted your stand is to your true market, the more effective your marketing will be, even at the expense of excluding or even irritating some players.

5   **If all your competitors are doing it, you have to do it too just to compete!** MYTH! You do not have to advertise in the local golf publication just because 50 of your favorite competitors do! In fact, it's plain

stupid to do so. Nor do you need to discount because they do! The less you act like your competition, the quicker you will define your own position in the marketplace!

Those are the five big myths we come up against again and again. Don't let your marketing decisions be influenced by these dangerous beliefs.

TOP 20 REASONS WHY MOST GOLF MARKETING FAILS

In the next few pages I'm going to save you hundreds of thousands of dollars and years of trial and error by detailing exactly why most clubs fail to reach their marketing goals. This is not subjective; this is not our opinion. It is based on over 20 years of research into the science of marketing and the analysis of several hundred golf club clients. (Some of these 20 reasons also relate to the five major myths I just covered. That's okay; this is a full list.)

Here are the top 20 reasons why clubs' marketing efforts fail. Read them, believe them and resolve not to do them!

1 **They don't collect enough data (golfers' names, e-mails, and so forth).**

2 **They don't do enough with the data they do collect.** This process works best when it's completely automated such as e-mails added automatically to your list. (See our Campaign Manager program as an example.)

3 **Their web sites are ineffective.** (If you need facts about why your existing site is ineffective please call and I will systematically destroy it for you!)

4 **They do not track their ad or promotional campaigns so they have no exact way of knowing which ads or promotions were really effective.**

5 **Their ads stink!** They have cute headlines, pretty pictures, and *impotent* copy.

6 **They run campaigns that people say "look good" rather than ones that actually get the phone to ring.** (This week we generated 200 membership leads for a client from a single sales letter.)

7 **There is no written sales process or scripting or training of the people answering the phones and in charge of memberships, outings, and banquets.**

8 **Follow-up to all requests is not automated or systemized, so follow-up is poor.**

9 **They do almost the exact same marketing as ALL their competitors; they are afraid to risk being different.**

10 **Brochures, ads, and letters are written in boring, generic corporate-speak and wouldn't motivate a drunk to leave his seat to get a free beer.**

11 **They discount green fees to get more business rather than look for ways to add more value.**

12 **Their budgets are based on a percentage of gross or a number someone handed down from head office instead of being based on the goals they are trying to meet.** In other words, the goals are pure fantasy with no consideration whatsoever of the income they need to generate.

13 **They do NOTHING to set themselves CLEARLY apart from other clubs in their marketplace.** Yet these clubs still say "We have the best course and great customer service"...yeah, yeah, yeah, tell it to the judge (as my 10 year old says!).

14 **Their service is really about 80 percent worse than they think it is!** They have no system in place for measuring service and they never run extensive customer surveys so they never really know how good or BAD their service TRULY is!

15 **They fail to thank their customers with letters, cards, and small gifts as is done in almost all other professional businesses.**

16 **They confuse "loyalty" programs with discount programs!** Loyalty is earned, NOT BOUGHT!

17 **They fail to outsource the things they don't do well (like telemarketing).**

18 **They don't capitalize on the automation that's available to help them maximize their operations.**

19 **They don't spend enough time studying or doing marketing.** (You tend to get the best results from the things you focus on the most!)

20 **They keep doing what they have always done because it's easier than changing to a more systematic approach that would actually work.** Meanwhile their market share is sinking faster than John Daly in quicksand.

SUMMARY

Now you have the key information why most clubs don't get where they want to go. You are ready to do things differently and get the corresponding successful result!

Chapter Three

Benchmarking and Measuring Your Results

All successful marketing begins with information. But information alone is not enough. You need insight and understanding into what makes your customers and prospects tick—what motivates them, what offers they are most likely to respond to, and what is the most effective way to communicate with them. But, first, a question.

WHERE ARE YOU NOW?

You may not have a clue as to where you are now. You may have just taken over a club, you may not be privy to past information, or you might just be lousy at keeping records—most people are! No matter how good or bad your information is, you have to start somewhere. The first step to achieving marketing success for your club is clarity—knowing where you are and where you want to be!

In this chapter, you will discover:

- ✔ What benchmarking is

- ✔ How to benchmark yourself

- ✔ Your strategic indicators

- ✔ How to measure your marketing results

- ✔ How to measure your status

We will start by benchmarking where you are now. Benchmarking is a process where you compare yourself to others. The simplest comparisons are to your direct competitors. However, benchmarking can be much more than that. You should also be comparing yourself to the best. And, by the best, I mean more than other golf courses. For instance, you should compare your restaurant to the best restaurants in town. You might study Disney World to determine what kind of entertainment experience your golfers want. And, you might compare your pro shop to Nordstrom or some other store that is known for great customer service.

Benchmarking is done in three stages:

1. Find tangible numbers about your current performance.

2. Measure intangibles like how you stack up to your competitors.

3. Take stock of your resources and programs you already have in place.

The benchmarking process we employ is very detailed. There are many worksheets and we constantly tweak them to make the data more useful (and, therefore, more valuable). You'll find examples below, but for the entire processs, visit www.LegendaryVault.com. I urge you to put in the work necessary to measure your real strengths and weaknesses.

To give you a brief idea of what's involved, use the following scales to rate your club and your competitors' clubs on the following scales:

1 = Lowest; 10 = Highest

How good is your course layout?	1 2 3 4 5 6 7 8 9 10
How good is your course conditioning?	1 2 3 4 5 6 7 8 9 10
How well known is your course in the area?	1 2 3 4 5 6 7 8 9 10
How do you compare against your competition in general?	1 2 3 4 5 6 7 8 9 10
How do you compare against your biggest competitor?	1 2 3 4 5 6 7 8 9 10
How do you compare against your second biggest competitor?	1 2 3 4 5 6 7 8 9 10
How do you compare against your third biggest competitor?	1 2 3 4 5 6 7 8 9 10
How well trained are your staff?	1 2 3 4 5 6 7 8 9 10
How loyal are your customers?	1 2 3 4 5 6 7 8 9 10

Finding out where you are now and where you want to be is an interesting, challenging, and eye-opening experience. Once you have completed these steps, you will have a far better understanding of how to measure important tangible and intangible data so that you can maximize your marketing efforts. Please take the time to do this.

The following pages contain a brief phone survey for benchmarking a daily-fee club against other local courses. If you're a membership club, you can easily modify or add questions to collect the appropriate data.

Sample Daily-Fee Club Phone Survey

Hello, this is Mary from Legendary Research, am I speaking to (name)?

Great. How are you today, (name)?

That's good, (name). The reason for my call is …

How often do you play a month?	1 2 3 4 5 6 7 8 9 10
How often do you play our course?	1 2 3 4 5 6 7 8 9 10

On a scale of 1 to 10, how would you rate (course), where 1 is the lowest, least favorable rating and 10 is the highest, most favorable rating:

Staff

	1 2 3 4 5 6 7 8 9 10
Overall friendliness & service of our staff?	1 2 3 4 5 6 7 8 9 10
The bag staff?	1 2 3 4 5 6 7 8 9 100
The pro shop staff?	1 2 3 4 5 6 7 8 9 10
The starter?	1 2 3 4 5 6 7 8 9 10
The ranger?	1 2 3 4 5 6 7 8 9 10
The beer cart?	1 2 3 4 5 6 7 8 9 10
The restaurant staff?	1 2 3 4 5 6 7 8 9 10

Conditions

The condition of the range?	1 2 3 4 5 6 7 8 9 10
The condition of the range balls?	1 2 3 4 5 6 7 8 9 10
The overall condition of the course?	1 2 3 4 5 6 7 8 9 10
The condition of the greens?	1 2 3 4 5 6 7 8 9 10
The speed of the greens?	1 2 3 4 5 6 7 8 9 10
The condition of the fairways?	1 2 3 4 5 6 7 8 9 10
The condition of the traps?	1 2 3 4 5 6 7 8 9 10
The pace of play?	1 2 3 4 5 6 7 8 9 10
How do you like the layout?	1 2 3 4 5 6 7 8 9 10

How difficult is the course?   1 2 3 4 5 6 7 8 9 10
(where 1 = not at all difficult and
10 = one of the most difficult)

Which three other courses in the area do you typically play?

Course #1 _____

How does (your course) rate overall against them? Not as good, about the same, better?

How would you rate the value you received for
your green fee *(where 1 = not at all a good*
value, and 10 = an exceptional value)   1 2 3 4 5 6 7 8 9 10

What do you like best about the facility? _____

What three things should they do to make your experience better? _____

_____

Course #2 _____

How does (your course) rate overall against them? Not as good, about the same, better?

How would you rate the value you received for
your green fee *(where 1 = not at all a good*
value, and 10 = an exceptional value)   1 2 3 4 5 6 7 8 9 10

What do you like best about the facility? _____

What three things should they do to make your experience better? _____

_____

Course #3 _____

How does (your course) rate overall against them? Not as good, about the same, better?

How would you rate the value you received for
your green fee *(where 1 = not at all a good*
value, and 10 = an exceptional value)   1 2 3 4 5 6 7 8 9 10

What do you like best about the facility? _____

What three things should they do to make your experience better? _____

MEASURING YOUR MARKETING RESULTS

Most club managers and owners would have a lot of empathy for the founder of Wrigley's gum, William Wrigley, Jr. At one time, Wrigley's was one of the largest advertisers in the world. One day a young reporter asked Wrigley if the huge amount of money he spent on advertising was a waste of money. He replied:

> Young man, I am sure that 50 percent of the money I spend on advertising is a total waste. The problem is, I'm not sure which half it is!

Things have come a long way since then. Today, every aspect of your marketing is trackable and accountable, but only if the proper system is followed.

You want your marketing to produce more leads and better-quality leads. This can only be accomplished if you meticulously track the results from each ad, direct mail piece, mailing list, billboard, and e-mail campaign. The results will help you to spend your marketing dollars where they are most effective.

Using paper systems and your SmartSite (if you use our web sites), you will be able to track and quantify all of your marketing efforts. This will lead to your making smarter decisions about your marketing, resulting in a dramatic increase in your return on investment.

THE IMPORTANCE OF MEASURING RESULTS

Legendary Marketing was recently asked to consult on a major golf real estate project. The client had just fired their "high falutin'" ad agency that happened to be one of the hottest shops around. The agency was well known for producing high-gloss, award-winning ads and collateral materials. Unfortunately, winning awards doesn't produce sales.

When we asked the client about the exact results of their previous campaign, they looked at us with a straight face and told us it simply hadn't worked. So we pressed further: "Of the $900,000 you spent on advertising last year, how many leads came from each of the magazines and each of the ads you ran?" The blank looks and nervous glances spoke volumes. Turns out their agency didn't use any tracking codes! So the client spent nearly $1 million but couldn't tell us if their meager response came from the *New York Times, Atlanta Magazine,* or the *Traverse City Record*!

How could this happen?

Simple. It's a lot easier to design pretty campaigns and talk about building an image than it is to put your company on the line and deliver the goods! If you start tracking all of your campaigns, you will quickly see what works and what doesn't. Unfortunately, very few people ever quantify their marketing efforts in detail.

Do you track all of your prospects and customers in a database management program such as the Legendary Customer Relationship Manager, ACT, or Outlook? (We have a custom tracker built into our SmartSites so every ad, e-mail, and phone call is tracked.)

Key questions

- ✔ What is your conversion rate of leads-to-customers? That is, of 100 people who call or visit your facility, how many buy?

- ✔ How much do they buy?

- ✔ What does it cost you to get a new customer? (That includes ads, phone calls, follow-up letters, commissions, and YOUR TIME!)

- ✔ How long does it normally take to turn a lead into a customer? How many times do you contact them?

✔ Do you have a written, structured process by which this process occurs?

✔ How could you shorten this time?

By taking the time to answer these questions, you can quickly spot holes in your marketing plan and find ways to maximize your response. The more you measure, the better your marketing will become!

WHAT YOU MUST TRACK

You MUST set up systems to track every single ad, e-mail blast, postcard, and promotion that you run.

You must have a tracking system so that you know your exact response to everything.

It's the only way to calculate your ROI (return on investment) and MAXIMIZE your marketing.

For example, we recently did an e-blast for Innisbrook Resort in Florida. The blast cost $1,500 and generated $28,000 of room-night revenue. We know this because the blast was set up with a unique contact point on the website and an 800-number that only appeared on that blast. Thirty days after the campaign, we were sure about the return on investment and whether we should use that list again.

List performance and ad performance

List and ad performance can be measured by the number of responses generated by the offer, publication, and timing.

Web performance

Web performance can be measured by factors like number of visitors, amount of data collected, tee times booked, and product sales.

E-blast performance

E-blast performance can be measured by the number of opens, the number of click-throughs, and the number of people signing up or taking advantage of a specific offer.

We have tracked the success of our own in-house e-mail lists for generating golf real estate leads on a cost-per-lead basis. In other words, rather than charging a lump sum to do a massive e-blast, we will charge the client only when a real lead is generated. (I know of no one in the golf real estate business willing to put their performance on the line like that. We similarly guarantee other responses from our e-mail blasts for rounds, memberships, and so on.)

MEASURING CUSTOMER SATISFACTION

All the marketing in the world is not going to help you in the long run if you fail to meet or exceed customer expectations. Customer satisfaction should be tracked regularly using surveys:

- ✔ At the counter
- ✔ At the 1st tee
- ✔ Off the 18th green
- ✔ Online
- ✔ In the mail
- ✔ On the phone

(See also the chapter on Customer Service.)

TELE-RESEARCH AND MEMBER SATISFACTION PROGRAMS

Have you ever been contacted by phone and asked to evaluate your golf experience? Probably not. A third party phone call like this to a recent player is by far your most effective tool in gauging customer satisfaction. The customer is far more likely to be open and honest with a third party.

Tele-research can also answer important marketing questions like why some people buy memberships or golf homes and others don't, or why some people support every club event and others never show up. The answers to these and similar questions can have a dramatic effect on the success of your club's marketing efforts and customer loyalty.

Tele-research programs will give you fresh insight into exactly what you should be doing to attract and satisfy your current and prospective members. Members and prospective members will speak more freely to a third party about topics like:

- ✔ Why they play or *don't* play your club more often

- ✔ What they are looking for in a club

- ✔ What they like and, more importantly, what they don't like about your club, your people, and your offerings

- ✔ Why they joined or bought somewhere else

Armed with these findings, you can enhance your marketing, your offers, your pricing, and your sales presentation to gain a competitive edge. You'll also increase member retention by offering exactly the types of products and services members want.

CONCLUSION

Benchmarking helps you compare yourself to the best and set goals for your performance. Then you must track and measure all your marketing results. It is critical to your long-term marketing success that you know exactly what your response is to each and every method you employ. Only then can you tweak your strategy and put every dollar where it is most likely to generate a profitable return every time!

Chapter Four

Defining Your Market

What types of people make up your customer base?

What motivates them to play or join your club?

Few clubs ever take the time to answer these critical questions in any detail. (Which is good news for you!) Once you have answered these questions, you will be in an excellent position to redirect your advertising and promotional efforts, refine your sales methods, and tailor your marketing to the specific segments most likely to respond. This will give you a significant advantage in your marketplace.

The more specific your target audience, the more effective your marketing will be. This is one of the hardest concepts for most people to grasp. After all, don't you want all the business you can get? The answer is: No!

For example, let's say you have a very long and tough Pete Dye-designed course. Do you really want to attract beginners and weekend duffers? If so, you are destined for six-hour rounds at the expense of angering your avid golf customers.

You should instead pinpoint your best customers so that you can target market to them. It's no surprise that seniors respond differently than business golfers. Social players respond differently than serious players. Women respond differently than men, and so on. The more you can segment your market into key groups, the higher your response rates will be!

In this chapter, you will discover:

- ✔ Who your perfect customer really is, including demographics and psychographics

- ✔ How large your potential market is

- ✔ Where your most likely customers are located

- ✔ How your customers segment into various target markets

- ✔ How to uncover hidden geographic patterns that affect your club

Be sure to complete the worksheet included in this chapter to nail down your best markets. By doing so, you'll be that much closer to increasing players or memberships, driving more play and boosting sales and profits!

DEFINING YOUR PERFECT CUSTOMER

Back when I taught karate for a living, Darren Willard was the most perfect client I ever had. He was an athletic nine-year-old boy with a photographic memory and a penchant for learning. He took private lessons, came to all the tournaments, and his parents ALWAYS paid on time. They supported all the promotional events, referred their friends, and constantly made glowing comments instead of complaining.

Ah, if only there were more Darren Willards in the world! The good news is that there are, but you have to find them.

Can you describe the qualities of a perfect customer at your club?

You probably immediately thought of someone at your club. That's great, because the first step in finding more perfect customers is understanding what they look like. These are the people who:

- ✔ Pay full green fees

- ✔ Bring guests

- ✔ Buy from the pro shop

- ✔ Take lessons

- ✔ Attend special events

- ✔ Play in tournaments

- ✔ Spend money in the bar and restaurant

These are your very best customers...the type of people you need more of. They're your "A" clients, the top 20 percent from which you derive most of your income. With more players like this...well, you wouldn't need more players!

Think of 20 people at your club who fit your description of a perfect member, player, or homeowner:

- ✔ What is their age?

- ✔ What is their income?

- ✔ What do they do for a living?

- ✔ Where do they live? Ten, twenty, thirty miles away, or more?

- ✔ What do they read?

✔ What kind of player are they—avid, social, business?

✔ What exactly are the qualities of a perfect customer for you?

Do this exercise with your staff (use the worksheet on the opposite page) and try to come up with 20–50 people who seem to be the perfect clients. Take a look at their profiles because from now on these are the only type of clients you want to attract!

SEGMENT YOUR CUSTOMERS

The basic universe of golfers includes males and females between the ages of 7 and 80—not very limited! To be effective with your marketing you need to segment clearly definable groups.

Why do people play golf?

Golf experienced explosive growth between the 1970s and the year 2000. Expansive television coverage and a few superstars by the names of Palmer, Nicklaus, and Woods played a key role in generating interest in the masses.

The number of people who now play golf is stagnant at around 26 million. When Legendary Marketing asked a cross section of golfers why they played, we received a wide variety of answers.

Let's categorize some of the more commonly expressed reasons so you can see what percentage of your market falls into each category.

✔ **The addict.** Loves to practice, play, compete, gamble.

✔ **Fitness.** Enjoys the moderate level of exercise.

✔ **Outdoors experience.** Likes the open air.

✔ **Social.** Likes meeting new friends or prefers the type of friends one makes on the course.

PERFECT CUSTOMER WORKSHEET

(Copy this sheet for each of your 4-8 primary markets)

Primary Customer # _____

Target Group Name: _____

Male/Female: _____

Age Range: _____

Occupations:

1 _____

2 _____

3 _____

4 _____

5 _____

Income range: _____

Lives in zip:

1 _____

2 _____

3 _____

4 _____

5 _____

Drives # miles: _____

Also plays at:

1 _____

2 _____

3 _____

Rounds played a month: _____

Responds best to which media:

1 _____

2 _____

Responds best to which offers:

1 _____

2 _____

3 _____

Target for: _____

- ✔ **Retirement Leisure.** Occupies one's retirement.

- ✔ **Business.** Combines business with pleasure. Golf is practically a necessity for the modern executive.

- ✔ **The fad golfer.** Watched on TV and decided to "give it a try."

- ✔ **Junior golfers.** Kids like fun; parents like safety.

- ✔ **Female golfers.** A growing group.

Each of these segments may be represented in your customer base. Although many people fall neatly into one of these categories, you must relate to each person as an individual and understand what makes him or her tick. It will make a huge difference between a high customer retention rate with maximum profits versus high attrition rate and minimum profits.

Now, let's take a closer look at each group.

The addict

The die-hard, addicted golfer is ready to try anything that might improve his game. Golf is a way of life, a crucial part of his psychological make up. Without it, he feels incomplete and unfulfilled. It's not unusual for him to relate to everything in terms of the sport.

The addict practices hard before and after rounds. He studies golf periodicals and instruction books, and frequently equipment specifications. Putters and drivers are the most commonly discarded former friends! The addict is a good customer and will be among your most loyal and supportive allies, but is likely to expect the same devotion from you. He or she is not necessarily a low handicap golfer.

The light-exercise fan or seeker of outdoor experiences

The golfers or would-be golfers who play for exercise or a love of the open air should not be ignored. The inherent beauty and attraction of the game turns many of these people into serious golfers or even addicts!

The social golfer

The person seeking social contact through golf may want to make new friends, meet members of the opposite sex, or spend more leisure time with a spouse or significant other who is already a golfer. The social golfer can develop into a more frequent player.

The retired golfer

People are living longer and staying active in their retirement years. This rapidly growing group is turning to golf as a form of recreation, exercise, and social opportunity. In fact, about 40 percent of all rounds are played by seniors.

Most seniors are on fixed incomes and are very concerned about their financial well-being. They are generally cautious with their money and always looking for bargains. Be very mindful of this when you market packages and specials aimed at this group. Seniors shop around and compare prices. You will need to be competitive to attract their business.

The senior golfer is often set in his ways. He doesn't want to change what he has for breakfast, his daily routine, his budgeted expenditures, and his backswing! Don't be discouraged by these peculiarities. Seniors comprise one of the largest groups of golfers and play more frequently than most. Their flexible schedules present you with a golden opportunity to drive more mid-week play.

The business golfer

This golfer is in a hurry, expects results, and demands value and an adequate return on his investment. He is usually constrained by time and will appreciate (more than most) flexibility in scheduling, prime tee times, and so on. Are you providing the business golfer the right setting for business deals?

The fad golfer

This individual may have become intrigued with the sport in any number of ways. Boredom with a current hobby may have set in. A change in lifestyle may have occurred. The precise reason need not concern you. The important fact is that you now have an opportunity to sell your services to this person.

Fad golfers usually don't stick around very long; but it doesn't necessarily follow that a student who seeks you out after watching a tour event on TV will quit. Some of them who enjoy the experience may eventually become dedicated players. You can also count on them to be an excellent source of referrals.

The junior golfer

Kids love to try anything that is new to them, anything their peer group is involved in, and anything that is fun. Additionally, parents often seek an activity for their children that is safe and enduring.

When you direct your marketing efforts to this group, emphasize the fun aspect to the kids and the safe, responsible aspect to the parents (who pay the fees!). Friends and playmates of youngsters in your program will often enroll too. With a little encouragement from you, these friends will in turn bring their friends and the cycle will continue. Summer programs can generate extra income.

The female golfer

Women comprise the largest, and possibly most significant, emerging golf market. Women represent all categories described in this module...addicts, businesswomen, and so on. Presently most are interested in the exercise and social aspects of golf. (Mixed foursomes are becoming more and more popular.) Nevertheless, the competitive instinct is definitely a factor, and can be easily observed in women's club tournaments and team play.

It's important to take into account this large and growing sector of the golf population when researching your area. The number of women who play and take lessons will only continue to grow.

OTHER POTENTIAL MARKET SEGMENTS

Other potential market segments include:

- ✔ League players
- ✔ Locals
- ✔ Out-of-town visitors
- ✔ Summer/Winter members
- ✔ Hotel customers
- ✔ Guests of major employers
- ✔ Students and faculty

The segments and motivations discussed in this chapter are by no means comprehensive. Take a look around to see how many of your customers fit these profiles. Knowing who your best customers are and understanding them is enormously valuable in aiming your marketing efforts accurately and effectively. When you have a better understanding of what motivates people to come to your club, you'll do a better job of attracting them.

USE YOUR WEB SITE TO DEFINE YOUR MARKET

The online survey is by far the most important and effective tool you can use to define and segment your market. You can learn more about a player and his playing habits in two minutes than your competitors will learn in a lifetime. What's more, your SmartSite Campaign Manager will be preprogrammed to follow up throughout the year with targeted promotions sent exactly to those people most likely to respond, based solely on their answers to these questions. Online surveys can be as simple or extensive as you wish. The sample below is a from a very extensive survey that has had great success. With SmartSite technology you can build a unique player history over time. Below is a list of the data that is collected and its use.

Online Survey to Define and Segment Your Market

First Name *(allows for personalized e-mails and postal follow up)*

Last Name

Address

City*(target a city or locals)*

State/Prov *(target a state/province)*

Zip/Postal Code *(target specific areas with different offers)*

Phone (tele survey)

E-mail (e-mail marketing)

What is the name of your company/ business?

Handicap

Does your spouse/partner play?

What is your age?

What is your approximate annual income?

Are you a member of a club? If Yes, which one? *(A yes answer tells you a lot about them based on the club)*

How many times do you play per month? *(tells you how avid and therefore how important they are to you)*

When do you usually play? *(indicates preference)*

Which course open to the public do you play most often? *(indicates what they will spend and also allows you to cherry pick your competitors one by one by preprogramming different offers to convert players from other clubs to yours)*

Which other course do you play?

What is your favorite course in YOUR STATE OR PROVINCE? *(use this data to trade with other courses)*

How often do you play at YOUR COURSE? *(how often do they play your course)*

About how far do you live from YOUR COURSE? *(helps define your primary trading area)*

Which other AFFILIATED COURSE have you played?

In season, what do you typically pay to play golf? *(important question lets you determine what price point they are most likely to respond to)*

How much per year do you think you spend on green fees?

Do you normally play as a team?

Do you ever participate in golf outings?

What are the names of the charity and corporate events you play in?

Which outings do you usually play in?

What month and where are those outing usually held?

How many lessons do you take a year?

Have you ever been to a golf school? If YES, which was the best you have attended?

Would you like information on our junior clinics and kids summer camps?

What brand of driver do you use?

What brand of irons do you use?

What model putter do you use?

What ball do you typically play?

How many golf shirts do you typically buy in a year?

What is your favorite brand of golf shirt?

What would you expect to pay for a golf shirt?

How much do you typically spend a year on clubs and equipment?

How many golf vacations do you take per year?

Where do you typically go on golf vacations? (check all that apply)

Would you like membership information on our exciting Club Max program?

YOUR PRIMARY MARKET

Your potential market

Consider a few general statistics.

In any given market, approximately 10 percent of the population in your immediate area will have some interest in playing or learning to play golf. A much smaller percentage, about 4 percent, are avid golfers who play more than 20 rounds a year. Using a population base of 100,000, that means the potential market of golfers in your area is no more than 10,000 (travelers excluded). The avid market would be around 4,000 people.

✔ How many clubs in your area are fighting for a slice of your market?

✔ How many players already belong to private clubs?

✔ How many are still up for grabs?

✔ How many single players made up your total number of rounds last year?

Your primary market

Your primary market is the key area from which most of your customers will come. At a typical club, that market falls inside a 30-mile radius. At some it may be as far as 100 miles. Within your primary market you could identify several key groups. You might also have two or three secondary markets, particularly if you have both a local and out-of-town base.

Do your homework

Buy a giant county street map and place a dot or pin representing the address of each player or member. Then draw a ring around your location just outside the largest concentration of players. This will give you a clear indication of your primary trading area.

If you take the time and effort to do this, you will likely uncover some interesting patterns. You will find small clusters of players residing in particular developments or zip codes.

Travel patterns

You'd be surprised at how often a river or major freeway stops people moving in a particular direction. In other words, people may drive 50 miles to your club from the West but only 15 miles from the East. In this case you will want to target more of your marketing to those players in zip codes to the West of your club.

Sometimes people don't like to cross state lines, county boundaries, or even city limits. A club located on a city's edge might draw very few members from another city just two miles away, yet members from the same city will gladly travel across town to join. Busy intersections and rush hour traffic can either work for or against your club's location. Identifying patterns like these can help you focus your efforts on zip codes most likely to produce results.

SUMMARY

Few clubs truly know who their market really is and thus waste untold millions marketing to people who will never visit their clubs. A small amount of time and effort spent researching your market will pay huge dividends. The more accurately you can define your "Perfect Customer" and the different segments of players to whom your club appeals, the quicker you can tweak your message. Tailoring your message to just the right type of player will deliver greater response from your marketing. Some simple market research using your SmartSite and a map will give you a head start.

Chapter Five

Legendary Budgeting

Marketing plans don't run on air. You need a plan in place to match your goals to the your marketing budget. A great many clubs dream about selling 50 lots with a $20,000 budget or 100 memberships for $15,000. Or they want a 20 percent increase in rounds with a budget that's based on five percent of last year's miserable gross!

You cannot increase business by spending less on marketing, although you don't always have to spend more to get the results you want. Often it's just a case of spending where the response is greatest and NOT spending it where there is no direct and tangible return.

You cannot set a marketing budget based on a percentage of your gross or net. You cannot set a marketing budget based on what your competition does. (Forget industry averages; there are none.) The only way you can set the right marketing budget is to reverse engineer exactly what you want to happen.

The step-by-step process outlined in this module will allow you to look at budgeting and meeting goals in a powerful new way. A way that directly connects everything you do in the name of marketing to a specific and tangible result at the counter.

In this chapter, you will discover:

- ✔ Why most marketing budgets make NO sense

- ✔ How to design the perfect budget that will increase your business

- ✔ How to make every single dollar pay for itself

- ✔ How to calculate your ROI on every campaign

- ✔ How changing your ratios can quickly boost response from your existing budget

MATCH THE BUDGET TO YOUR GOALS, NOT THE OTHER WAY AROUND

Here's the perfect way to discover your marketing budget. If you want to sell 100 memberships, you cannot do it by arbitrarily picking a number for your marketing budget. You have to think in terms of the answer to the following question: How many leads must you generate to sell 100 memberships?

To answer that question, you need to know what percentage of leads your membership director closes.

If the membership director only sells one out of five prospects, that means you need to generate 500 leads to sell 100 memberships.

So how many leads does your $4,000 glossy ad bring in...seven or eight? Not enough. Perhaps you should look at direct mail. At a 1 percent rate of response you will need to send 50,000 letters to generate 500 leads; at a 2 percent response rate it's 25,000 letters, envelopes, stamps, and time. Let's say it comes to $25,000 or a dollar apiece when all is said and done.

This is $10,000 more than the proposed budget and you still have no idea if the membership director can actually sell! All you have done so far is generate the number of leads needed to sell 100 memberships. However, this is a step taken only by about 0.1 percent of courses.

We're not saying you have to spend more, just that you need a realistic plan. Measure the cost of every piece of marketing you do to generate leads. Then know how well your lead conversion process works.

BUDGET PLANNING WORKSHEET

Before you can set a realistic marketing budget you must establish your closing ratio. Only then can you come up with a budget number. You may find this a difficult exercise, but without benchmarking you can NEVER maximize your marketing dollars.

> **WARNING:** Before you start, you should know up front that you may not like the answers you come up with. That's because for the first time you will have a TRUE picture of how many leads you REALLY need and what you have to spend to reach your marketing goals.

Most clubs exaggerate their true closing ratios. They remember all the successes and quickly forget the failures. Very few close more than two out of every 10 leads. Even the world's best salespeople don't get more than eight out of 10. (If you can close 8 out of 10 leads, call our office at once; I have a great job waiting for you!) Back in the real world, if you don't know what your closing ratio is I suggest you consider one out of 10 as a starting point. Two out of ten is probably better than average, at least in membership sales. Outing and banquets could be quite a bit higher, but it pays to err on the side of caution. Golf real estate sales are often based on one in 500 leads! When in doubt, make an educated guess. Even that is better than mindlessly spending money hoping you are getting a return. Fill out the following worksheet and you'll have something to start with.

BUDGETING WORKSHEET

Your Market

How big is your club's potential market? (It might be 10% of the area's population. But if you are talking avid golfers, you are down to about 4%.)   _____

What percentage of that market are "ideal" prospects for you?   _____

What percentage of your potential market do you reach with your current marketing plan?   _____

MARKETING DATA

Memberships

How many total membership inquiries did you get last year? (Phone, Internet, referral, walk-ins, e-mail, etc.)   _____

How many of them bought memberships?   _____

Membership closing ratio (Example: 100 inquires, 10 sold would have a closing ratio 1 in 10. 200 leads would be needed to sell 20 memberships, 400 leads to sell 40 memberships, and so on.)   _____

This year's goal for number of memberships?   _____

Number of membership leads needed to meet goals based on the above closing ratio?   _____

How many membership leads do you expect from member referrals?   _____

At what cost? (gifts, etc.) $ _____

How many membership leads do you expect from your web site?   _____

Proportionate cost? (i.e., 25% of web site cost) $ _____

How many membership leads do you expect from
mailing to past inquiries?   _____

What exactly will this cost?
    Postcard $ _____
    Brochure $ _____
    Letter $ _____
    Envelope $ _____
    Postage & Mailing $ _____
    Design/Creative $ _____
TOTAL $ _____

Now, add up the total number of membership leads. Is it enough to meet your goals? If yes, move to the next area. If not, include another tactic to increase the number of leads. (This could be the Legendary Marketing Membership Success Telemarketing Program, which typically generates at least 400 membership leads.)

Outings

How many total outing inquiries did you get last year?
(phone, Internet, referral, walk ins, e-mail, etc.)   _____

How many of them booked outings?   _____

Closing ratio?   _____

This year's goal for number of outings?   _____

Number of outing leads needed to meet goals based on the
above closing ratio?   _____

How many outing leads do you expect from repeat business?   _____

How many outing leads do you expect from referrals?   _____

At what cost? (gifts, etc.) $ _____

How many outing leads do you expect from your web site?   _____

Proportionate cost? (i.e., 25% of web site cost)   _____

How many outing leads do you expect from mailing
to past customers?   _____

What exactly will this cost?
    Postcard $ _____
    Brochure $ _____
    Letter $ _____
    Envelope $ _____
    Postage & Mailing $ _____
    Design/Creative $ _____
TOTAL $ _____

Add up the total number of outing leads. Is it enough to meet you goals? If yes, move to next section. If not, include another tactic to increase the number of outing leads. (This could be the Legendary Marketing Membership Success Telemarketing Program, which typically generates at least 400 outing leads.)

Banquets

How many total banquet inquiries did you get last year?
(phone, Internet, referral, walk ins, e-mail, etc.)   _____

How many of them booked banquets?   _____

Closing ratio?   _____

This year's goal?   _____

Number of banquet leads needed to meet goals based on the
above closing ratio?   _____

How many banquet leads do you expect from repeat business?   _____

How many banquet leads do you expect from referrals?   _____

At what cost? (gifts, etc.) $ _____

How many banquet leads do you expect from your web site?   _____

Cost? $ _____

How many banquet leads do you expect from mailing
to past customers?   _____

What exactly will this cost?
    Postcard $ _____
    Brochure $ _____
    Letter $ _____
    Envelope $ _____
    Postage & Mailing $ _____
    Design/Creative $ _____
TOTAL $ _____

Add up the total number of banquet leads. Is it enough to meet you goals? If yes, move to next section. If not include other tactics to increase the number of banquet leads.

Tee Time Bookings

How many people who call the shop actually book tee times?   _____

How many people who visit your web site book tee times?   _____

How often do your existing customers play your course in a year?   _____
    Examples:
        11,000 players 1 time   120 players 4 times
        4,000 players 2 times   87 players 5 times
         230 players 3 times   - and so on -

Average number of times a golfer plays your club?   _____

Total number of rounds divided by number of individual players?   _____

Based on the average number of times a golfer plays, how
many players do you need to attract to your club this year to
meet your financial goals?   _____

MARKETING EXPENSES

Newspaper Ads

Annual newspaper ad cost? $ _____

Number of coupons/offers redeemed?   _____

Dollar value of this business? $ _____

ROI   _____

Magazine Ads

Annual magazine ad cost? $ _____

Number of coupons/offers redeemed?   _____

Dollar value of this business? $ _____

ROI   _____

Yellow Pages Ads

Cost of Yellow Pages ads? $ _____

Dollar value of this business? $ _____

ROI   _____

Billboards

Cost of billboards? $ _____

Dollar value of this business? $ _____

ROI   _____

Postcards

Cost of postcards? $ _____

Dollar value of this business? $ _____

ROI   _____

Tee Time Bookings

Cost of sales letters $ _____

Dollar value of this business? $ _____

ROI   _____

Rack Cards

Cost of rack cards? $ _____

Dollar value of this business? $ _____

ROI   _____

Direct Mail Campaigns

Cost of direct mail campaign #1? $ _____

Dollar value of this business? $ _____

ROI   _____

Cost of direct mail campaign #2? $ _____

Dollar value of this business? $ _____

ROI   _____

Cost of direct mail campaign #3? $ _____

Dollar value of this business? $ _____

ROI   _____

Add up the totals. Is this enough leads to meet your green fee goals? If yes, move to next step. If not, add other tactics to generate enough leads.

Now, let's review a couple of web-based tactics you may have used to generate leads.

INTERNET MARKETING

Automatic Monthly Newsletter

e-newsletter #1 _____   e-newsletter #4 _____
   Impressions _____   Impressions _____
   Click-throughs _____   Click-throughs _____
   Bookings, inquiries _____   Bookings, inquiries _____

e-newsletter #2 _____   e-newsletter # 5 _____
   Impressions _____   Impressions _____
   Click-throughs _____   Click-throughs _____
   Bookings, inquiries _____   Bookings, inquiries _____

e-newsletter #3 _____   e-newsletter #6 _____
   Impressions _____   Impressions _____
   Click-throughs _____   Click-throughs _____
   Bookings, inquiries _____   Bookings, inquiries _____

e-newsletter #7 _____
    Impressions   _____
    Click-throughs   _____
    Bookings, inquiries _____

e-newsletter #8 _____
    Impressions   _____
    Click-throughs   _____
    Bookings, inquiries _____

e-newsletter # 9 _____
    Impressions   _____
    Click-throughs   _____
    Bookings, inquiries _____

e-news letter #10 _____
    Impressions   _____
    Click-throughs   _____
    Bookings, inquiries _____

e-newsletter #11 _____
    Impressions   _____
    Click-throughs   _____
    Bookings, inquiries _____

e-newsletter #12 _____
    Impressions   _____
    Click-throughs   _____
    Bookings, inquiries _____

Targeted e-blasts

Specific promotions that you used throughout the year to drive extra play:

E-blast promotion # 1
    Date   _____
    Offer   _____
    Impressions   _____
    Click-throughs   _____
    Bookings, inquiries _____

E-blast promotion # 2
    Date   _____
    Offer   _____
    Impressions   _____
    Click-throughs   _____
    Bookings, inquiries _____

E-blast promotion # 3
    Date   _____
    Offer   _____
    Impressions   _____
    Click-throughs   _____
    Bookings, inquiries _____

E-blast promotion # 4
    Date   _____
    Offer   _____
    Impressions   _____
    Click-throughs   _____
    Bookings, inquiries _____

E-blast promotion # 5
    Date   _____
    Offer   _____
    Impressions   _____
    Click-throughs   _____
    Bookings, inquiries _____

E-blast promotion # 6
    Date   _____
    Offer   _____
    Impressions   _____
    Click-throughs   _____
    Bookings, inquiries _____

E-blast promotion # 7
  Date _____
  Offer _____
  Impressions _____
  Click-throughs _____
  Bookings, inquiries _____

E-blast promotion # 8
  Date _____
  Offer _____
  Impressions _____
  Click-throughs _____
  Bookings, inquiries _____

E-blast promotion # 9
  Date _____
  Offer _____
  Impressions _____
  Click-throughs _____
  Bookings, inquiries _____

E-blast promotion # 10
  Date _____
  Offer _____
  Impressions _____
  Click-throughs _____
  Bookings, inquiries _____

E-blast promotion # 11
  Date _____
  Offer _____
  Impressions _____
  Click-throughs _____
  Bookings, inquiries _____

E-blast promotion # 12
  Date _____
  Offer _____
  Impressions _____
  Click-throughs _____
  Bookings, inquiries _____

NOTE: Collateral costs from brochures, creative, etc. should be divided by campaign. For example, 10,000 brochures cost a total of $7,000 (including printing, shipping and creative). Each time you use one for membership it costs 70 cents.

Using your data

Based on adding up the numbers on the worksheet from all of the typical marketing you do for your club, are you going to generate enough leads to meet your goals in each category?

Take a look at how many leads you are short in each category and increase your budget to match the anticipated response needed. (Or, increase your efficiency!)

For example, printing and mailing a postcard to a list of 10,000 golfers might cost $5,000. The anticipated response might be .5 percent if it's lead generation for membership.

That's generating 50 leads at a cost of $200 per lead. If you close one out of 10 leads for a $5,000 membership, you will have made $25,000. A very good ROI. If you close two out of 10 you will have made $50,000.

If you are just looking for daily play, the response will need to be much higher. This depends a great deal on the offer. Let's say you get a 5 percent response on a strong offer that would give you 500 leads at $40 a round. That would generate $20,000, another great ROI.

HOW TO PRODUCE MORE LEADS

Here are four ways to generate more leads:

- ✔ **Increase your closing ratio.** Easy to say, but it takes a commitment to training or an investment in developing better scripts and systems.

- ✔ **Increase the amount of money you generate from existing customers.** A no-brainer. Details on this will follow.

- ✔ **Increase the number of referrals you generate.** Another no-brainer.

- ✔ **Increase the amount of marketing you do.** There are many ways you can spend your existing marketing budget more effectively. Nevertheless, most clubs do not have a marketing budget in line with the number of leads they must generate to achieve their goals.

The most important aspect of your budgeting is actually outside the "budget" itself. It's finding methods that work most cost effectively. Armed with data that directly correlates money spent and money made, it's easy to justify increasing you marketing budget by ten, twenty, or even a hundred thousand dollars. It's also the reason why nearly all successful marketers use direct response advertising.

SUMMARY

Don't set your marketing budget based on an arbitrary number like five percent of gross. Set your marketing budget for the year based on performance. Base your budget on the financial goals you want to reach, not on a percentage of last year's income or some mythical number that someone in management happens to conjure up. Then work to make your performance more efficient so you exceed your marketing goals.

Chapter Six

Perfect Pricing

Few clubs take the time to determining exactly what their products and services are, what they could be, and what they intend to charge for them. Yet pricing is the area of marketing that offers the quickest and easiest way to dramatically increase your income in a very short period of time; therefore, it's one of the most exciting concepts.

There are only three ways to make more money, assuming your overhead is fixed.

- ✔ Attract a more new business

- ✔ Charge higher prices

- ✔ Get existing customers to buy more often

Many in the golf business look to others, their competitors, members, or boards to dictate pricing policy with little thought as to the long-term effect of these decisions. Perfect pricing is all about maximizing revenue. It's about making your product appealing to the largest segment of your particular market while leaving little or no money on the table. It is about creating a value proposition in your customer's mind.

The biggest mistake most clubs make is to underprice their green fees, joining fees, or membership dues. With excess capacity and competition in many areas, the temptation is to discount your fees. Don't get caught in that trap! By using the material in this book on setting yourself apart (your USP), and by adding value and service, you won't have to discount. Your goal should be to differentiate, not discount! That said, there will be times when special pricing is useful in order to maximize response to your marketing effort or to take into account different seasons and changes in your local market conditions.

In this chapter, you will discover:

- ✔ Why discounting is dangerous for all but one type of course
- ✔ When it's okay to discount
- ✔ How to discount without destroying your price point
- ✔ The most logical way to set your prices
- ✔ How to increase transactional business
- ✔ How to package for greater profits

RUSSIAN ROULETTE—PLAYING THE DISCOUNT GREEN FEE GAME!

Too many clubs think that the only way to react to their competitors is to cut prices. In the low-price game there is only one winner—the company that can sell at the lowest possible price. People who shop only by price have no loyalty. As soon as another course in town lowers prices, they switch and play somewhere else! In the retail business, low-cost stores like Woolworth's, Ridgeway, and Montgomery Ward are already gone even though their prices were low! Many of the rest are dying a long, slow death.

In the car business, Kia has won the low-price game at the expense of Yugo, Lada, Daewoo, and a host of other car companies you already don't remember! (Even Kia had problems and was bailed out of bankruptcy by Hyundai purchasing it.) You only have to look at the jokes about low price to know that's not where you want to be:

How do you double the price of a used Yugo?
Fill it with gas!

Now let's look at the top end of the car market: Ferrari, Porsche, Mercedes, Aston Martin, Maserati, Lamborghini, Rolls, Bentley, and the list goes on and on. Lots and lots of companies are not only surviving but, even in bad economies, enjoying some of their best years ever!!!

How can this be?

Because they are not selling on price! They are selling luxury, speed, sex, dependability, prestige, and other tangible and intangible concepts.

Now, back to golf...

Think about why you are in business. You shouldn't operate as an assembly line, pushing as many golfers through your course (or lessons) as possible. Instead, develop a value philosophy. (See the chapters on USP, Customer Service, and Experience.) How much is it worth to a golfer to be greeted by name? For staff to be sincerely happy to see him? Think of the service you receive at a fine restaurant. People can buy food in thousands of places but are willing to pay more for great ambience and service. Everyone wants to feel special. If you can do that for *your* customers, you can be their favorite upscale course.

In any discount war there can only be one winner, usually the business with the deepest pockets. When you're competing by discounting, you are overemphasizing price. Other intangibles like service and building relationships with customers are ignored. The more price becomes the focus of your club's marketing efforts, the less attention any other factor gets and price soon becomes the only dimension on which you are judged. Instead, look for other ways to get an edge over your discounting competitors—like service, ambiance, tournament history, great greens, food, follow up, quality, design, and fun.

By not focusing on factors that would differentiate you in your marketplace, you become a commodity judged solely on price. Discounting is easy!!! Being creative, REALLY increasing service, and building relationships is not! It takes time, it takes effort, it takes work! (A great deal of relationship building can be automated nowadays with your web site.)

Discounting works fine; in fact, it is a great strategy if...

- ✔ You have lower costs than all of your competitors. Is your club is paid for?!

- ✔ You have a much larger database of customers than your competitors.

- ✔ You have some kind of back-end strategy that will allow you to up-sell something else to your golfers once they've been to your course. A resort might give away golf to sell rooms. Myrtle Beach has been doing this for years! A real estate development may give away golf to sell lots or homes.

- ✔ You have much deeper pockets than your competitors and can wait a few years before you need to see a profit.

Obviously, I don't recommend discounting!

Before considering jumping into the discount game, do the math

First of all, your odds of long-term success are low. For instance, in the Orlando and West Palm Beach markets several clubs have closed in the past year and several more are about to. All were discounting heavily. Most were the lowest price in town.

There is usually only one winner in a discount war! If you are not absolutely certain it will be you, forget it!

Second, consider this, 100 clients at $25 is the same as 50 clients at $50, or 25 clients at $100. It's a lot easier to give great service to 25 golfers than to 100 and you make the same money with less wear and tear on the course. Is there another option that might net you the same profit other than discounting?

Third, have you exhausted all the possible positions and marketing strategies that would give you an edge in your marketplace without discounting? Like adding service, value, ambiance, and follow up! (See the chapters on USP, Service, and Creating a Legendary Experience.)

When is it okay to discount?

You can sometimes use cunning and guile to make your offer appear at least as good, albeit different, without discounting. For example, offer a two-for-one green fee at your regular rate but make the second round only usable in less popular time slots. You keep your price integrity in that the customer still paid the same 50 bucks like he always did. You may think I am splitting hairs but I assure you there is a significant psychological difference between paying $50 and getting a second round free or paying $25 twice. It's a difference that can have a huge effect on your club's future.

As you can tell, I'm against the growing practice in the golf industry of discounting yourself out of business, i.e., you log 40,000 rounds and lose $200,000 in the process. Discounting frequently destroys your club's price integrity in the marketplace. The $100 club only has to offer a $50 rate a few times before it's not regarded by the golfing public as a $100 club anymore.

Here are a few additional times when discounting is acceptable:

✔ Off-season you can discount without fear of destroying your price integrity. Everyone knows that golf in Florida and Arizona is cheap in July and August.

✔ You can discount when you have a legitimate reason for offering lower prices that is credible to your customer— like the greens have just been punched or it's cart path only!

✔ You can discount all you like if your positioning is to be the lowest price, highest volume club in town. Someone has to be the cheapest and as long as you can survive and make a profit taking this stand, so be it!

✔ You can discount anytime if you are making the money up-selling something else like rooms or real estate! But remember, one day the real estate will run out!

Do NOT get caught in the vicious circle of discounting just because the course down the street dropped their rate ten bucks! It's a suckers' game and one you cannot win unless being a low-priced course is your positioning—and even then you need low debt, low overhead, and deep pockets just to play the discounting game!

HOW TO COMPETE WITH DISCOUNTERS THROUGH VALUE-ADDED PRICING & PACKAGING

Before you even consider resorting to discounting, work on as many combinations of value-added pricing as possible.

The best way to compete with cheaper clubs is to offer clearly superior value. You charge more, but you're worth it for your kind of golfers. Note that you're not trying to appeal to everyone. You must have a clear position and communicate your advantages to your segment of the marketplace (for more, see the USP chapter).

Offer premiums rather than discounting

It is far better to hold your price integrity and "bribe" your customers with a free gift than to get caught in the downward spiral of discounting. Depending on your area and price point, some offers will undoubtedly work better than others. Track them all and see what works best.

- ✔ Free cart
- ✔ Free range balls
- ✔ Free lessons
- ✔ A dozen balls
- ✔ Free glove

- ✔ Golf cap
- ✔ Golf instructional video
- ✔ Free lunch
- ✔ Free dinner
- ✔ Free guest

(See the Promotions chapter for other ideas.)

Before jumping on eBay to sell your tee times to the "lowest bidder" consider your options. Get your staff involved; brainstorm for ideas.

The millionaire and the plumber

There is an old story about a millionaire who wakes up in the middle of the night to find his toilet overflowing and water seeping down the hallway. He goes to the phone and calls the first plumber in the book who offers 24-hour service. Fifteen minutes later the plumber arrives and is escorted straight to the offending bathroom. After quickly surveying the scene, he grabs a large wrench from his tool kit and slams it down on top of the pipe just behind the overflowing unit. With that, a loud gurgling sound is emitted and the water quickly disappears down the pipe and returns to its original level. The millionaire, amazed, thanks the man and asks for the bill. At once, the plumber says $500.

"That's outrageous," says the millionaire, "you just pulled that out of the air. All you did was hit that pipe with a wrench, it only took two minutes. I want an itemized bill."

"Certainly," says the plumber, reaching into his overalls for a pen and scribbling on a tattered invoice.

Emergency plumbing service itemized bill: "$5 for hitting the pipe with the wrench. $495 for the 20 years of training and experience that taught me where to hit it! Total $500."

The moral of the story, of course, is that you are selling value. If you market correctly, you can reap the type of rewards you truly deserve. Maybe you can raise your green fees and offer a bad-weather discount. That way, people pay more for a great day. Or if you're selling lessons you could offer a handicap-reduction package for a fixed price. Wouldn't some people pay $1000 to cut five strokes off their game? Or a club can offer a "lesson" round with the pro for three times the green fee and split with the pro.

PRICING YOUR PRODUCTS AND SERVICES

In order to run a successful business you must be able to price your products or service so that you can make a fair profit after expenses. There are a lot of different ways to do this. At my seminars, I am amazed that when I ask attendees why their courses charge the green fess they do, nobody ever seems to come up with what I would consider the right answer. I usually get answers like "That's what my market will bear" or, "That's what everybody else is charging." These answers *are* the way most courses (or pros) set their prices, but they are not the *best* way. You cannot ignore the fact of what your market will bear, or what other people may be doing in your market. But you should not let these considerations be the deciding factors in determining your prices.

How much do you want to make?

Most course owners are so focused on what everyone else is doing that they never stop to think what they should be doing to run their own businesses the way they prefer. They are letting others dictate their terms for them.

The first thing you should determine before asking the question, "How much should I charge for my product or service?" is, "How much money do I want to make?" Now, *this* is an interesting question. Instead of focusing the discussion on what everyone else in town is doing, let's start at the most important place, your place! What do you want to have happen? What do you want to earn?

Let's suppose, just for argument's sake, that you want to gross $2,000,000 a year. There are lots of different ways you can arrive at making that income. For instance, that's 100 rounds a day at $100 a round for 200 days a year. And that doesn't count banquets, food, and other income.

You should also consider the stress and hassle factors of dealing with an increasing number of employees and golfers. The lower your price, theoretically the higher your volume, but also the more maintenance and the employees you need. The higher your price, the more limited your market, but also the fewer employees you will need to offer superior service. (See the Budgeting chapter for more information on backwards-based budgeting.)

You set your own prices

Why do some golf pros charge $200 an hour and others $30? Why do some attorneys charge $100 an hour and others $500? Why do some accountants charge $40 an hour and others $200? Why do some stores sell a cotton dress at $40 and others at $400? In my seminars, whether the group is club owners or golf pros, I often make a point of asking what three or four of my audience charge. Let's say that a group of golf pros answered that they charge 40, 50, and 80 dollars an hour for lessons. My next question goes to the low man on the totem pole.

"Are you good at teaching?" I will ask.

"Yes," he will reply.

"Do you think then that Mr. Golf Pro over here charging $80 a hour is twice as good a teacher as you are?"

"No, I don't," he will reply.

"Then why is he making twice as much money as you?" Sometimes he will answer that it's the club, the area or some other factor, but for the most part, regardless of industry or profession, the dominant reason why one professional can charge more than another boils down to this: **That's what they decide to charge!**

WHEN TO RAISE PRICES

Raise your prices!

Through proper service, pricing and packaging, it's possible to significantly increase your income in a very short period of time by raising prices and offering extra value. This situation is made all the easier by the fact that most courses, golf schools, and resorts charge far less than they are really worth! After all, how long did it take you to gain the knowledge you now have? To build your course? To maintain it? Now spend some time to find the golfers who will appreciate what you offer—and will pay for it! (Part of the secret is to target the right type of players for your club, not just anyone who swings!)

There are two times to raise your prices. The first and most obvious time is when you are too busy or approaching capacity at your present price. This is the good old law of supply and demand. If you are at capacity and don't get too greedy, it surely will work. And it will give you more money and more time to plan your expansion.

The second time is when you want to differentiate yourself from others in your area or industry. The prices you charge relate to your quality and status in most golfers' minds. Find out what perceptions exist in your area for golf. Where are the price breaks in the minds of your prospects and clients? At what point does a high-end value become expensive? At what point does a low price encourage a perception of low quality? Where is the middle ground and what can you do to move to one end or the other?

How to raise dues

Many clubs are deathly afraid of raising prices for fear of losing what they already have, but rarely does this fear translate into a mass exodus, unless there are other problems. Members may bitch and complain, but few who were not going to leave anyway will quit if the cost of dues goes up 5 or 10 percent. (My club doubled it's dues last year and hardly anyone blinked!) Most people will simply accept price increases and after a couple of weeks of discussing the clubs shortcomings around the bar will go back to daily life. Even if a dozen people leave, the extra fees will still reap greater rewards, but let's look at how to soften the blow.

One way is a letter simply outlining where the operating costs have increased, or the proposed improvements you plan to make with the additional revenue. When people think they understand your motives, they tend to be more accepting of increases.

Another way I have used successfully is to invite members to pay their current rate for a year or in some cases more as long at they pay in full before a certain date, that is, lock in last year's rate by paying for next year in full by November 30th. Or take double advantage and pay for two years now!

There are of course more creative ways like this one from Todd Smith of Lynwood Lynks (no—that's not my spelling again!) One of the great rewards of dealing with 300 different clubs on a daily basis is the feedback and ideas that you get from clients. Todd's creative letter to sell annual memberships not only grabbed my attention but also delighted everyone at my office.

He sent a letter to his annual pass holders as usual asking them to renew but instead of the usual 10 percent discount for acting before November 30th he came up with a much more clever idea. The headline says it all.

Join Before November 30th And If It Snows On
Christmas Day, Your Membership Is Free!

Now here is the clever bit; he took out insurance against it snowing which cost him just 8 percent of the annual membership! (To avoid all controversy, it had to snow a certain amount and be documented by the National Weather Center at the Moline, Illinois facility!) BRILLIANT!

INCREASING THE SIZE OF THE AVERAGE TRANSACTION

It's not even necessary to raise prices in order to make far greater profits. In some cases it's just about increasing the average sale. Your player pays a $65 green fee. You hand him back a ONE-DAY-ONLY gift certificate worth $10 off any shirt in the shop. For convenience, let's say the average shirt is marked $40 and you paid $20 for it. If you sell four shirts typically on a Saturday, you make $80 profit. With the gift certificate, you sell 15 and make $150 profit.

How to raise big money instantly

Do you have a low-end course and need $100,000 for course improvements? Simply offer ten lifetime memberships at $15,000 instead of your yearly $1800. Have a higher-end course? Sell five lifetime membership at $50,000 and you just raised $250,000 without going to the bank!!! It sounds simplistic because it is, but it works if you package the deal right.

GETTING CUSTOMERS TO BUY MORE OFTEN

Let's say your most profitable source of business is daily fee players. If you had good data, you would know how many rounds each player at your club played last year. This data is a very important tool in helping you price your rounds. Surveys like the ones included on our SmartSites also help you by telling you how many rounds a player plays and at what other courses.

Let's say I played 15 times at $50 per round. The first time I stand in front of you at your golf shop counter this year, you sell me a $1,000 pass to play 20 times or even 30 times. Your income from me has increased at the very least by 25 percent and that's without counting carts, beer, and balls! A single sale to me could easily result in 50 percent greater revenue on the first day of the season if it is a custom package that appeals to my needs—my needs as an individual player. And therein lies another great and often over looked truth— you build a successful business one sale at a time.

MEMBERSHIP FEES—TO BE OR NOT TO BE?

Another common practice among clubs trying to sell memberships is to discontinue the joining fee! In the majority of cases this is a big mistake! Instead of doing away with the $5000 joining fee they should instead send out a mailing with a $5,000 check towards joining enclosed. You may think I'm splitting hairs but the difference between the two strategies in customer perception is often staggering.

REFER FOR A FEE

If you are constantly asked for a service you cannot or don't want to provide, set up a network of other clubs in your area and charge a referral fee or a booking fee of 10 or 15 percent for sending the business to them. This works very well when you are doing a good job of booking outside events, wedding and banquets. Why not develop a relationship with a competitor and hand your extra business off to them for a 15% booking fee instead of just telling the customer you are booked? I have one client that made an extra $20,000 last year by doing exactly this, booking events at other courses on days where his was already booked!

KEEP TESTING PRICES AND PACKAGING

Test, test, test and keep testing offers, bonuses and value-added promotions to increase the number of players who come and the average spent by your players. If you do 40,000 rounds, and the average spend is $6, an increase of just 10 percent will result in $24,000 more in income. And remember—golfers are already your customers. It costs you nothing to collect the extra revenue.

A NOTE ON PRICING PHILOSOPHY

When running price promotions, you must sit down and consider how you can use the promotion to make more money, not just increase traffic. If you discount, how will you make a fair profit margin back? Can you expect to make it up by selling additional full-priced items? Will you lower the perceived value of your memberships, rounds, and so on?

When it comes to packaging and pricing, it's very, very important that you don't get caught up in the trap of doing what you've always done. Because if you do what you've always done, you'll get what you always got. Don't follow the herd in your industry. Set prices based on what you want to make and the value you are willing to offer. Consider the multitude of different packages and prices you could offer to get where you want to go. Then narrow your offerings down to no more than three clear options at one time.

SUMMARY

In general, I recommend that you not price discount except in very controlled circumstances. For instance, in the off season. Or offering free weekday rounds with weekend promotions. An ideal promotion will increase your income without cheapening you in the long term. Look for ways to add value to your memberships, daily play, and outings, so that you are not reducing the dollars you take in. Involve your vendors in special events and discounts. Create so many interesting goings on at your club that people always feel they received more value and entertainment than they paid for.

Chapter Seven

Developing a Legendary USP
(Unique Selling Proposition)

How important is a USP? So important that without a great one your golf business will always be an "also-ran."

The Unique Selling Proposition (USP) was first described more than 50 years ago in the classic book by Rosser Reeves, *Reality in Advertising*. While given much lip service, the concept of USP is seldom understood or operationalized well. Reeves said that your USP must meet three criteria to be complete and powerful:

- ✔ It must say to your consumer, "Buy this and you will receive this specific benefit."

- ✔ Your USP must be one that your competition does not, or cannot, offer.

- ✔ It must be strong enough to attract new customers to you.

Your USP is the basis for your marketing and advertising efforts. It is your unique advantage you use to sell your club, your lessons, outings, and so forth. Your USP should be so strong and memorable that it will both distinguish you from other clubs *and* attract new business. It should also be memorable enough to generate word of mouth to drive referrals. Some select courses have obvious and powerful USPs: Augusta—the Masters course; Saint Andrews—the home of golf; or Pebble Beach—unique coastal beauty. Since your course is likely to be among the 99 percent that are less famous than the few like Augusta, you'll need to work harder to develop your USP.

In this chapter, you will discover:

- ✔ Why your USP is so important to lower your costs and increase your income
- ✔ Why most courses have no USP
- ✔ How to develop possible USPs
- ✔ How to gather input for your USP development
- ✔ Formulas for possible USPs
- ✔ Sample USPs
- ✔ How to test your USP for effectiveness
- ✔ How to best use your USP

LEGENDARY USP

No matter who you are or where your course is located, your club's reputation precedes you in your market. The more positive and solid your reputation for whatever your unique selling proposition is, the easier it will be for you get players, members, students, or outings. More players will seek you out, pay you more money, and happily refer you to others.

While some clubs have taken decades to build their legacies and reputations, others have done it much faster. In today's world of the Internet, direct mail, and targeted magazines for every audience, the opportunity to build a reputation quickly has never been greater. The challenge is to accurately define your unique selling proposition (USP)—the essence of what your club offers that is superior and unique.

DON'T BE A "ME-TOO" CLUB

Most managers have never heard of a USP. And while a select few instinctively emphasize their uniqueness, *most clubs have done nothing to set themselves apart in the marketplace.* Except for custom pictures, you could take one of these clubs' names out of their ads and replace it with a competitor's and the ad would be just as accurate.

The importance of accepting this challenge to differentiate yourself from your competition is that without a USP you can waste millions of dollars marketing the features of your golf club—features that every other club also has, or that no one cares about. You will be another me-too club with 18 holes, a pro shop, and a driving range.

By taking the USP challenge, you will, with a few words and concepts, set yourself apart from all of your competition. You will find yourself more focused and your message more on target, while attracting a far greater number of the right type of players for you.

Let me give you a clear example of what I mean. Pebble Beach sells a once-in-a-lifetime experience, not a round of golf! Using some non-golf examples, a Saturn dealer and a Rolls Royce dealer both sell cars, but they are hardly in the same business. A Saturn dealer sells transportation; a Rolls dealer sells luxury. A Timex dealer sells watches that tell time; a Rolex dealer sells jewelry and status.

Most clubs don't have a USP and therefore they don't ever build a strong marketing program on a secure foundation. Instead they bounce from idea to idea without a consistent theme. In fact, I've had clients who proudly showed me the twenty different ads they had run over the last five years—each touting something different! This approach wastes lots of time, lots of money, and a great deal of effort!

In order for your club to attract the maximum number of prime clients in your market, you must determine exactly whom you are trying to reach and what message from you will resonate with them. Then you must shape your club's performance to deliver this unique experience.

"RESTRICTING" YOUR MARKET

You might argue that if you focus your club on one USP, you will limit your market, but, that, my friends, is the very idea. *You focus your market on the people who value the one thing your club can do best.* Then you harp on it for all you are worth and develop your own niche market within a much broader category.

It turns out that this new focus doesn't limit you as much as it attracts more play. Your USP also produces a tag line on your business card, a slogan on the bottom of your ads, and is attached to your name like a double-barreled surname (the club where the pros play; the hardest course in town; the club for family play; the highest-rated course in town; the most water; the most exclusive, and so on).

Without a position around which to build your marketing, you are just another commodity that no one thinks is special! With a strong USP, you lower your marketing costs, increase word of mouth, focus your efforts to do a better job for your golfers, and increase your income.

What comes to mind when you hear Domino's Pizza? "Domino's delivers in 30 minutes or less." That was their unique selling proposition and it fueled one of the most rapid business success stories ever. Domino's wasn't really selling pizza, what they were selling was fast delivery. There are hundreds of different chains around the country that sell pizza. But when you think of Domino's, you think of of their 30-minute delivery guarantee. You might be interested to know that those ads haven't run in over a decade, ever since a driver was killed trying to get his pizza delivered on time. Yet the 30-minutes-or-less perception remains because that 30-minute USP was so strong!

The same is true in the shipping business. There's UPS, there's the US Postal Service, DHL, and a host of other services that claim to get your package delivered directly to your customer, across the country, overnight. But when you absolutely, positively must have it there overnight, whom would you use? If you said the Post Office, move to the back of the class! (They lose 100,000 packages a day!) If you absolutely, positively must have it there overnight, the only company to use is FedEx. That perception has survived even through their name change from Federal Express. They have a legendary reputation for fast and reliable delivery and practically own the word "overnight." You must do the same—own a concept in your marketplace that defines what your club is all about. This will attract people to you like a magnet!

USP DRIVES INCOME AND OPPORTUNITIES

Why can Doral or Pebble Beach get plenty of players to pay several hundred dollars a round? Because they are among the world's best courses you say? While Pebble boasts spectacular ocean-front scenery, if the truth be known, Doral is a pretty average golf course, yet they can still command almost $300 a round. Why? Because it's the "Blue Monster" that's why! Because they have water on 14 holes and some very clever guy early on dubbed it "The Blue Monster!"— despite the fact that the water isn't a real hazard on more than half the holes!

It doesn't matter! Doral has done a brilliant job of getting people to believe that when in Miami, it's the place to play and stay. Sure they had some help from the PGA Tour, but there are plenty of second-rate courses that host PGA events that you or I would never dream of playing, let alone paying $300 to play! Think Eagle Trace—that has lots of water, was home to the PGA Tour's Honda Classic for many years, yet stands for nothing. You see my point. Despite the fact that they host a PGA Tour event, no one is going to pay $300 to play there!

WORLD'S LEADING TEACHER?

Marketing is not merely having a great layout or teaching talent! You need to **own** a key thought in a player's mind so that when he picks up the phone to call three buddies to go play this weekend he's already thinking about your course!

Who is the world's leading expert on the "short game?" Tiger Woods—he's pretty good? Jack Nicklaus—he's got the wins to back up almost any claim, but, no, bunker shots and chipping were never Jack's strong suit. Perhaps it would be a really great player like Moe Norman was, who never played the Tour because he didn't like all the publicity? No, I think not. In fact, the person generally regarded as the world's leading expert on the short game is an ex-NASA scientist who rarely if ever breaks eighty!

Does that bother you? It bothers many of my PGA friends, but it shouldn't because Dave Peltz is first and foremost a master marketer and that is what it's all about.

Marketing! Selling your uniqueness!

How did Dave Peltz, amateur enthusiast for many decades, with no particular talent for the game, became the world's leading expert on the short game?

Dave Peltz did several very interesting things to build his Unique Selling Proposition:

✔ He used his NASA background to gain credibility for his golf theories.

✔ He wrote a book—always a great start to building credibility.

✔ He noticed that while there were plenty of swing gurus pushing a method, no one seemed to be focusing on the area of the game that offered the greatest potential return in terms of score, the short game!

✔ He told everyone who would listen that he was the world's new short-game expert and that he—unlike others—had approached the problem scientifically!

✔ He wrote magazine articles on his theory.

Bingo! Dave Peltz, a 50-something ex-NASA employee with no teaching credentials, no tour players winning majors in his stable (when he started), and no personal playing history out-marketed 50,000 other golf instructors because of his superior USP.

SOME USP EXAMPLES

Let's look at some more examples by studying the USPs of two of the top equipment companies. To see what kind of job they are doing, take a simple test to see if you can match the companies' USPs with their names.

What company's equipment is:

For Those Who Want To Play Their Best!

The Number One Ball In Golf!

If you answered Ping and Titleist, kudos to you, and to the companies as well—their marketing stayed in your mind (and in a great percentage of other players' minds).

Interestingly enough, *Ping For Those Who Want to Play Their Best!* is a good slogan, but not a USP! Originally Ping had some technological differences which they could use to back up a claim that they improved your game (differential weighting, heel-toe weighting, and so on). However, they've lost that uniqueness. Because their slogan was catchy, it is still useful; but everyone wants to play their best, so it is not a good USP.

Titliest, The Number One Ball In Golf! Simple and tough to argue with!

Now tell me what does Yonnex stand for...quick...come on... Okay, they did have a little run about 20 years ago with a graphite-headed driver, but now what? What have they done for me lately?

For most of the last decade, Yonnex had one thing going for them—the world's undisputed best left-handed golfer. (Kudos to Mike Weir, but I'm talking Phil here!) I spent almost a year trying to convince them that their USP should be *"The world's best left-handed golf clubs."* Statistically 10 percent of the 27 million people who play golf are left handed. (In Canada, a greater percentage of the population is left handed, but I digress.) No one in the world had ever claimed to be the world's best left-handed golf clubs, so the position was open!

AN OPEN UNIQUE SELLING PROPOSITION in this over-crowded marketing world!!!!

This is a serious marketing opportunity!!! But the wise people of Yonnex thought that .000000001 percent share, or whatever they have of the right-handed market, was better than total DOMINATION of the left-handed market!! They just couldn't see pigeonholing their market like that!!!

Why be the undisputed leader in a US market of 3 million left-handers, and a worldwide market of 30 million or so, when instead you can be a nobody in the worldwide market of 150 million right-handers?

Okay, so you get the idea. Let's get back to talking about *your* club and *your* marketing.

WHAT DO YOU WANT <u>YOUR</u> CLUB'S REPUTATION TO SAY?

The first step in building a legendary reputation in your community is to determine how you want people in the marketplace to perceive your club. Your USP will be the basis for getting your marketing message across and building your reputation. It will be what they remember about you and pass on to others. It will be the foundation on which all your marketing is based, from your web site to your customer-service training!

If you have a strong and memorable position in golfers' minds, it will carry over into other areas. They will also think you are good in other ways.

In contrast, if you try to advertise your club as all things to all people, they will think you're a "Jack of all trades and a master of none." A strong USP doesn't limit you, it opens up your options!

Throughout this discussion, I will continually emphasize that you must pick one USP and stick to it. However, if you have distinctly different audiences, it *is* possible to have different USPs for each audience. For instance, individual golfers are a different audience than members or outing planners. Your members may be most interested in the status of the club as a place to bring business associates. Day players may be most interested in a challenging (or nonchallenging!) course. And outing buyers may be most interested in price, or doing minimum work while looking good for their bosses! If you know your submarkets, you *may* develop different USPs aimed at each group. Of course they should not be contradictory.

HOW TO DEVELOP YOUR USP

There are several factors to consider when designing your USP. The best way to start is to gather input from your staff and golfers. If possible, get your staff together and ask them as a group to come up with individual words or phrases that define your club. Make a list of at least 10 to 20 key words or statements. Do the same thing with your customers, either in a group (like the board) or individually. You could even send out a quick e-mail to members asking them what they think the best thing about your club is. Ways to ask about a USP include phrases like:

- ✔ Our members tell us that what they like best about us is

  _____ .

- ✔ We are the only course in our area that does

  _____ .

- ✔ We are the best course/club because _____ .

- ✔ The thing we are proudest of is _____ .

- ✔ We're better than anyone else at _____ .

- ✔ The thing people remember us for is _____ .

- ✔ The most unusual thing about us is _____ .

If you heard people talking behind your back about your club, what strengths of yours would you want them to be mentioning?

What is it about your course that people use to describe you (the quality of the course, the history, the status, the exclusivity, the value, the pricing, the attentive customer service, the scenery, the ambiance)? Specifically, what is it that your club does better than anybody else, or what is it that you have to offer that no one else can offer?

Try to avoid generic answers like quality or value. You can't be everything to everyone. You should therefore select one main perception that you want to convey in your marketplace, and back it up with a couple of subsidiary points.

Take some time to carefully consider the questions and write down your answers. Even "silly" answers can sometimes stimulate useful material. For instance, if your club has a nickname it may suggest a USP (like the Blue Demon).

Normally, the answers to these questions will involve your golf course. But they could also involve your people, your general location, your price or value, your service, your clubhouse, your restaurant, and so on.

After you have collected information, develop variations and combinations and narrow the list down to three or four of the very best possibilities. Once they have been defined, these answers should be synthesized into a possible defining statement. This may take you a while, and that's okay. This is much too important a decision to rush, but make sure you follow through and come up with just a single sentence, preferably one that offers a clear benefit to the customer.

Focus on one key trait!

Let's take the golf pro as an example. Is a golf professional in the golf business, the service business, the entertainment business, the retail business, the instructional business, or something else? Your answer to this question can have a serious impact on marketing decisions, customer perceptions, customer satisfaction, and your reputation.

At a typical country club, the golf pro may be in all of the above businesses, but sales and marketing decisions must be based on a single underlying philosophy. No one since Tommy Armour (several decades ago) has had a reputation as a great champion and also as a great teacher. It's equally tough to have great member service and play a lot of golf. You can't play a tough guy and a comic at the same time, just ask Sylvester Stallone. Every movie in which he didn't put up his dukes or didn't blow up half the world flopped!

Cadillac keeps trying to make smaller and cheaper cars and loses millions in the process every time! Remember the Catera? Don't worry, neither does anybody else despite a $100-million ad campaign! Cadillac means big and luxurious, not small and sporty. They would have had better results if they sold their smaller sports cars under another brand, a strategy Toyota used very successfully with Lexus for the opposite reason. I mean, who in their right mind was going to buy an $80,000 Toyota? The Toyota branding of inexpensive and reliable was too strong.

Speaking of branding, lately some of the discussion about these USP issues has also been in terms of *branding*. You brand your club, and so forth. Another concept closely related to USP is *positioning*. Positioning focuses a bit more on you compared to the competition, not on your uniqueness. For our purposes here, however, both positioning and branding mean the same thing as USP.

You will only be remembered in one key area, with perhaps a couple of subthoughts at most. Once you choose that area, you must use as it as your central focus in making future decisions. This means focusing on one particular area and spending less time and effort on others.

It's very important that you decide what your image should be in the golf community. If you try to be everything to everybody, it won't work. And once you have developed your reputation label, it's nearly impossible to shed it. Good or bad, your reputation ultimately will depend on a few words, so choose the statement that represents your club wisely for it will stick with you for a long time.

MORE USP EXAMPLES

Cleveland makes fine irons and, I am sure, great woods, but when I think "Cleveland," what comes to mind? Putters? No. Wedges! Great wedges! Wedges that PGA Tour players use! Cleveland built its reputation on wedges and parlayed it into something more, but without their success and recognition for wedges they were just another second-tier company. Their positioning as the maker of the best wedges gave them the leg up that they needed.

Let me give you a personal example: I am the world's leading authority on golf marketing. There are several reasons that I can make that statement and not blush:

- ✔ I wrote the only book in the world on how to market golf on the Internet. (And, obviously, I've written this book.)

- ✔ I have delivered more than 100 full-day seminars on golf marketing for the PGA, the Golf Course Owners Association, Club Managers Association, and others.

- ✔ I have written a book on how to make money teaching golf.

- ✔ I have over 20 years experience in marketing.

- ✔ I have hundreds of testimonials from people who will back up my statement that I am, in fact, the world's foremost authority on golf marketing—or at least the best person they know.

- ✔ I have a track record of success on which to draw with a very diverse range of hundreds of golf clients.

✔ I am a scratch player with a passion for the game, so I can talk your language.

✔ Most importantly, no one else has claimed this position; therefore, on top of everything else, I win by default!

My company could do marketing work for lots of other types of businesses, but we don't. We just do golf, and because of that focus and commitment our business has grown 800 percent in two years!

Common (though faulty) wisdom will tell you that a market of everyone is better than a market of just one type of client. Common wisdom is wrong! The same is true for your club. The more clearly you define what you're all about, even at the exclusion of some types of players, the quicker your marketing will pay dividends.

"Central Florida's Best Greens"

Here's an example of one of the USPs we developed and how we came up with it.

Stoneybrook West is not the best golf course in Orlando; it doesn't have the best holes, has little or no elevation, and is surrounded by homes. That is not to say it's a bad golf course; it's just that it's a lot like every other golf course in Orlando. We needed an edge. After brainstorming with head pro Ian Shepherd, he came up with a list out of which we crafted the statement "Orlando's Best Greens." We later modified this to "Central Florida's Best Greens." This has worked out very well for several reasons.

✔ People from out of town want to have good greens above anything else so it helped attract out-of-town play.

✔ Since we made the claim "Orlando's Best Greens," media (including the *Orlando Sentinal* and two local golf magazines) all chose to use that as headlines for articles they wrote about the course (which is nice)!

✔ No one else claimed to have the "Best Greens" so we were first in the market to do so, making it very hard for anyone else to take that title away from us.

"Michigan's Most Beautiful Resort"

Garland Resort in Northern Michigan had plenty to shout about with four great courses, natural beauty, cross-country skiing, and a host of other activities, but nothing was pulling the marketing message together. We solved the problem by designating Garland as Michigan's Most Beautiful Resort! Everyone enjoys beauty whether it's golfers, riders, skiers, diners, meeting planners, or families!

SOME COMPONENTS OF USPs

Here are some other ideas to get your creative juices flowing.

Preempting the truth for your USP

While it's better if the USP you design is something nobody else can claim, it's not essential. You can choose to highlight some aspect of your club that your competitors may also possess but have failed to exploit. By being first, you lay claim to the particular benefit that you're promoting. Jack Trout and Al Ries, the originators of the term positioning, call this "preempting the truth."

Miller Brewing Company built its business on 'lite beer,' but they didn't invent the category. Coors did that more than a decade earlier. But Coors failed to position its beer as a light beer, and lost out to Miller (who exploited the position to the tune of hundreds of millions). You don't have to invent it; you merely have to claim it!

Back when courses like Pine Hill or Pine Barrens in New Jersey were both among the best public courses in the world, either could

Four magnificent courses to choose!

Monarch

Swampfire   Reflections   Fountains

Visit Our Website For A Free Round Of Golf At Garland, Michigan's Most Beautiful Resort.

"Quite simply, it's the best combination of golf, accommodations & value in Michigan!"
– Ken Mehall, Kalamazoo, MI

Visit PlayGarland.com, fill out the online survey and then discover why people travel from around the world to seek out and play Ron Otto designed courses, which is lucky for us, since we have four. In fact, this reclusive genius designed only four courses before retiring to universal acclaim.

At Garland You Can Play Them All! With four of the most beautiful and well conditioned championship golf courses in the nation, Garland offers guests an exceptional golfing experience.

The natural backdrop of 3,500 acres of unspoiled wilderness provides a perfect setting for our four courses, Fountains, Swampfire, Monarch, and Reflections. Ron Otto's sweat and blood are in Garland's soil. He personally designed and oversaw construction of every yard of our 72 holes, and his passion and dedication can be seen in every inch. Each hole has its own unique character and design including rolling meadows, lakes, streams, mature hardwoods, and dramatic elevation changes. These innovative designs offer a variety of challenges to delight golfers of all abilities, while multiple sets of tees allow each player to select a distance that best suits their game.

Visit our website NOW!

Visit www.PlayGarland.com For Your Free Round of Golf

GARLAND
R E S O R T

The USP "Michigan's Most Beautiful Resort" brought together Garland's many multi-seasonal activities.

have been positioned as "The Second Best Course in New Jersey, But the Best One You Can Actually Play!" (You don't even have to claim to be best to have a great USP.)

Standing out from the crowd

Let's say that you are one of ten daily-fee courses in town. You have a typical 18-hole, par-72 golf course. It's better than some, not as good as others. How are you going to make your mark?

First, look at what your competitors are doing—what do they specialize in? Take a look at their web sites, brochures, print ads, Yellow Pages ads, and any other literature you can find to determine what positions they are claiming. Fortunately for you, in most cases there will be nothing significant! However, their random claims may give you a few ideas and help you spot their weaknesses.

Have you got a great skins game Friday afternoons? I know several courses whose success is due to the number of players who show up on specific days to play in games. Encouraging such games can turn a mediocre course into a winner! **"Home of the best games in town!"**

Is your course amenable to a fast-paced round? **"Play in under 4 hours or your money back!"** That's a bold statement, but I'll tell you what—I'd pay an extra $10 to get that guarantee. With the right course, proper instructions to the players upon check in, and a good ranger program, it can be done! If you took over four hours to play a round in Scotland—and that's without the aid of a cart—they'd hang you from a lamppost!

When I lived in Southern California, I used to ski in Big Bear where I had the choice of two resorts. Both were more or less on the same mountain and one was ten dollars a day more than the other was. Where would you ski? I skied Snow Summit, the more expensive of the two.

Why? Because they limited ticket sales and had a 10-minute lift-line guarantee! If you were not on a lift in 10 minutes they gave you a ticket for another day free! It never happened. The two or three times I tried the cheaper place, Bear Mountain, I waited as long as 30 minutes to get up the mountain—NO THANKS!

Think about the free publicity you could get, **"Just say NO to 4 hour rounds!"** Think T-shirts, *Golf Digest* reporters at your door, and a big pat on the back from the USGA. You could run different types of speed tournaments and marathons. Or charge people on slow days by how long they spend out on the course! In fact, the promotion possibilities are endless.

Does this exclude certain people from playing your course? YES, SLOW PLAYERS, players who eat up your daylight, and upset the 20 groups behind them!! GOOD RIDDANCE!! The extra space and publicity will more than make up for the loss of Bernard Langer disciples who play slower than wounded snails!

Okay, I'm on a roll. Let's say your course is the worst of the ten aforementioned competitors. What then? *Don't* market the course as your key feature! Market something else. When the new GM of the New Jersey Nets basketball team took over in the mid-Nineties, he had on his hands the very worst team in the NBA. Not only did they have a terrible winning record, but the players had bad attitudes and the few fans who did show up hated them! So how did the new GM manage to go from a stadium that was not even half full to selling out every game in just a few months—while the team continued to play as badly as ever?

Brilliance, that's how! Brilliance and a change in his Unique Selling Proposition. He stopped trying to sell his team. It was pointless— the Nets were terrible and everyone knew it! He couldn't change the team play without some serious personnel changes and time to work on things. But he could change the USP and turn the team into a profitable business instead of a money pit. Instead of marketing *his* team, he started to market the stars of the opposition teams!

Come see Michael Jordan and the Chicago Bulls!

Shaq and The LA Lakers!

Larry Bird and the Celtics!

In his favor was the fact that many of the stars he was promoting were nearing the ends of their careers, so he added some of that into the mix. *"This might be your last chance to see Jordan play in New Jersey!"*

He bundled the good games into packages of five, tripled the ticket prices for those games and threw in all the mediocre games for free. He sold out the stadium in a matter of weeks while the Nets continued their mediocre play. But it didn't matter—he was no longer selling his team. He was instead selling the superstars on the *opposing teams* as the reason to come to the game.

Brilliant!

Your USP doesn't have to relate to your course

So, what can we do to help the worst course in town in our earlier example come up with a USP? Change the focus from golf to something else. Here are a few extreme examples to stimulate your thinking.

Consider the USP "An Ordinary Course Where We Treat You Like Royalty." How can you treat customers like royalty when you only charge $25 a round? How about offering a free car wash while golfers play! That's a nice touch that saves the player time and fifteen bucks, while it only costs you two guys on minimum wage! Picture this: a guy wakes up thinking, where should I play today? Umm...well, the car needs washing, let's go to YOUR CLUB!!!

Here's another idea. Turn the 19th hole into a haven of golf memorabilia, like a theme restaurant. Then people will bring their friends just to look at all the cool stuff you have on the walls. (This can be done fairly cheaply.)

Make your 19th hole the best place in town to hang out after a round. Satellite TVs, free salsa and chips, a waitress with large..., well, you get the idea!

I know some country clubs that make it on the strength of their junior swim team! Anything that makes you outstanding can make you a winner.

TESTING YOUR USP

Like other parts of your marketing, your USP can be tested. You can use focus groups to compare different USPs. You can use surveys. You can test headlines in e-mails using different USPs. You can test USPs as direct mail or advertising headlines. Just don't fall in love with the first clever idea someone comes up with. As famous advertising man David Ogilvy used to say, you don't want your ads to win awards for creativity, you want them to make you money!

YOUR USP STRENGTHENS YOUR MARKETING MESSAGE

With a USP in mind, your logo, ads, web site, brochures, and other marketing material can all be designed in a very cohesive manner. This is called integrated marketing, where your different pieces reinforce a consistent marketing message and convince, rather than confuse, the customer.

All too often, course owners bounce from one message to the next, hoping in vain to be everything to everyone. It doesn't work. Once you have decided to be a tough course for serious players, don't shoot for women and seniors—stay focused. Develop your campaigns around strong images. Use strong colors that carry the feel of your USP throughout everything you do!

Confused prospects do not make good customers because confusion causes doubt. Doubt leads to fear of making a poor decision, and fear leads to paralysis or procrastination. Use your USP as a roadmap for your marketing materials. When completing any new marketing tool, ask yourself the following simple questions.

Are the graphics and copy congruent with your message?

A client recently brought me a marketing piece in which he claimed in his copy to offer both the finest and the cheapest service in town. But you cannot be the cheapest and the best. People simply won't buy that concept. They have been preconditioned to believe that the best of anything is always more expensive. The cheapest may offer good value, but you hurt your credibility, never to regain it, if you also try to claim that you are the best! The best is never the cheapest. On the other side, words claiming that you are the best club in town would not be supported by printed material that was cheap looking.

Does it enhance your position in the minds of your customers?

Check if each marketing effort stands out and brands your course's name clearly and uniquely in the minds of your prospective customers. If it's only as good as anyone else's effort, don't do it.

Stand out and be bold—or save your money and invest it in bonds!

Is your delivery consistent?

With your marketing materials in complete harmony and building on your USP, the next question to ask yourself is how consistent you are in delivering your message. In many cases, business owners develop a winning concept and then become bored with it, thinking that others must surely have tired of the concept as well. So they move on to a different and far less effective concept, just as the other one was taking root in the public consciousness.

In my golf consulting, I frequently design ads for clients that they instantly proclaim to be the most effective they have ever used. Eight weeks later, they are back on the phone asking me to design a new one, even through the original one is still pulling far better than anything else they have ever done. I ask them why they want a new ad.

They tell me because everyone has seen it already. Good ads can go on working indefinitely. Sure, you might rest them for a few weeks and then bring them out again, or perhaps change the picture, keeping the copy much the same, but the fact remains that a good ad will work far longer than most people have the patience to keep running it!

Consistency is the key to building a long-term image that allows you to dominate your marketplace. Most great marketing campaigns last for years, even decades, as has the Marlboro cowboy, the Energizer Bunny, the twins in Wrigley's Double Mint Gum ads, and Budweiser, the King of Beers.

I'm sure that in your town you can think of at least one particular business that has made an impression on you just because they are so consistent, even if their marketing is consistently bad. The Crazy Greek Mattress Shop, the car dealer who always wears a ten-gallon hat on late-night TV, or the attorney who pitches injury law with a cast on his leg. Consistency is no substitute for great marketing, but great marketing done with consistency will produce the best results of all.

SUMMARY

Trying to be everything to everyone is a sure way NOT to conquer your market. You must decide on what your core business is and build a unique selling proposition around what you do best. To define your USP you must answer at least two questions:

✔ What is the word or statement you want to "own" in the minds of your customers?

✔ What one thing do you do better than anyone else around?

Once you have answered these questions and decided on a USP, you must stay focused and use your position as a guide to both marketing issues and business decisions.

You must make your marketing congruent with your USP message so it builds and grows in the minds of your customers. Finally you must remain consistent *within* your marketing message. Resist the temptation to change for change's sake. Once you find a good marketing message, ride it for all it's worth, over and over again, until it's burnt into the collective consciousness of all the players in your market.

Chapter Eight

Legendary Lead Generation

The most important information that you will ever have is the contact data (names, addresses, phone numbers, and e-mail addresses) of your customers and potential customers. This is true whether you are selling daily fee golf, memberships, resorts, or real estate.

Marketing to your existing customers is ALWAYS the single most profitable and cost effective way to boost your business. Instead of this relatively simple task of collecting and storing data, many golf clubs would rather spend $50,000 a year running coupons and ads trying to get new clients.

Take a golf club that does 40,000 rounds a year. How many names and addresses do they typically have in their computers—30,000, 20,000, or at least 10,000? Wrong. Despite the fact that many clubs have been doing 40,000 rounds a year for decades, the average club has a pitiful 3,000 names in their database and less than 1,000 good e-mails. (Most of these have never been mailed to anyway.) You must focus your energy on generating the largest possible list of golfers in your area as quickly as possible. That means getting their names, addresses, phone numbers, and e-mails plus whatever other data you can glean on their playing habits.

Ten thousand names is a start; 20,000 is better. Aim for 50,000 or more if you are in a metro area or are a destination-type facility. Once you have this data you are OFFICIALLY in control of your own destiny.

If you are really serious about marketing your club successfully, collecting names is the key. It will increase your sales and reduce your long-term marketing costs. Once your mailing list and e-mail lists are large enough, you can target market other media while your competitors waste money. (All of your data can be managed effectively through your Legendary Marketing SmartSite.)

In this chapter, you will discover:

- ✔ The seven steps to effective marketing

- ✔ Why most golf marketing is an insane waste of money

- ✔ How a simple paradigm shift will instantly give you a huge advantage in your market

- ✔ How to leverage this new concept into more outings, banquets, and membership sales

- ✔ How to collect 20,000 names, addresses, and e-mails this season

A REVOLUTIONARY CONCEPT

We all love instant gratification. We all want to book more tee times, sell more memberships, and generate more income. But if you are willing to make that your secondary goal, you will not only make more money in the short term, you will take a quantum leap towards securing your club's long-term future. If you can get yourself to look at marketing as a seven-step rather than a one-step process, you will enjoy significantly better results.

7 STEPS TO EFFECTIVE MARKETING

✔ Step 1: Lead generation

✔ Step 2: Lead segmentation

✔ Step 3: Lead qualification

✔ Step 4: Lead conversion

✔ Step 5: Maximizing the relationship

✔ Step 6: Customer loyalty and retention

✔ Step 7: Testing and tweaking the marketing so the system works even better!

HE WITH THE BIGGEST DATABASE OF PLAYERS WINS!

In any market, only so many people play golf. Let's say that within a 30-mile primary trading area of a golf course there are 200,000 people. And let's say 10 percent of them will play golf at least once or twice a year. That's a potential market of 20,000 people. Avid golfers make up about 4 percent of the population, meaning 8,000 people in this market play 80 percent of the rounds.

PARADIGM SHIFT

Instead of trying to get more people to play golf at your club over the next 90 days, what if your primary aim was simply to identify all 20,000 potential customers in your market?

Lead Generation

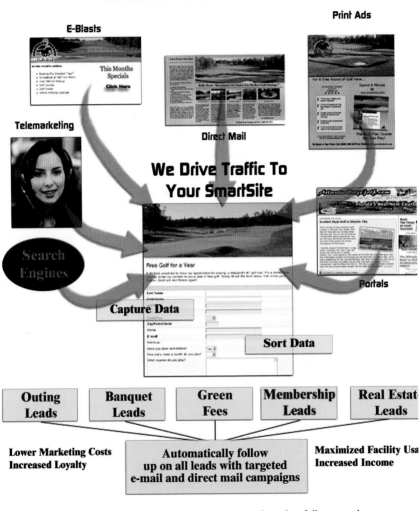

The first stage of lead generation is to capture data; then follow up with mail and e-mail to drive sales.

Think about that for a moment. What if you, and you alone, owned the name, address, phone number, and e-mail address of every single player in your market? What if you also had detailed information on their preferences for play, courses, lessons—even vacations?

You would never have to run another print ad except to "top up" your data maybe once a quarter. Your Yellow Pages ad could shrink, your billboard could disappear. In fact, you wouldn't need any of them because you'd already own the name, address, and phone number, and e-mail address of every player in the county!

You could mail or e-mail them at will...guaranteeing that 100 percent of the people who see your marketing massage are at the very least GOLFERS! Depending on your club, you would want to qualify and segment your lists, but that's Phase Two.

An insane waste of money

Why do clubs insist on running ads in the local newspaper when 90 percent of the readers DON'T play golf? Why don't they direct those funds to buying or renting the names of people who *do* play golf? If you really think about it, it's insane!

Just as insane is buying mailing lists of new homeowners, 90 percent of whom don't play golf. Or running a campaign on local radio or TV (with the exception of golf shows) where only 10 percent of the viewers and listeners play golf! Or running an ad in a non-golf magazine for your golf real estate development!

You must focus all of your energy on generating the largest possible list of potential customers (golfers!) in your area as quickly as possible.

The same concept holds true for outings, banquets, or membership leads.

✔ How many organizations hold golf outings in your primary trading area?

✔ Who are the people running them?

✔ When and where do they hold their events?

✔ How many players are there in these events?

By telemarketing to organizations and charities, it's possible to build a detailed list of over 400 groups in less than eight weeks! (We do it regularly for clients.)

Case history

Eagle Sticks Golf Club
Zanesville, OH (rural market)
High-End, Daily-Fee, $65 a round

Goal: To build a database of 20,000 players in 90 days.

Offer: A free round of golf in the traditionally slow month of April in exchange for filling out a 22-question survey about golfing preferences.

Tactics:
✔ Tradeshow flyers
✔ E-mail blast to in-house list of 750 names (very high pass-around)
✔ Local print ad, driving players to the survey for a free round

Results:
✔ Every tee time in April booked!

✔ Income up $15,000 compared to the previous April, even with the free green fees. Over 18,000 players registered on the web site!

Follow Up: Automatic bounce-back offer brought 900 players back at full fee the following month. A $25 gift (that cost the club $2) was given to each player.

Leverage: Entered their 20,000 names in the optional Legendary Marketing Data Alliance and got the use of 40,000 other names in Ohio!

LEGENDARY LEAD GENERATION STARTS AT HOME

You have to make a *commitment* to collect golfers' names, starting with your own players. Collect data at your counter and on the first tee using contests, drawings, and prize giveaways. Not occasionally, not on weekends, and not when your staff feels like it. DO IT EVERY SINGLE DAY!

Collecting names from your web site is painless once the system is set up. For example, announce on the home page of your web site an **"Enter to Win a Free Year of Golf"** contest. Periodically add free golf book downloads. Various special promotion coupons of their choice are programmed into our clients' SmartSites. (See the Promotion chapter for details.)

You can also trade your data with others in your area such as golf shops or golf leagues to grow your database quickly. (The chapter on building your e-list will give you lots more ways to do this.)

HOW TO GATHER GOLFERS' NAMES

Here are ten steps you can take to start dominating your market with your database of players.

1   **Get serious about collecting customer data.** Set goals for how many names and e-mails you will collect in a week, a month, a year.

Give prizes, discounts, rewards, and free information to people who are willing to give you the data. Reward frontline employees for making the effort to collect the data.

Check out the player survey on the LegendaryVault.com web site. It is loaded with key questions about playing habits. Auto responders are in place to acknowledge every player and send back proof of completion. Use free golf and the dates and rules outlined (also see the Promotions chapter.)

Rent or buy opt-in e-mail addresses of every golfer in your area (usually a 30-mile radius, more if you are a resort or destination). Call your local list broker or Legendary Marketing for details of lists available in your area.

Send an e-promo to each of theses lists, driving people to your web site to register for your offer. The offer must be compelling! We have several that deliver spectacular results.

TEST which e-lists work best. Buy or rent more of these names and repeat the process.

Buy or rent a mailing list of every golfer in your market. Lists are readily available of *Golf Magazine* subscribers, mail order buyers, responders to golf TV offers, club members and a host of other golf, income and demographic sorts. Lists usually rent for between $75 and $200 per thousand names depending on how good they are. Call your local list broker or Legendary Marketing for details on lists available in your area.

Send your list an offer-driven sales letter, postcard, or self-mailer directing them to your SmartSite. (See the Promotions chapter for more details.)

TEST which mailing lists worked the best. Buy or rent more of these names and repeat the process.

Design new response-based print ads for use in local media. These will probably look NOTHING like what your competitors are doing. They will be response driven. (See the Advertising chapter.)

All ads should drive people to your web site to register for a promotion or participate in an offer at the counter. The offer is ONLY VALIDATED when the player parts with additional data!

ADDITIONAL TIPS FOR OUTING & MEMBERSHIP LEADS

When you go fishing, fish for whales, not minnows. Ten extra outings a year is a lot more profitable than 100 extra players.

Telemarket local charities and organizations to build a list of at least 400 outing prospects. (Legendary Marketing has had huge success with this program. See the Outings chapter for program details.)

Add the FREE Outing Success Guide to your web site to encourage planners to sign up and download the booklet.

Telemarket local business professionals to generate a list of hot prospects for corporate memberships.

Develop and implement a formal referral program to increase membership, outings, and real estate sales.

We have additional proprietary material on selling outings and memberships. Check our web site or call us for details.

SUMMARY

He with the biggest database wins! Read it, believe it, LIVE IT!

Make no mistake, the long-term success of your club depends on the amount and quality of the data you collect. The more you collect, the easier it will be to drive players, find members, and fill tee times. The better the quality of the information you collect the easier it becomes to build customer loyalty.

Build a great database of players in your area and all your marketing headaches will disappear! You will be the only club in town working on the timeless 80/20 rule and you will be the clear market leader in your category.

Chapter Nine

Legendary Promotions

OVER 50 PROVEN STRATEGIES TO GENERATE LEADS AND DRIVE MORE BUSINESS FOR YOU

Promotions are special offers or activities designed to bring people to your course, lessons, or other services. The important thing to remember about promotions is that different people respond to different offers. Some people use coupons whenever they can; others wouldn't use a coupon if you paid them. Some like free information, golf books, or tips; others couldn't care less. Some will enter every contest; others wouldn't take the time if you guaranteed a prize. Some will jump at a sleeve of balls; others won't respond unless the balls are a certain brand. Only by trying and testing different types of promotions in your market can you get a true idea of what your response will be.

Offering a free $20 golf cap may only motivate 30 people to show up and pay full green fees. But it will very likely be 30 different people than will show up for $20 off your green fee. It's the difference between a discount mentality and a value-added mentality.

In the same way, the player who enters your contest to win a Free Year of Golf will often not be the same person who signs up for a free download of your bestselling golf book *Shanking for Distance*!

With this in mind, you need to take a varied and segmented approach to promotions. As your database grows, you will increasingly segment your market so that you are only sending offers to the players most likely to respond. (We have a tool, the Legendary Campaign Manager, that does the work for our clients.)

There are two types of promotions that we are interested in: those that generate leads and those that generate immediate income. Lead generation promotions are primarily used to help you collect data and identify prospects, but they very often result in extra business as well.

In this chapter, you will discover:

- ✔ More than 50 tried-and-tested promotions
- ✔ Web-site lead-generating promotions
- ✔ E-mail promotions
- ✔ Creative valued-added promotions
- ✔ Community promotions
- ✔ Pro-shop promotions

WEB SITE PROMOTIONS

Win a free year of golf

Prominently placing a contest on your home page can quickly and painlessly increase your database. The chance to win a free membership or year of golf produces the best results.

The average club will generate 1,500 to 3,000 entries a year using this promotion alone. Some clubs would rather give a free foursome or driver, but usually these lesser prizes do not produce the desired response.

After you pick the winner, ask for a photo so you can show that someone really won. We had 100 percent response to an e-mail telling players to go to the club's site and check the names of the winners to see if they won!

Free coupons

Coupons can be offered effectively online. Upload a number of coupons with offers from each segment of your business. For example:

- ✔ Cart
- ✔ Dining
- ✔ Pro shop
- ✔ Range

Send an e-mail blast offering $50 of money-saving coupons at XYZ Golf Club. Once they register for the coupons, the SmartSite automatically e-mails them to the player.

Free golf e-book

As the introduction pointed out, some people are contest people, others coupon people, and still others information hounds. Adding a PDF download of a book or booklet can have excellent results. At one site 7,000 people downloaded *Traits of Champions* in a single week. At another site a 20-page booklet on lowering scores was downloaded by 1,800 people in a week.

If you are a destination or a real estate development you can also offer a download of a golf guide or complete brochure on your property.

Downloadable pdf books (e-books) are very effective in both collecting data and selling prospects on a future business relationship.

Electronic licensing rights to books usually cost between $795 and $1,595, giving you unlimited download rights.

E-Books we have used successfully include:

- ✔ Golf joke book
- ✔ *The Traits of Champions*
- ✔ Golf architecture book
- ✔ *Tales of the Road Hole*
- ✔ *Lower Your Score 20%—Guaranteed*

Join our discount or e-club

Invite visitors to sign up for your discount or e-club. Be sure to let them know that only e-club members get the best deals and watch your e-list grow!

Provide discounts, tee time privileges, and other special offers only to those who register online. The benefits of registering should be mentioned throughout your site. People are cautious about giving out their e-mail addresses, so make sure you offer compelling reasons to register on your site. Assure them that you won't sell their name and you will use it only for your e-zine and special offers from the club.

Once they register, MAKE SURE your site sends an automatic "thank you" letter. Take this opportunity to restate the benefits of registering. Ask them to refer the site to a friend. By making registration on your site rewarding and easy, you can quickly build your e-mail list and slash your marketing costs. (All the Legendary Marketing SmartSites are equipped to do this.)

E-zine newsletter sign-up

Invite your visitors to sign up for your electronic newsletter to keep informed of tournaments, news, and special offers at your club.

Your newsletter should be more than discounts. It should include fun and useful content like tips, jokes, and golf anecdotes. The more value your newsletter offers, the more likely people will stay subscribed and pass the information on to other players (see samples at http://LegendaryVault.com).

Win a golf outing for you and 50 friends

A headline offering the chance at a golf outing for 51 people is a great way to generate daily fee and outing leads. The contest can be announced on the front page of your web site or as an ad in local golf magazines.

You can further target the response by offering the deal only to charities or fund raisers. You will quickly build a list of outing prospects.

Make a big deal of the event (which you can hold during off-peak time) with the local newspaper. Send them a press release announcing the offer and the winning organization. This will help generate more response and interest next year!

E-MAIL & DIRECT MAIL PROMOS

Free golf when you participate in our survey

The results of this promotion have been astonishing in both the amount of data gathered and the additional income generated at traditionally slow times.

Online surveys are a great way to gain feedback and insight into your market. They can mine amazing amounts of data if the incentive is attractive. Quite frankly, there is nothing more attractive than free golf to motivate players to respond.

At one club, 1,250 golfers completed the survey in less than 48 hours and over FIVE HUNDRED (yes 500) tee times were booked for the week—that's just Monday through Thursday!

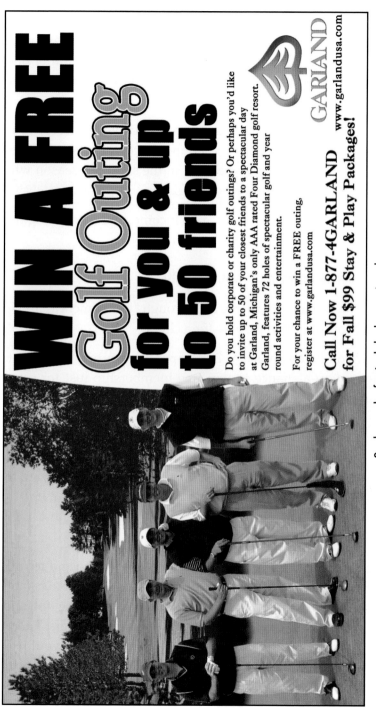

Good example of a simple lead generation ad.

When players showed up at the club they were also invited to participate in a one-day spring sale with 20 percent off almost everything. The income and traffic was very welcome after a horrible winter, but the real gold as always was in the information that was collected about players.

Additional revenues are generated by cart fees, food and beverage, pro shop sales and bounce back offers. Remember, these promotions should only be used in the shoulder season when the weather makes normal play marginal.

That way you gain data, gain income, and do nothing that will negatively affect your P&L bottom line!

Enter our tournament & win free golf!

A promotion to win free golf through "tournament" participation drove lots of midweek play for a client.

If you had a choice of 20 comparable courses but one of them offered you a chance to win free membership just for turning in your card, where would you play?

Here's how Twisted Dune Golf Course did it:

> Every time you tee it up at Twisted Dune between now and June 15, Monday–Thursday, you will be playing for more than just the lunch tab. Our FREE tournament gives every player a shot at FREE golf for the rest of the season!

> Simply book your tee time at Twisted Dune and tee off before 3 PM, Monday thru Thursday at our regular rates. Play from the designated tees, hole everything out, and have your card signed by your playing partners. Then hand it in at the pro shop upon completion of your round.

Gross and net winners in each flight win free golf for 2004 (Flights: 0–7, 8–14, 15–22, 23–30, and 31–40). Plus we will have an open division for all golfers who don't have a legitimate USGA handicap.

Winners in each flight will receive free golf at Twisted Dune from June 15th to December 31st, cart fees not included.

The more you play, the more chances you have to win! Enter as often as you like Monday thru Thursday. The more you play, the more chances you have to win!

Buy X number of rounds in advance and get X bonus rounds!

Prepaid sales are a great way to raise cash up front (and many rounds are not even used). You can restrict rounds from Monday to Thursday if you wish. Always put an expiration date on these rounds.

Suggest in your e-mail that customers:

✔ Split the cost and share the rounds with friends

✔ Use them for business incentives or employee rewards

✔ Just take advantage of this amazing deal themselves

The grand-opening special

"Grand Opening Special"—these words alone will attract attention. But here is one that will really appeal to the male ego: When opening a new course, whomever finishes the course first will (by default) be the course record holder! Who doesn't want to tell his buddies about that! Run a contest for the privilege of being the first to play and frame the card in the locker room.

VALUE-ADDED PROMOTIONS

While occasionally it does pay to use discounting, I always favor testing value-added promotions first. A cautionary word on discounts: Discounts do work, but—and it's a big BUT—if you keep discounting, players will wait for a bigger and better discount rather than play your course on a regular basis. For this reason you should mix up your offers with value propositions, not just discounts. Here are some examples:

- ✔ Pay for three and the fourth player is free. Actually, you are cutting the green fees by 25 percent.

- ✔ A free box of balls. Sounds like a $30 deal, but it really only costs you $12 and can be used instead of slashing your green fee.

- ✔ A free cap is an $18 value, but costs you just $8. Plus it gets others to serve as walking billboards for your course!

The more you mix up and test your offers, the less likely you are to build a discount mentality in your players and the more likely you are to hit the right combination of offers. Timing is also an important factor. If an offer works one Labor Day, chances are it will work next Labor Day as well. So be sure to make a note not only of what offers work, but when they worked.

Double your e-mail response

Here is a quick and simple tip to seriously increase the reach of any of your e-promos. Simply instruct the reader to forward the offer to a friend at the bottom of each of your promotions. You'll be amazed at the additional response you can generate by adding this one simple line of text.

Play this week and get a FREE $XX gift!

There are many ways to use this value-added promotion. Test what works best for you, including:

Swampfire   Reflections   Monarch   Fountains   *www.GarlandSummerGolfing.com*

Play Michigan's Only Ron Otto Designed Signature Courses!

People travel from around the world to seek out and play Ron Otto designed courses, which is lucky for us, since we have four. In fact, this reclusive genius designed only four courses before retiring to universal acclaim. **At Garland You Can Play Them All!**

With four of the most beautiful and well conditioned championship golf courses in the nation, Garland offers guests an exceptional golfing experience. The natural backdrop of 3,500 acres of unspoiled wilderness provides a perfect setting for our four courses – Fountains, Swampfire, Monarch, and Reflections. Ron Otto's sweat and blood is in Garland's soil. He designed and oversaw construction personally of every yard of our 72 holes, and his passion and dedication is there in every inch of it. Each hole has its own unique character

and design including rolling meadows, lakes, streams, mature hardwoods, and dramatic elevation changes. These innovative designs offer a variety of challenges to delight golfers of all abilities, and multiple sets of tees allow each player to select a distance that best suits their game.

"Quite simply the best combination of golf, accommodations and value in Michigan!"
– Ken Mehall, Kalamazoo, MI

To add to your golfing experience, the sights and sounds of natural wildlife abound with nesting bald eagles, deer and fox.

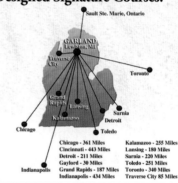

Chicago - 361 Miles	Kalamazoo - 255 Miles
Cincinnati - 443 Miles	Lansing - 180 Miles
Detroit - 211 Miles	Sarnia - 220 Miles
Gaylord - 30 Miles	Toledo - 251 Miles
Grand Rapids - 187 Miles	Toronto - 340 Miles
Indianapolis - 434 Miles	Traverse City 85 Miles

TAKE ADVANTAGE OF OUR SPECIAL GOLF PACKAGES & RATES

Couples Package - This package caters to couples who love to golf together. Includes two nights lodging in any accommodation. 18 holes with cart, $100 in Garland Bucks* that can be utilized for dinner and breakfast for two people. For a two night stay on this package, you will receive a complimentary round of golf for a total of three rounds per person. Based on two people for a one night stay. **From $297.00**

Mulligan Package - This package is for golfers who like a fine meal after 18 holes. Includes one nights lodging, 18 holes with cart, $50 in Garland Bucks* that can be utilized for dinner and breakfast for one person. For a two night stay on this package, you will receive a complimentary round of golf for a total of three rounds. Based on one person for one night stay. **From $130.00**

Unlimited Golf Package - This package is for the die-hard golfer who wants to play until he drops.

Includes two nights lodging and all the championship golf you can handle with cart. Based on one person for a two night stay. Surcharges apply for the Fountains Course. **From $257.00**

72 Hole Package - This package is not for die hards but for avid golfers wanting to experience each Ron Otto designed course. Includes two nights lodging and 72 holes of championship golf with cart. Based on one person for a two night stay. Surcharges apply for the Fountains Course. **From $216.00**

54 Hole Package - This package is for those of you who want a little time to spare and enjoy all that our award winning resort offers. Includes two nights lodging and 54 holes of championship golf with cart. Based on one person for a two night stay. Surcharges apply for the Fountains Course. **From $185.00**

Hole-In-One Package - This package is for the golfer who only wants one round a day. Includes one nights lodging and 18 holes of championship golf. Surcharges apply for the Fountains Course. **From $80.00**

Couples & Parent Child Tournament Packages - Two nights lodging plus three rounds of golf (two tournament rounds and one practice round). Leisure dinner on Sunday night. Cocktail reception and dinner Monday night. Luncheon and awards presentation on Tuesday. **From $557.00** **Based on two person team.**

CALL NOW! 1-877-583-5368 and
Ask About Our Special Golf Packages.

Notice not one—but three different value-added offers at the bottom.

✔ Golf book

✔ Club cap

✔ Club towel

✔ Golf glove

✔ Sleeve of balls

✔ Golf shirt

Free lesson before you play!

Everyone wants to play better, but only 13 percent of golfers in any given year ever take a lesson. Here's a painless way to add value, help a customer, and get more people interested in your lesson programs.

✔ Free video lesson

✔ Free putting lesson

✔ Free chipping lesson

✔ Free bunker lesson

U.S. open-style championship

Pick three players, add their Sunday score to your net score and win valuable prizes. This tournament-based promotion works well with avid players. The value of the prizes will also dictate participation.

Free car wash with green fee this weekend only!

Out-market your competitors by offering players a time saving and value-added service like a car wash. This can help you attract more players even though your green fee might be higher than the course down the street.

This works especially well in busy urban areas. Simply hire some kids on your own or call a local detail shop.

Demo day—hit the very latest equipment!

Players of all abilities love to try out the latest equipment. You should organize several demo days throughout the year with your equipment reps.

Demo day—every weekend all summer long only at xyz golf club

Since demo days work, why not continue the concept all summer long? You would quickly establish yourself as the club with the latest equipment! We're talking extra play, extra range revenue, and plenty of club sales.

Putter-only demo day—over 100 different putters to try!

A different twist on a popular concept. Everyone likes trying new putters. They don't even have to be new—just clean out your garage!

Who said there's no such thing as a free lunch?

There is at XYZ Club when you play Monday through Thursday. Throw in a free burger and fries and you're sure to satisfy some appetites.

DISCOUNT PROMOTIONS

You play free when you bring three other players

Phrasing the promotion this way is simple and works to varying degrees depending on the day and time you make the offer. By carefully tracking the results you will see when it truly helps you increase business.

Two for one

A standard discount promotion that can bring in extra play midweek. Use judiciously.

Play now...get a free round later!

This has worked well for many of our clubs in the Northeast to drive mid week business in the summer by offering a free round in the shoulder season when the weather and business are marginal.

Play free on your birthday!

Most people don't play alone on their birthdays, so you gain by getting three paying players. This program can be run all year. Once you have the player's birthday, your Legendary SmartSite Campaign Manager will automatically e-mail him the birthday offer every year two weeks ahead of his birthday. It will also send him an e-birthday card on his birthday—a nice touch, indeed!

Register yourself and your friends for free!

Register yourself and your friends for our free birthday gift package. Package includes:

- ✔ A free round
- ✔ Free golf e-book
- ✔ Personalized e-greeting

Kids play free with a paid adult

This is a simple but effective way to drive play at off peak times and lay the foundation for future revenue. It can also be used in conjunction with your range!

Father-son or mother-daughter day

Do this on your own or in conjunction with one of the national events sponsored by the PGA, NGCOA, or others.

Become an XYZ staff player

How about creating a special bond between your club and your customers? Put together a staff package: tour bag, golf shirts, cap, and several rounds of golf. Offer it at a very attractive price and get 20 to 30 players on your staff. Work out some additional perks for them throughout the year. (See Chapter 19 on Loyalty Programs for more details on Opinion Leader Programs.)

Team colors

At Legendary Marketing we are far more interested in results than image. But that doesn't mean image and branding should be ignored. Here is a promotion to get you some real branding in the community. Pick a team color—say, purple—then order 1,000 low-cost purple shirts with oversized logos on the breast or arm. This is now your team identity, like silver and black is for the Oakland Raiders. Your goal is to get at least 5,000 players all over town wearing your colors.

Display the shirts in your shop with a $39.95 price tag, but offer them to everyone who plays that day for just another $10 on top of their green fee (assuming you can buy your shirts for $10).

"Sir would you like one of our XYZ club staff shirts for just an extra $10, that's a savings of $30?"

SEEKING OUT NEW PROSPECTS

Car wash booth

Nobody coming to your club? Then go to them! This may seem like a strange promotion for a golf club, but you'd be amazed at how successful it can be.

I came up with the idea partly by accident. I walked into one of my karate schools in California on a sunny Saturday morning to find it totally dead. I asked the manager what was going on and he joked "Everyone's at the car wash."

His words hit me right away! I had just passed the car wash on my way in and it was jammed. There were people with expensive cars and SUVs, people with absolutely nothing to do for at least 20 minutes while they waited for their cars.

I immediately went down there and asked for the manager. I offered him free lessons for himself or his kids in return for us putting a table outside his office where I could promote my school.

On a good weekend 1,500 people a day went through that car wash. We never spent a day there where we did not sign up a new student, and karate only appeals to 0.5 percent of the population. At 10 percent for golf, that means 150 of them would have been golfers with nothing to do for 20 minutes!

How many of these bored golfers could you get interested in your club in a single day? How about every one of them! Depending on how upscale the area is, you can do everything from collect data to generate leads for lessons and membership.

Mall booth

This next idea is an upscale version of the previous one, and can be used at Christmas. Ninety percent of all retail shopping is done between Thanksgiving and Christmas. That's great if you are located in a mall, not so great if you are a golf course far away from a mall. But here's a solution. Rent one of those little handcarts in the middle of the mall walkway. That way you get all the traffic at a fraction of the price and with no long-term commitment.

Load up the handcart with brochures, information kits, booklets, flyers, gift certificates, and promo items. Play your course video on TV. Hand out surveys, take names, have drawings. Sell rounds, lessons, memberships, and generate leads with contests and giveaways. Give away water bottles, pens, T-shirts, key rings, or whatever makes sense for your club. Have a special "Christmas present package" that includes a gift-wrapped product or ornate gift certificate.

Lead boxes

A lead box program is certainly not a new invention, but rather the result of many years of trial and error. The original lead boxes were put out by health clubs in the early 1950s. The purpose of a lead box program, of course, is to get people to put their name, address and phone number in your box to win a prize. Follow up by offering the prospect a free coupon or a prize with the goal of getting the prospect to become a permanent customer.

Important things to consider about using a lead box program:

- ✔ It's an incredibly low-cost source of prospective new clients.

- ✔ Your lead boxes will act as mini-billboards everywhere they're placed.

- ✔ Lead boxes give you something to do during the slow times. It's a great way to train new salespeople and it forces your sales team to follow up and get on the phone.

- ✔ Finally, lead boxes can create lots of new clients and referrals. Of course, lead boxes don't work if you don't work them. They must be serviced constantly or the leads will deteriorate. Often, you'll find that the pen has disappeared, or there are no more little slips to put in your box. Sometimes you may find graffiti or someone else's stickers on your lead box, so it's very important to service your boxes weekly.

Sometimes when you service your boxes you will find that Mickey Mouse, Donald Duck and a host of other assorted characters have put their names in your lead box. Don't let this discourage you. You will find at least one or two names out of every 10 are serious prospects with a real interest in golf. The more boxes and locations you have, the more leads you'll get, and the greater chance you'll have of filling up your business.

A few ideas on how to place your lead boxes in as many locations as possible:

- ✔ You can make arrangements to put lead boxes in many stores, malls, gas stations—any place. You can have a dozen lead boxes out in the community at no cost to you. First, start by asking all of your friends and existing clients if they would mind putting a box in their places of business.

- ✔ Hit up different fast food locations and service locations in your area.

- ✔ Go to additional malls and businesses that you frequent. These should make them easier targets. Since you are supporting their businesses with your money, they should be a little more receptive to placing your lead box at their businesses.

The best types of businesses to put your lead boxes are in high traffic areas. Video stores, pizza parlors, hair dressers, and liquor stores are a few examples.

I suggest that you empty your lead boxes at least on a weekly basis. Make sure you don't interfere with the flow of business. Simply walk in and replace your existing lead box with a new lead box that reflects well on your club.

While it's illegal for others to steal your lead boxes or your leads, it's a good idea to put a dummy name and address and phone number in your lead box. Not only does this encourage other people to put leads in your lead box, it's also a way to catch someone who's stealing your leads.

Once you've gathered all of your leads, you'll want to enter them into your SmartSite CRM for easy follow-up and tracking. The next thing is to mail-merge the letters so that every one of them is personalized. The letter you send will announce to the prospect that they have won something; a free lesson, cart fee, or promo item. The key is that while only one person wins the grand prize, everyone who actually enters wins something!

Follow up with telemarketing

Once you've mailed the letters, wait 48 hours before you start calling. You will find that one out of 10 of the letters will reach a hot prospect who will call you. For the rest, you must initiate an outbound telemarketing campaign to follow up on the letters. Be sure you don't miss a single prospect.

The real success of your lead box program lies in a competent telemarketing follow-up. If you have a cheerful, enthusiastic person following up on your leads, you're going to have great response. If you have someone who's uncomfortable, someone who doesn't like to sell, or someone who sounds monotone or boring, your lead box campaign is doomed to fail.

Experts say you have less than 15 seconds to capture the attention and interest of the person you are calling. The telephone is a very interruptive medium, so it's crucial to immediately identify who you are, why you are calling, and the potential benefit to the person for taking the call. This information must be presented in a clear, concise, and timely manner. The quality of your voice pitch, inflection, tone, and enunciation is critical. (See Chapter 21 on Outings for more on telemarketing.)

TARGET MARKET PROMOTIONS

The more targeted and exclusive your offer is, the greater your response will be! Seniors don't want ads for kids' camps and avid players don't want to receive promotions for the nine-hole ladies group.

- ✔ Headlines should qualify the group.
- ✔ Offers and copy should speak to that group's unique needs and motivation.
- ✔ The offer should be of interest to that specific group.

Locals-only day!

Locals-only days work well in areas with high tourist traffic. Give locals or state residents a special rate during specified days or months.

Beginner's day!

Stress a no-pressure, quiet day at the club. Provide free tips on the range. Let them know that beginners are welcome at your club.

Ladies day!

Simple things like changing colors can have an effect on generating additional response. Think pink, or at least more pastel colors when marketing to women. Offering a free rose on ladies day might well work better than a sleeve of Pro V1s!

Seniors day!

Since seniors are far more flexible as to when they can play, you can designate a Seniors Day that fills a hole in your schedule. Seniors typically respond well to value. That often means discounts but it could just as easily mean including the cost of a hamburger in their green fee! Also consider providing a weekly prize from the pro shop. Like anyone else, seniors respond to personal attention.

Feeling lucky?

Try a simple promotion that randomly lets one out of 10 players play free on any given day. This only amounts to a 10 percent discount and generates more extra business than that. Require them to register on the web site to qualify.

ON-SITE PROMOTIONS

Monster day!

A Halloween promotion can be used to drive play to a midweek day near October 31st. The course could be set up super-tough and prizes given for the best scores, closest to the hole, and so forth. Add a few decorations and some eerie noises and you're in business.

Sell gift certificates that double in value if they hit the green

Have the ranger or cart girl stationed by a par three. Offer the players a chance to double their money in pro shop script if they hit the green. Let them decide how much to "wager," from $5 to $20.

GET LOCAL BUSINESSES TO ATTRACT NEW CUSTOMERS FOR YOU

Have stores give out (free) gift certificates from you to their customers. Your certificates are a free bonus for the stores' customers. The first step is to seek out compatible stores for your particular club. Golf courses typically target local golf shops, dry cleaners, video stores, and so forth. How many gift certificates you give the store is entirely up to you, because the purpose is to get your gift certificates in the hands of prospective customers who meet your demographic profile. The gift certificates should look valuable, not like some second-rate photocopied coupon. (These businesses in turn can give you prizes for your tournaments or promotions.)

How to solicit the help of other businesses

Ask the person in charge of your target business, "How would you like to provide your best clients with an extra bonus of X amount of dollars for every purchase they make, say over $100?" Either wait for his response or let the person know at once that you're not trying to sell him anything, just offering him a win-win deal. Once he agrees to the concept, you can offer him as many gift certificates as you wish. Make sure that the merchant understands this is a no-strings-attached offer for him and his clients and you will more often than not meet with success.

How about going to all the dry cleaning stores within 10 miles of your club and giving each of them 50 free $10 gift certificates that they can give to any client spending over $50? How many new faces will that bring to your club? Plenty! Then it's up to you to treat them right and turn them into full-fledged customers.

The key is to remember that this is not merely a discount coupon, but an actual gift certificate that is being added to the store's sale in recognition of a substantial purchase or customer loyalty. This creates a huge difference in whether or not the certificate is redeemed and avoids a discount look. (Of course, you can make the gift certificate good for only green fees or only carts or only lessons or whatever you choose.)

What about the cost?

If the thought of giving away your product bothers you, look at it this way. If you run a full-page ad in your local newspaper, it's going to cost you $600 or $700 (or even more), and you still can't guarantee any new business. If you give away sixty $10 gift certificates to your dry cleaner, you are virtually assured of getting some new business. Second, it only costs you $10 for the certificates that actually come back. And third, it's not real money that you're spending, just a discount on extra business you might not get!

Let's say that half the certificates are redeemed by people who are already customers and half are new customers. That means it costs you $20 per new customer, which is not bad over the lifetime of a typical customer. Think of this type of program as an alternative to advertising with far better results since you only pay for the leads you actually get!

FRIENDS AND FAMILY

Another way to distribute gift certificates is to get your existing clients to distribute them to their friends and family. Every Christmas, I used to send all of my karate school students two free $80 gift certificates, the price of a month's lessons. Along with the cards was a letter letting them know that the gift certificates could be passed along to friends as a gift and would be treated as such when their friends arrived at the school. The letter also pointed out that the certificates were only redeemable for lessons and that they could not be used by existing students. Sometimes the students asked if the certificates could be used by another person in their family, which of course was allowed, because after a month they became regular paying clients.

SELLING LESSON PROGRAMS

Take a look at this sample letter:

This Holiday Season Give Gifts That Last A Lifetime!

There's no better feeling than finding a perfect gift for that special person on your list. Not just another gift that will be forgotten in a couple of days, but something that will be remembered and appreciated for years to come. However, it isn't easy to find something special and different, something that can really make the recipients feel great about themselves and you.

This year, Beech Creek Golf Club offers golfing gifts that last a lifetime: Confidence, Satisfaction, Enjoyment, and the wonderful feeling that comes from knowing you are in control of your golf swing. All these gifts can be developed through our unique teaching program.

The game of golf is more than just a way to pass the time. It gives you the ability to look inwards and know yourself. Playing well improves your self-image and your whole outlook on life, and it brings you a new circle of friends and business acquaintances. Much more than a tie or gift certificate to a restaurant, the instruction we offer at Beech Creek develops mental and physical vitality and can be life changing. Surely you know of others who would benefit from a gift like this.

For more information on the benefits and lessons programs available, call us at (803)499-GOLF and be sure to take advantage of our Holiday Special!

A happy and healthy holiday season to you from all of us at Beech Creek Golf Club

CHARITY REQUESTS

Most golf clubs are regularly solicited by charities and organizations to donate a free foursome. The smart clubs let it be known that they can always be counted on to respond to such requests with the following understanding:

> "We will be happy to donate X to your program with the understanding that next year you give us a shot to hold any golf event at our club."

At the very least you pick up the name and address of the event and event planner. At best you book the event next year!

MORE IDEAS

Golf swap meet

This is probably best suited for a daily fee club, but it can work anywhere. Set up a golf swap meet in your parking lot once a month or even once a week on your slowest day. Charge a small fee for each table. You will make money on table rental and on players sticking around before and after to play golf. As an alternative you could offer a free table with the purchase of a green fee.

You could have your staff run it. Players show up and drop off the clubs they want to sell at a table. Your staff tags and prices everything. The player goes off to play and your staff makes the sales, keeping 15 percent of the sales price for your efforts.

18 members will have a hole named for them

Here is a neat way to get your first few members to pony up that initiation fee! Name a hole after them!

Daily fees: Have a hole at xyz club named in your honor!

Even at a daily fee you can use this concept to drive extra play. This could be done yearly.

Double your income and double your players' fun by playing golf at night!

Why limit your club's profit and your players' fun by playing only in daylight? It's relatively easy to set up your course to play at night. One company, NiteLite, has specialized in helping clubs run evening tournaments. With over 200,000 successful tournaments worldwide, they've shown it can be fun for your members or guests. And it's largely extra profit for your club. NiteLite is a commercial service that you can work with, but you can also arrange your own evening events with lighted balls and other available material. How about flashlights with your logo for every player? Or a bonus for players who use regular balls?

An evening golf tournament can:

✔ Increase your green-fee revenue

✔ Drive cart-fee revenue while other fleets are parked!

Evening golf tournaments are also ideal for fundraising. They have raised millions of dollars for charities of all kinds, including hospitals, medical groups, churches, schools, Rotary Clubs, fraternal organizations, foundations, fire departments, police departments, sports teams, and more!

For details, you can contact NiteLite Golf at: 800-282-1533, ext 21 or visit their web site at http://www.nitelitegolf.com.

Tie-in promotions

Create excitement on and off the course by tying in with the hottest shows and movies. Use a theme and decorations for a special event or weekend. For example, Sponge Bob is great for junior events. When every big new movie comes out, local golfers will think of your course.

On-hold phone marketing

In today's world of cost cutting and shrinking staffs, being put on hold is simply a reality of business life. A simple, effective, and low-cost way to market your upcoming events or ongoing specials is to have an on-hold message that continually repeats. On-hold machines can be picked up very inexpensively at Radio Shack. You simply insert a regular cassette tape, which should be changed on a weekly or even daily basis depending on the message. This is an excellent way to give customers the special message you want and to increase response to your events. If you add a little humor, it's also a way to keep them entertained and less irritated while on hold.

Promoting social events and club tournaments— automatic marketing

Your web site can be programmed to automatically send out promotions all year long. It can also send out customized promotional material based on visitors' answers to questions on your site. For instance, our Legendary Marketing Campaign Manager can preprogram an entire year's worth of golf and social programs into your SmartSite. E-mail promotions can be triggered by date or by the player checking a specific box in a survey. This way, members get the right promotion for their unique interests at the right time.

High school golf day

Talk to the local high school golf teams. Have a fund raiser for them. Let them sell tickets for a special tournament and gift certificates for other times. You can add lots of touches:

- ✔ Ask your members to bring in equipment to donate to the team
- ✔ Have your ground crew collect balls for them.

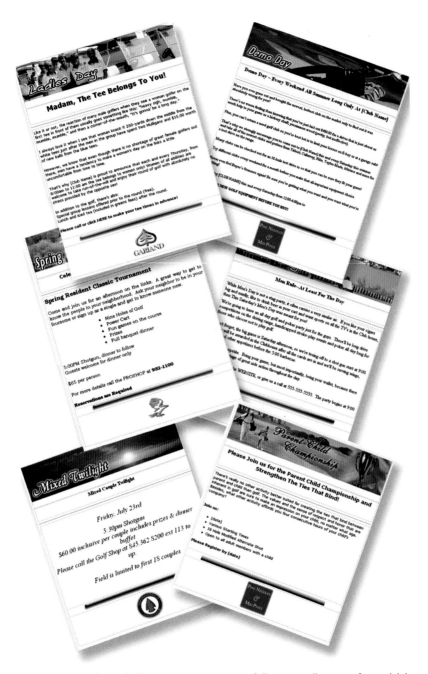

The preprogramed e-mail offers in Gampaign Manager follow up on all aspects of your club by sending e-mails only to those most likely to respond to the offer.

MEMBERSHIP PROMOTIONS

Member for a day

Bring prospective members to your club for a day and make them feel special. If they come alone put them in a friendly foursome with some existing members.

VIP executive outing

This is a great way to identify membership prospects and give them a little taste of what to expect at your club. We can provide more complete consulting on this program but here are the basics:

First, using the power of the Internet, build a database of leading professionals within a certain socioeconomic bracket (depending on your club's unique needs). Typically you would target attorneys, doctors, executives, business owners, and entrepreneurs located within a 30-mile radius of your club.

Make 10 calls for every lead you want to generate. So you need 4,000 calls in order to generate at least 400 prospective members. During the initial call, invite the prospective members to come to the club for a special VIP Executive Golf Outing. This will include breakfast, a 15-minute presentation on the benefits of memberships, 18 holes of golf, and a short awards ceremony.

SUMMARY

There are many special promotions you can use for your course. As you experiment with them, you'll find the ones that work for you and they can repeated every year (or more frequently). As you develop a routine, events will get easier to run; you just have to get started.

Chapter Ten

Legendary Print Advertising

HOW TO DESIGN A GOLF AD THAT WORKS

Frankly, most golf print advertising is a giant waste of time, money, and trees. That is not to say that print publications are not worthy of your ad dollars or that they're not an integral part of your overall marketing plan. The problems lie largely in how the ads are done.

For starters, most ads fail by not grabbing the readers' attention in the headline. Research shows that 90 percent of readers never get beyond the headline. The text of the ad frequently fails by not expanding on the headline and by not turning features into real benefits. People buy for emotional reasons backed up by logic. The ad fails if it doesn't spell out benefits clearly.

Misuse of graphics is also common. Many ads feature pictures or graphics that are indistinguishable from their 50 closest competitors. Poor layout of the ad components often draws the reader's eye away from your sales message instead of towards it.

Failure to ask for specific action can turn an otherwise good ad into a waste of money. The whole purpose is to lead the reader to action, yet many ads do not spell out the action.

WHAT MAKES A GOOD AD?

An advertisement is not necessarily good just because it is funny, clever, or even easily remembered. A good ad effectively motivates people to ACTION—to sign-up for your offer, visit your web site, book a tee time, inquire about membership, or buy a shirt. In other words, a good ad gets response!

In this chapter, you will discover:

✔ Why most golf ads fail

✔ How to capture your readers' attention

✔ How to write response-driven copy

✔ Which "gimmicks" can help you garner additional response

✔ How to prove your value

✔ How to create compelling offers

✔ How to test your ads for effectiveness before they run

With these ideas in mind, let's look at ten factors that will determine the success of your print advertising.

TEN KEY FACTORS TO PRINT ADVERTISING SUCCESS

First, let's look at what printed material can and cannot do for your club. Print ads can educate, qualify, generate leads, and even handle some objections. In some cases, ads can sell your product or service. Ads cannot interest a 69-year-old woman in buying a golf membership to your Pete Dye golf club. Nor can they realistically attract a member of an exclusive country club to play an $18 municipal course!

Ads can only attract and heighten the interest of someone who wants to buy your product. You do not design printed pieces to be everything to everybody. You design them to attract either people who are already buying your product or people who may be thinking about your product.

In the golf business, you can figure that about 10 percent of the readers of any given newspaper have some interest in golf. It matters not whether your ad is brilliant, the number of people who glance at it stays roughly the same.

The key is to increase the number of people who actually read your ad

Recent studies have shown that of the thousands of ads people are exposed to each day, only 4 percent gain more than two or three seconds of attention.

While each different print vehicle obviously has its own nuances, these factors will hold up for all vehicles: Yellow Pages, direct mail, magazines, newspaper ads, and brochures. Ignore one of these 10 key factors and you instantly decrease the power of your marketing message!

1   **Respect every inch of printed space.** The biggest reason that most printed material is a waste of trees is that most people treat printed matter as a challenge to fill up space. Logos are too big, pictures don't relate to headlines, and worthless copy explains the club's history rather than your sales message, benefits, and call to action!

To increase the effectiveness of each piece you print, you must treat each inch of each ad, flyer, letter, and brochure with the respect it deserves. That innocent piece of white paper is going to cost you lots of green paper, so make it work for you for all it's worth. Never make a casual decision about even an inch of space. Make your paper into the best salesperson your club has by committing to maximize its full potential. That means doing your ads well in advance of any deadline!

The simplest way to maximize your ad is to remind yourself constantly that people buy for their reasons, not yours! This is Sales 101, but for some reason when people try to sell someone on the idea of visiting their club or inquiring about a vacation, logic goes out the window. They suddenly spew a host of mind-numbing statements like "committed to excellence," "in business for twenty years," and "we're the biggest resort in town." The reader doesn't care. Use space to sell, not to build your ego!

2 **You must capture the reader's attention in three seconds.** Your headlines have just three seconds to capture a reader's interest. If they don't, you're doomed to failure. This is just as true for a two-cent flyer as for a $10,000 brochure. There are several methods you can use to accomplish this, but by far the most predictable way is to make sure your headline states a clear benefit to the reader. What can your course offer him? How will it benefit his life or his work? Here are some examples:

- ✔ Play in Less than 4 Hours Guaranteed!

- ✔ Play the Number One Course in Maryland!

- ✔ Never 3-Putt Again!

- ✔ Play a Great Scottish Links without Leaving New Jersey! Spend What You Save on Airfare at the Bar!

Each of these headlines would grab the attention of anyone looking to play quickly, notch up another #1 course, or stop three putting! The benefits of reading further are obvious from the headlines.

Another way to create a good headline is to pose an intriguing or thought-provoking question like:

Why Is the Back Nine at XYZ the Best Nine Holes of Golf in Virginia?

Yet another way is to make a bold and provocative statement that grabs attention, similar to what you see in the supermarket tabloids, "Martians Land in London!" While the last two approaches are both acceptable ways to use a headline, they are harder to test than simply offering real benefits. Start with benefits before you test "fancier" approaches.

③ **You must capture your reader's attention with the picture you use.** Pictures should capture your readers' attention and show your course in effortless, happy, exciting, and wonderful use! With a few exceptions such as fashion merchandising, pictures do not sell your product or service; rather, they attract readership and complement the copy. By all means, use a photo of your best hole. But be warned: if it is not something spectacular—think 18th at Pebble Beach—it's just another golf hole.

You will do far better in attracting readership, especially in a golf magazine, if you add an element to stop the reader dead in his tracks. For example, a man or woman in a swimsuit playing golf on your signature hole would get people to STOP and look at the ad, read the headline, and then decide if they want to read the copy. We're not saying to do something like this just for shock value; the picture MUST relate to the copy and the offer. In this case, perhaps the theme might be how relaxing your resort is or how close the course is to the ocean. The point is that by adding an extra element you can greatly increase how well your ad stands out.

Use graphics to point out features and benefits of your product or service. People believe what they see. Show how fun your course is to play. Show how much enjoyment it brings; show how your readers' lives will be enhanced if only they buy!

For the most part, headlines work better if they are placed below a picture, not above it or next to it.

Very often readers will scan captions to determine whether they want to go back and read the copy. Never waste caption space by describing what's in the picture—the readers can see that. Instead, use that space to remind them of key benefits, or restate your offer in different words.

4. **Learn the difference between benefits and features.** People tend to list lots of meaningless features rather than opting for a handful of potent benefits. A feature tells you about a product, a benefit explains how the prospect can benefit from it.

Most ads contain short bulleted phrases like "convenient location." By using more words, you can take that simple feature and turn it into thought-provoking benefits that connect with readers:

> Our convenient location next to I-95 makes our club
> easy to get to when you feel like a fast nine or just want
> to hit some balls on your way home from work!

Now the reader can't help but think for a moment about the proposition you have put before him.

You may think that if you list lots of features the prospect will put two and two together and figure out how that feature will benefit him. He won't. Instead he will scan the feature and move on to the rest of your copy without ever having made the connection. Had he scanned copy with real benefits, he may well have stopped, re-read a key point, and been enticed to buy.

Other than poor headlines, the greatest waste of money in printed matter is generated by volumes of text that say absolutely nothing about what your club will do for the reader. Most people are so afraid of filling their ads up with words, they opt instead for meaningless features or bulleted highlights that don't tell the reader much of anything.

Words sell! They sell your reader on the concept of picking up the phone or driving down to your club. They sell the reader on the need he has for what you offer, on the pain he will feel if he doesn't see you, and on the joy she will feel upon joining your club!

Do not be afraid to fill your ads with copy. There is no such thing as copy that is too long, only copy that is too boring! The biggest myth in advertising is that people don't read. Book and magazine sales are at an all-time high despite 300 channels on TV and the lure of the Internet. *People do read things that are of interest to them.* The most successful print material of all time is full of long, interesting, benefit-filled copy. Write as much as you can about your product or service. Write two or three times more than you need, then go back and pick the very strongest statements that make your offer sound exciting, reliable, the best in town.

5   **Back up all your claims with proof.** People are very skeptical of advertising. That's why it pays to back up all your claims. Use quotes from magazines, statistics, charts, study findings, and testimonials. Show people that you are giving it to them straight by bringing in third-person endorsements for your club. Quote satisfied members, outing customers, and wedding planners, and use their real names and titles. Use well-known people in your community to heighten awareness and build your credibility.

6   **Do not assault the reader's eye or make your ad hard to read.** Do not confuse the reader with off-the-wall type styles, fancy designs, and strange layouts. Some graphic designers understand the principles of effective advertising as do some advertising sales reps. About as many understand the principles of nuclear physics! Please remember that neither graphic design or advertising sales have anything in common with designing printed material that increases your business!

People read from top to bottom and from left to right. If you make their eyes jump around too much they will give up. If you make the type too small, they will pass. If you print your flyer on

No Homes, No Freeways, No Noise

When You Play CrossCreek Golf Club, You'll Enjoy A Pristine Arthur Hills Design That Defines The Way Golf Was Meant To Be Played!

If you enjoy pure golf, clean air, natural wildlife and the sound of birds singing instead of freeway noise, CrossCreek Golf Club is the place for you! Although it's just 5 miles from I-15 in the heart of the Temecula Valley, you'll feel a million miles away!

Relax and enjoy our spectacular canyon layout as it winds its way through running creeks flanked by mature sycamore and oak trees. Designed by world renowned architect, Arthur Hills, our traditional layout is among this master's finest work.

"I can hardly believe that golf this good, this beautiful, this quiet, yet this affordable still exists anywhere in Southern California. Add it to your MUST-PLAY list at once!"
– Andrew Wood, Golf Writer

You'll find GPS on every cart for your added enjoyment, fine practice facilities on which to hone your game before or after your round, plus a cozy club house and veranda for settling up your wagers and enjoying a cold one after your round.

Our staff shares your passion for the game and is eager to make sure your time at CrossCreek is memorable for all the right reasons. You'll find our club an excellent location for your next golf outing with a professional event staff to handle all the details for you, including helping you promote your event!

CrossCreek is special as much for what it doesn't have – like homes, adjoining freeways or exorbitant green fees – as for what it has. In addition to reasonable daily fee rates, yearly memberships are also available and surprisingly affordable.

Come discover golf the way it was meant to be played. Come play CrossCreek today!

Book your tee time TODAY and experience superior golf at surprisingly affordable rates.

CALL NOW! 800-818-4398
or visit us online for rates and directions at www.CrossCreekGolfing.com

43860 Glen Meadows Road, Temecula, CA 92590

Don't be afraid of lots of copy—just make sure it's interesting to your TARGET reader.

bright red paper, they will give it a miss. By all means be creative, but never at the cost of making your piece difficult to read.

Using colored paper is good, unless it prevents or handicaps you from reading the material, as many colors do! Also, if you ever need to fax any of your printed material to customers, keep that in mind when choosing background colors. Red, for example, reproduces as black, making it impossible to read if faxed or photocopied.

7. **Use all known gimmicks to increase customer response.** There are a great many little tricks you can use in a printed piece to greatly increase its effectiveness. On their own, each may seem insignificant, but put them all together and you can increase the effectiveness of your ad ten-fold or more!

- ✔ End the headline where you want the reader to start reading, not at the far side of the page.

- ✔ Always use a caption under a picture. It's the second place everyone looks.

- ✔ Make sure the caption sums up your key benefit or offer—you may not get another chance!

- ✔ Make sure all photographs with people have the people oriented looking towards the text so the reader's eye follows the picture and begins to read. Photographs of people who appear to be looking off the page take the reader's eye to the next ad.

- ✔ Use a graphic of a phone next to the phone number, it can increase response by up to 25 percent.

- ✔ If you want readers to clip a coupon, show scissors— you'll get up to 35 percent more responses.

08 **Always ask the reader to do something.** Not asking the reader to take action is the biggest sin of all. Surprisingly, it is often committed by people who up to this point have passed most of the key tests. They have grabbed their readers' attention, expanded on benefits, used the right pictures, and have their readers salivating like Pavlov's dogs. Then, their copy ends. Readers are left lost, empty, and wondering what to do next. Should they file this information for future use? Should they throw it away, or should they pick up the phone and call right now? Better still, why not ask them to get into their vehicle and drive right on down, because you are ready and waiting to see them?

Use strong calls to action, such as:

✔ Go to our web site right now and claim your coupon.

✔ Pick up the phone right now and call!

✔ Don't wait another minute to get the rewards you deserve. Clip out this coupon and mail it today!

Never end a printed piece without direct and specific instructions for what you want the reader to do next. Don't blow it by arousing their interest in what you have, and then letting them go to a competitor first.

09 **The more compelling the offer, the greater the response.** Much retail advertising in golf is price-based. Yes, some people are drawn to this, but if you want to build a real reputation in your community, make a statement about who you are and why people should do business with you.

If you compete only on price,
someone can always do better!

Use your copy to make statements about your experience, your service, your selection and your reputation. Then tie each statement into a clear and specific benefit to the customer.

10 Put all printed matter to the test before allowing it to leave your office. All printed material should be put to the test before it ever gets to print. By all means, use family, friends, other business owners, graphic designers, and ad reps to gain feedback. But be warned. If you have followed any of our advice until now, they may tell you that you have too much copy (you don't). They may tell you to use fancier type styles or, worse yet, put your headline in reverse type (which makes it 35 percent harder to read). They may encourage you to use a picture of yourself or to make your logo bigger. Resist the temptation. Instead, do the Legendary Print-Ad Test below.

LEGENDARY PRINT-AD TEST

Use the following tests to evaluate the design-readiness of every print ad:

Headline test

Does the headline promise a clear benefit to the prospective customer, such as:

Be the First to Play XYZ Club!

Alternatively, does the headline make a provocative statement or pose a very interesting question? If your headline does not pass the above criteria, it stands a 99.5 percent chance of failing.

Picture test

Look at each picture in your ad. Will it capture your prospects attention?

Does it CLEARLY differentiate itself and stand out from the host of other ads it is competing against?

Does it show people just like your target reader having fun?

Copy test

Is the copy written specifically for your most probable prospects? Does each line state what's in it for the client with clear, compelling benefits?

The classic test we have developed is this: Read two sentences of any printed piece, then ask, "So what?" If one of the previous two sentences did not answer that question go back and rewrite them. Of course, the answer to "so what?" must relate to the customer's point of view, not yours.

Gimmick test

Have you used all the gimmicks you can to incrementally increase your response?

Have you used the captions underneath each picture to sum up your offer, rather than merely telling the reader what he can already see in the picture?

Are coupons flanked by a graphic of scissors?

Is there a picture of a phone next to the phone number?

Does your ad avoid hard-to-read type styles, colored paper, all capitals, and reverse type?

Is your ad designed so that the eye follows a natural path from the top left to bottom right?

Call to action and offer test

Have you asked for action? What do you want the customer to do? Be specific!

Tracking test

Have you used a unique web address and a unique phone number to track all response to this ad?

Media test

Is this the right media to run your ad? Sure, they may have lots of readers, but how many of them fit into your "Perfect Customer" category?

MATCH THE MESSAGE TO THE MEDIUM AND DON'T BE SEDUCED BY NUMBERS

Even taking all of the above 10 key ad-design factors into account, an ad can still fail. Many club owners are unwittingly seduced by the lure of large numbers. They think, "Well, if 100,000 people see my ad in the newspaper I am going to get X number of calls. Or if I mail out a flyer to 10,000 people, I ought to get X response." Ad reps love to seduce you with the power of large numbers, but a smaller number of the right target group will always beat a larger number of just anybody. Choose your media with care. Don't waste money on people who are not your prospects.

Ninety thousand people who see your ad but don't play golf won't make you a dime! Nor will people who read your ad and play golf, but only make $55,000 a year, join your $100,000 golf club.

SUMMARY

The sole purpose of your print ads is to get people to take action—for example, to drive them to your web site to register for an offer. Once you have their information you do not need to run ads to reach those people again—they are yours! Let your competitors squander their money building their images! Design your ads to elicit response.

Most print advertising by golf courses and clubs is poorly done. Use the rules and guidelines from this chapter to design effective ads. When you are preparing ads, run them through the Legendary Print-Ad Test and make sure they pass muster before proceeding with them.

Garland, Michigan's Most Beautiful & Flexible Meeting Facility!

Receive complimentary meeting space if your organization holds an event with Garland in 2005!

Come discover Garland and inspire your attendees to greatness. You'll find Garland's meeting space and staff to be incredibly flexible. Our facility is yours to use as you see fit! No dumb rules and policies to make your life difficult – just a "can do" attitude!

Garland Resort offers: **Incredible Lodging** – The largest log lodge east of the Mississippi must be experienced by your attendees to be fully appreciated. Once they do, they will talk about our cozy rooms and our golf course cottages forever! **Outstanding Food** – Our chefs are featured on the Food Network and among the finest in the U.S. And our banquet food is just as good! **Magnificent Golf & Outdoor Activities** – You'll have multiple choices for social and company bonding activities with four magnificent championship golf courses. Also enjoy tennis, swimming, fishing, and canoeing. Snowmobiling, cross-country skiing and sleigh rides are available in winter. Plus you'll find live entertainment in our lounge every weekend. **Convenience** – Unlike many mega resorts today, you'll find everything at Garland is in one place – accommodations, meeting rooms and dining. Our four golf courses are just steps from the Main Lodge. To add to your convenience we are also the closest resort to Metro-Detroit!

CALL NOW! 866-995-0309 to Book Your Next Meeting Or Event! Visit www.GarlandMeetings.com

A promo outings piece. Notice how a strong photograph draws your eye to the headline. The copy highlights benefits. The call to action is clear and strong at the bottom.

A diamond ring.
A four-diamond resort.
What a perfect match!

Share your special day with family at Garland Resort.

A diamond ring is the ultimate symbol of commitment. The AAA four-diamond rating assures you that Garland is committed to making your special day as flawless as your diamond — without the cost.

Congratulations on your engagement! Now leave the planning to us. From your bridal shower to your 50th anniversary dinner, our wedding planners will fuss over the details like you're one of our children walking down the aisle.

Garland Resort — Michigan's most romantic four-diamond, four-season resort!

For more information contact:
Brian Smith, Wedding Coordinator
Brian.Smith@GarlandUSA.com

CALL NOW!
(989) 786-2211 ext. 1442
1-877-583-5367

GARLAND
R E S O R T

Visit www.GarlandWeddings.com TODAY and download your FREE Wedding Planning Guide.

A sample event promo piece. Note also the offer of a free wedding guide at the bottom (the free guide is pictured on page 124).

GARLAND Michigan's Most Beautiful Resort

No matter what the season, Garland Resort has everything you are looking for. From 72 holes of Ron Otto designed championship golf, to exhilarating cross-country skiing or snowmobiling. Enjoy horseback riding, mountain biking, swimming, fishing, or canoeing down the beautiful Ausable River. Join us for a romantic getaway, mystery dinner or Zhivago Night. Garland is also a favorite choice for meetings, banquets, weddings and special occasions of all kinds. With easy access from metro Detroit and our own private airstrip, getting here is a breeze.

Explore our 3,200 acres of pristine wilderness and spectacular gardens. Enjoy great food, cozy accommodations and a staff that treats you like family. With all this, it's easy to see why Garland is Michigan's most beautiful resort.

Call today to book a room, make a tee time, plan your next corporate meeting or just getaway and have some fun!

CALL NOW
1-877-583-5371
www.GarlandUSA.com

For a FREE DVD Go to www.GarlandDvd.com

A general promo piece for a golf club designed to introduce the club to prospects. The offer of the free DVD both gets more information to prospects and allows the club to capture interested prospects' names and e-mail addresses.

Chapter Eleven

How to Design a Direct Mail Campaign that Works

Other than the Internet, direct mail is by far the best form of advertising for golf clubs, resorts, real estate, and golf schools. Yet many clubs have tried and failed with direct mail. There are usually two reasons for this: poor lists and the absence of a sales-oriented message. Instead, they hope pretty pictures and a few *"impotent"* features will sell. They will not!

Direct mail is the most scientific form of advertising. The majority of factors, such as lists, timing, offers, copy, and space, are all in your hands. Each variation can be precisely tested for effectiveness. There are proven techniques that boost response. Unfortunately, many people ignore proven techniques and try to be "creative!" Instead, you should be testing each incremental improvement in the copy, layout, and design that can have a far-reaching effect on the success of your campaign.

No other type of advertising lets you target market so specifically with income ranges, demographics, gender, even occupation. Direct marketing is not cheap. But if systemized, the results can be quite astonishing.

In this chapter, you will discover:

- ✔ Why most direct mail campaigns fail
- ✔ What makes an effective direct mail campaign
- ✔ The most effective lists to generate response
- ✔ The importance of the offer
- ✔ The keys to copy and design success
- ✔ How to test properly

LEGENDARY DIRECT MAIL

Why most direct mail campaigns fail

First, let's explain what I mean by a mail campaign. At Legendary Marketing, we frequently talk to course owners who've just run a direct mail campaign with terrible results. Upon questioning, we learn that their idea of a mail campaign is a 2×3 coupon included with 50 other coupons in a shotgun mailing to anybody with a mailbox. That is not what we mean by a direct mail campaign!

We also talk to many course owners who eagerly rent a mailing list of everyone who just moved to town. They print a one-sided flyer with no letter, no offer, no headline, no sweetener, and then send it to four thousand people. They are shocked when the phone doesn't ring. That is not a direct mail campaign, either.

Sending a one-page John Doe invite letter to a list of golf magazine subscribers doesn't cut it either!

Creating your campaign

There are no hard rules about what a mail package should contain. It could be as simple as a one-sided sales letter or be as complex as a 14-page letter complete with a color brochure. However, if you take a look at the type of mail you receive, you'll find 70–80 percent will contain the following:

- ✔ An envelope with teaser copy that entices you to open it and find out what is inside
- ✔ A 3- or 4-fold brochure
- ✔ A 2–4 page letter
- ✔ A clear, compelling offer
- ✔ A reply card or other response device

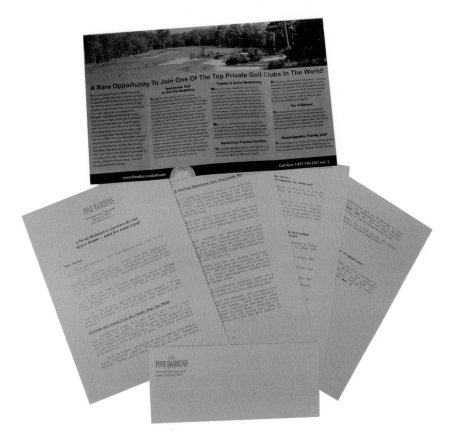

A typical direct mail package with an envelope,
four-fold brochure, and four-page letter.

Mailing lists—the first key to success

The best direct mail package can fail miserably if you don't send it to the right people. If you're not careful, your letters will end up in the hands of old people, dead people, and people who can't afford your services. Lists can be ordered and sorted in almost unimaginable combinations. You can rent lists of people categorized by race, income, zip code, property value, business, or a thousand other identifying factors.

Even with golfers there is a huge difference between the performance of good lists and poor lists. For example, if your club is high end, you will need a clear income qualifier.

First, figure out what your ideal prospects look like. (See Chapter 4, Defining Your Market).

What characteristics do they have?

- ✔ Do most of your customers live in the same zip code or same part of town?

- ✔ Do they have a certain level of income?

- ✔ Do they have children, drive a Corvette, or root for the Redskins?

Once you've pinpointed the characteristics of your ideal prospects, check to see what lists are available with those exact criteria.

Lists are usually available in minimums of 5,000 names and can be rented for one time or multiple uses. I suggest a one-time use and asking for a credit if you want to reuse it within 60 days. By then you'll know what the response rate was. Make sure you use a reputable list broker or call us; there are plenty of sharks!

THE MOST EFFECTIVE LISTS TO GENERATE RESPONSE

While good lists can be found from third parties, the most effective lists you will ever use are the lists you build yourself. All the data you collect from your web site and at the counter will pay off big time with direct mail. These are people who already have had contact with your club and that will translate into far greater response rates than any cold list you buy or rent. (That's providing their experience with your club was positive.)

The first trick is to get your mail opened

When a prospect gets a letter from you in the mail the VERY FIRST CHALLENGE is to get your letter in the interesting pile! Fail to do that and I don't care what you spent or what you sent, your campaign is DOOMED!

Have you ever watched someone open their mail? It's a very interesting study in human nature; take me for example, I'm a sorter.

First I look through the stack for checks and bills. That's the accounting pile—pile A. Pile B is anything for my wife. Pile C is the "later pile"—catalogs that might be of potential interest (golf, car stuff, and, at Christmas at least, possible gifts for my wife) and periodicals. They get put on my magazine rack for later reading at night or for my next plane trip. Pile D is my favorite. That is the interesting stuff—a handwritten letter from a friend, books or tapes I ordered, brochures for interesting vacations, and direct mail offers for things that interest me (books, tapes, cars, golf, and so forth). Catalogs and mailing pieces of no interest to me (credit card offers, insurance solicitations, stock pick newsletters, car dealerships of brands I don't care about) get instantly trashed.

Which brings me to pile E. Pile E is direct mail offers which might be of interest to me—only pile E almost never exists because very few pieces make it through the sort and trash process.

For sure there are other methods of sorting your mail but they all have one thing in common, some stuff gets thrown out without a glance, some gets saved for later reading, and some actually gets OPENED and READ!!!

So how can you massively increase your chances of getting our letter opened and read?

How about an envelope with a handwritten address and a Bobby Jones golf stamp affixed, and a tee, pencil ball marker, or some other lumpy trinket inside the letter to create some interest? I have used everything from ball markers to tea bags and seed packets to divots! They are not going to trash that letter like the rest of the "Junk Mail"!

They are going to first put it on the interesting pile.

Grab readers' attention with your headline

When they open it to see what the lump is, a giant headline is going to grab their ATTENTION at ONCE! If you don't grab them by the throat with your headline, 95 percent won't make it past the first paragraph. (Which means no matter how long or short your letter is it won't work!)

Just as in print advertising, writing good headlines is critical to the success of your direct mail campaign. Without good headlines everything that follows is a waste of time and money for it will most likely never be read.

With direct mail you have more space than a print ad and traditionally see much longer headlines. Longer headlines give you a better chance to hook the reader.

Some of the more effective ways to write good headlines are:

✔ An expose-type headline that gets people to look!

> **Amazing True Story: How a Mentally Tortured Woman Found Peace and Happiness through a Golf Outing at GlenEagles**

✔ "How-to" headlines also work well.

> **How You Can Be the Hero of Your Next Golf Event with This Incredible Limited-Time Offer!**

> **How I Talked My Wife into Buying Property at My Favorite Golf Resort**

✔ Put the key benefits of your product in the headline or, better still, put the key benefits *and* the offer in your headline.

> **Designed by Golf Professionals for Golf Professionals—Starters Hut, The World's Most Powerful, Easy to Use Electronic Tee Sheet...**
> **And It's Yours FREE for Six Months to Put It to the Ultimate Test...in Your Pro Shop!**

✔ Put your guarantee in the headline

> **You Will Cut Your Handicap by at Least 20% or Your Money Back!**

✔ Offer secrets

> **The Inside Secrets to BOOKING 10 Extra Outings This Month**

Whichever method you choose, you must work and re-work you headlines until the promise created in them motivates your reader to dig into the copy that follows.

Make sure the person writing your copy is a DIRECT RESPONSE MARKETER, not a typical agency copy writer. Based on my search for copywriters, such a person can be found in about one in 200 people who call themselves copywriters!

Go back and READ the letter in Chapter Two that starts on page 18 for an excellent example of GREAT COPY!

Long, relevant, interesting letters sell

Once you have your prospect's attention, the letter needs to tell an INTERESTING story AND make a COMPLETE SALES PITCH as to why the reader should act NOW!

Which brings me to my favorite topic, long copy. Almost all successful direct response packages have a lot of copy. Most letters are 2–4 pages or more. Now, you might think that is too much to read. This is the biggest fallacy people have about direct marketing.

For those who are truly interested in golf and your club, the more information, the better.

Long copy always outsells short copy! Yet ask anyone and they won't believe it! In fact they will flat out tell you that nobody reads anymore BUT...

If people don't read anymore, why were there more books printed last year than in any year in the history of the world?

If people don't read anymore, why are there more magazine titles on the newsstand than at any time in history?

If people don't read anymore, why has the size of a local bookstore grown from 1,500 square feet to 20,000 square feet (and that doesn't count the cappuccino bar!)?

If people don't read anymore, why is the number one complaint of web surfers that they didn't find enough information when they got to a site?

I'll tell you why—because despite what the amateurs tell you, people do read but they ONLY read things that are of strong interest to them!

At the very first marketing seminar I ever conducted, I asked 40 small business owners whether they thought people would read letters that were 4, 8, or even 12 pages long. They all said no. I then asked how they learned about the seminar they were attending and they all said they received an 11-page letter with a four-page brochure and a personal note, a total of 15 pages of text. I asked them how many had read the entire letter before committing $600 for the seminar along with airfare, rental car, lodging, and meals. All but one said that they had read the entire letter before making the commitment. Some even admitted to reading it twice, including a husband and wife who had driven 2,000 miles from Houston!

Has time changed anything? No, last year I repeated the experiment, this time attracting 93 people to my Golf Marketing Boot Camp at $1595 a head with an 11-page letter! When the group was asked if anyone would read a 11-page letter every single one said NO!!! But when I pointed out it was the only way the seminar was marketed most agreed to having read every page, with some admitting to reading the entire package three times before making their decision to buy! What people say they do and what they *actually* do is often different!

Don't be generic

Make your copy of great interest to your readers. Get them emotionally involved in what you have to offer! Do not settle for generic descriptions of what you have at the club.

- ✔ Make it LIVE, make it breathe, make it real!

- ✔ CONNECT with the reader in a personal way!

- ✔ PAINT a picture with your words, with them in it!

  - ✔ What will it feel like to hit the ball 20 yards further?

  - ✔ What will it feel like to play golf with your son every evening when you buy a golf course home?

  - ✔ How will your wife feel after a day at the resort's spa?

Ninety-nine percent of all copy in the golf business is impersonal corporate-speak with no passion, no connection with the reader, and no reason to act now. Therefore it FAILS! (In fact half the text in the golf business is obviously written by people who don't play golf. I saw one recently that compared a course in New Jersey to the great ones in Scotland like Ballybunion!!!!! I saw another at a very high-end real estate development that gave the approximate length of the fairways in feet! I mean what do they want to do land a plane on it?)

To sell golf, speak like a golfer, think like a golfer, act like a golfer, relate like a golfer, quote golfers, and tell golf stories! All of which should happen as part of the natural sales presentation you are making in your letter.

People need reasons...they need benefits...they need proof...they need motivation—and it takes more than a few lines of puff to connect on a meaningful level. Don't be afraid of writing letters long enough to prove your case. There is no such thing as a letter that's too long, only one that is too boring! If people are interested in any given subject they want more information, not less.

- ✔ Why is your course or resort better?
- ✔ What are the other members like?
- ✔ Why is your teaching philosophy different and more effective?

Remember, when developing a direct mail campaign, design the letter, brochure, and everything else NOT for the people who will regard it as junk mail and just throw it away, but for the ones whose attention it will catch and whose interest it will pique. Inspire them by providing more benefits and reasons to pick up the phone and take advantage of the unique offer you have made.

Have a conversation with your reader

The letter copy should be written as you would write a letter to a friend. It should be conversational and use simple, explicit language, free of technical jargon. It should excite the reader to want to learn more about your club, resort, real estate, or teaching program. It should be laced with benefits, testimonials, and true life stories that will categorically back up your position.

Tell your reader a story about someone who's really benefited from a particular service, someone who saved their sanity, made a business deal, or beat the odds and vastly improved their lives...thanks to you. Back up your story with lots of testimonials...fill them up with benefits, benefits, benefits. Add that real-world touch to your letter. Make it down home and folksy, like you've helped the person next door and can help them.

Grab readers' attention, then tell them a story

Here is part of a letter to event plannerd that goes with one the the dramatic headlines mentioned earlier.

Amazing True Story

How a Mentally Tortured Woman Found Peace and Happiness Through a Golf Outing at GlenEagles

Dear Event Planner:

Glenda (not her real name) worked for a demanding doctor. This particular doctor was a big philanthropist in the community and head of a well-known local charity. Anyway, one day right out of the

---

blue he had a great idea, "Let's hold a golf event to raise some money!" he said to Glenda.

That's where the problems started for Glenda. You see, Glenda did not play golf, so she didn't have a clue about how to run a golf event.

How To Survive Your First Outing

What she did know was that the doctor, all his friends, and the charity's major donors did golf, and all eyes would be on her performance! She was petrified.

The first night she tossed and turned in bed waking up in a cold sweat as one horrendous golf outing disaster after another (all starring Christopher Lee) filled her mind with images.

On day two she started looking on the Internet for a venue, biting her nails to the bone as she surfed the web.

Wow! She had no idea there were this many courses. They couldn't all be good ones, could they? They all seemed to offer outings but none had very much information.

It was the third day now, and poor Glenda was no closer to booking her event. She was paralyzed with fear.

GlenEagles Makes It Easy

Fortunately for her, a caring friend intervened before it was too late and suggested she simply call GlenEagles. Glenda thought this was particularly odd since while surfing the Internet, she had found the club was located in Scotland and did not want to add booking 144 plane tickets to her already full plate. Her friend filled her in...

(Continued)

As the letter on the opposite page shows, run your text to the next page so that the reader will have to go there to finish the sentence. Underline, circle, or highlight key words and phrases. Indent key paragraphs and double space your text to make it easy on the eyes. Use lots of bold headlines to break up the text and to allow your reader to scan your letter just by reading the headlines. Sometimes that's exactly what people do first to decide if they will read your letter. Once their attention has been gained and points scored with benefits and testimonials, the real object of the direct mail letter must be revealed.

The following page contains another example of a direct marketing letter. Again note the headline, breaking the text mid-sentence at the bottom of the page, and the various devices used to highlight key words and phrases.

YOU NEED A GREAT OFFER

I want to expose the truth to you, one that no one else in the advertising industry dares to tell you—99 percent of all your marketing is doomed to FAIL because of one KEY missing ingredient: The lack of an irresistible offer!

The truth of the matter is you can take an average list and average writing ability and still make a success of it if you have an irresistible offer! However, most do not.

This is where it gets tricky. You see, most people in the golf business have a totally distorted view of what it takes both physically and financially to get a new client.

This makes them very reluctant to devise an IRRESISTABLE OFFER since they think that ANY offer is giving away or cheapening their product!

An Invitation to Experience
the *Golf Club of Your Dreams!*

Dear Golfer:

This invitation to join Pine Barrens Golf Club is not for everyone.

It is reserved for a select few who appreciate magnificent golf and pristine, awe-inspiring surroundings. It's for those who wish to play, entertain, and relax in the friendly ambiance of other successful professionals just like you.

At the same time, it's for people who yearn to belong to a world-class golf facility <u>without</u> the huge up-front fees, assessments, and politics so often associated with stuffier clubs.

If I am correct, <u>you</u> are one of those people. If so, I'd like to share with you more about Pine Barrens and give you a glimpse of the privileges that await you as a member.

<u>Solitude and Tranquility Are Closer Than You Think</u>

Carved from sandy soil and dotted with pines, Pine Barrens sits in scenic Jackson, New Jersey--just 90 minutes from New York City, 55 minutes from Atlantic City and 75 minutes from Philadelphia. It has the virtue of easy access plus a mild maritime climate that makes year-round golf possible.

"The staff here treats you like family and the course and membership just keep getting better every year!"
         - Mike Jensen, Member, Since 1999, Brielle, NJ

From the moment you arrive at our gorgeous, Adirondack-style clubhouse, you'll know you're in for something special. First, you'll notice there are no

(continued)

What is a player, member or home buyer worth to you?

If you get a new player to show up at your club for a $50 green fee, you make $50. But if you get that player back 10 times this year, that player is worth $500; get him back 20 times and he's worth $1,000! And that does not include pro shop or F&B revenue, referrals, and so forth! That player's true value as a client might well be $2,000 for which you should gladly pay $100 or more to get him in the door.

Now, let's say you spend $12,000 on a direct mail campaign to 10,000 golfers in your area. What will the response be?

I could tell you the typical response to a good list, with good copy is 0.5 percent, but even that would be a stretch.

What's a great offer?

The truth of the matter is that, all things being equal, the number of people who respond will be based on the quality of your offer!

You can get 1 percent, 3 percent, or even 5 percent response rates and higher BUT ONLY TO IRRESISTABLE OFFERS:

- ✔ Offer a $5 discount to your green fee and the response will be lukewarm at best!

- ✔ Offer a dozen Pro V1s and you'll do way better than 0.5 percent!

- ✔ Offer a FREE lunch and response drops back to alarmingly average.

- ✔ Offer a FREE green fee and watch response SOAR!!!

- ✔ Tell people to come see your golf homes in Florida because they are exclusive...yawn.

- ✔ Offer two nights in the Ritz, a round of golf, and a property tour at a very attractive discounted rate and, BOOM, they are already on SouthWest.com booking their flight!

In order to determine your optimum offer you have to track your leads, conversions, and up-sells. It may well be okay to give away $600 worth of gifts per person to attract 30 new members as we did recently at a club in California.

Sure it's a loss leader, but it's one that pays off VERY QUICKLY in the form of monthly dues!!!

What works?

We had an amazing response to an $80 tee package in closing over $150,000 of outing business in just 30 days at one of our resort clients.

We have had excellent response to books, DVDs, and Audio CDs as premiums.

Property discover packages, free room nights, and replay rounds all work in the right situation.

Like most effective marketing, the key to finding effective offers is to test, test, test.

Spell out the action you want from the reader

What do you want the reader to do? What is the offer they should act upon at once? The more compelling your offer, the greater your response will be. Whatever you decide to offer, be sure to emphasize the value. For example, if you're offering a free room night, be sure you let your people know that it is a $200 value. The higher the perceived value, the more response you will generate. In addition to the actual offer, direct mail campaigns often include some kind of sweetener or bonus if you act now. You might want to offer a T-shirt or free golf glove, a free book, or some other kind of inducement to get people to respond immediately.

Your letter has to create a sense of urgency, a sense of loss if they don't pick up the phone and act right now. Here's a letter for the club where I live:

"Where to Live If You Live For Golf"

Dear Golfer:

There are obviously lots of great places you can choose to make your home in Florida if you like to play golf.

But...if you truly love golf, there is simply no better choice than **Black Diamond**. Our facility features 45 holes of spectacular, un-crowded, Fazio golf. Great weather all year round, luxurious, yet affordable homes and a diverse and active membership that is always ready to invite some new blood into their games. No matter what your scorecard looks like you'll find a group to match your game. Unlike many top clubs you don't have to bring your game with you at **Black Diamond.** In fact you'll find year round play with a group that's a perfect match for your game!

Of course, once you are a member of our **"Top 100 Club"** that boasts (according to noted sports writer **Dan Jenkins)** *"The best five consecutive holes in the world,"* you might find plenty of friends flying in to see you as well!

You'll find our clubhouse facilities an excellent place to conduct business and entertain friends. While our world class fitness center, tennis and swimming facilities will help keep you in great shape.

For a very limited time we are offering the opportunity for you and your spouse to experience the spectacular beauty of Black Diamond, our world class golf courses, cuisine and accommodations for the nominal fee of just $495 per couple.

Here's how it works: Fly to Tampa, Florida where you will be met and welcomed by the Black Diamond limousine. Then just sit back and relax as you enjoy the tranquil beauty of Florida's Nature Coast on your journey to **Black Diamond**. Once on property you will be shown to your spacious cottage accommodations. Next it's time to take a tour of the property before you experience the beautiful rolling terrain of our **Ranch** course. In the evening enjoy a sumptuous dinner in our clubhouse and meet some of our friendly members. Tour the area once more in the morning before an early afternoon round on our famed **Quarry** Course.

To take advantage of this spectacular offer go at once to www.GolfBlackDiamond.com and register now. This offer is for a very limited time so even if you plan to visit us later in the year please register now to avoid disappointment. If you have any questions please feel free to contact me directly at **888-328-8099**.

Yours sincerely,
Ken Breland
Director of Sales

P.S. Will Rogers once said he loved investing in real estate because "*It was the only thing they weren't making any more of.*" Nowhere is that statement more true than in the pristine beauty of Black Diamond. We are in the final phase of development and soon it will all be gone! Don't wait too long to come and see us and take advantage of our special offer today at www.BlackDiamond.com.

The importance of your P.S.

Many people read the headline of the letter and then go straight to the end to see who signed it and read the P.S. For this reason it is extremely important that you use both your headline and your P.S. to state your case as succinctly and powerfully as possible. Excite the reader and promise him specific and tangible rewards for taking his valuable time to read through the body of your text.

THE BROCHURE

Your brochure should be a graphical representation of your club and should expand on the major points of your letter. The majority of direct mail campaigns use either a 4-page format (an 11 × 17 page folded in half) or a 3- or 4-fold format that is 8.5 × 11 or 11 × 17, printed on both sides.

Use the front cover for a good clean photograph or graphic that demonstrates the end result of your service. If you sell a vacation experience, show relaxed people smiling. If you improve players' golf games, show their score cards. The better you can visually demonstrate the end result of your services in your lead photograph, the more effective your brochure will be. And don't forget to promise a clear benefit in the headline.

The inside of your brochure is where you repeat your story. Use a less personal approach that is full of facts and benefits. Make every line read from the golfer's perspective. If your benefits are unclear, remove that copy at once. To break up your text, use descriptive headlines, graphics, pictures, and charts. Always use captions under pictures or graphics to sell yourself or your service, never to describe what is in the picture. (Many brochures stupidly don't use captions or headlines with their photos!) Use facts, figures, statistics, surveys, comparisons, awards, and anything else to prove that you will do exactly what you say you will. Use the back panel or back page for summarizing all your benefits point-by-point, a brief biography dripping with benefits, or a new set of testimonials elevating your reputation. Also include a strong call to action.

The envelope

There are two different strategies when it comes to the envelope. One is to leave the impression that this is important and personal. That means using no copy, a first class stamp, and at least a laser-printed address. (Handwritten is always better!)

A Rare Opportunity To Join One Of The Top Private Golf Clubs In The World!

I t is a rare opportunity indeed to be able to join a private club with a course so highly acclaimed as Pine Barrens. Most clubs of this stature have a waiting list back to the Mayflower and therein lies your opportunity. Our club, designed by architect Eric Bergstol, recently named the **#1 Public Golf Course in New Jersey** by *Golf Week* is going private. Opportunities like this don't come often and don't last long especially when you consider what a surprising value membership at Pine Barrens offers. Our low, refundable initiation deposit and reasonable golf dues not only give you full membership at Pine Barrens but incredibly provides access to seven other top clubs in the Empire Golf network including; Pine Hill, Twisted Dune, New Jersey National, Minisceongo, Branton Woods and Hollowbrook.

To Find Out More About Membership At Pine Barrens Golf Club Call Now!

Spectacular Golf Is Just The Beginning

Carved from the sandy soil of the New Jersey Pine Barrens, from which it derives its name, the course gives the appearance of having been there forever, so naturally does it blend with it's surrounding land. Stretching to 7,112 yards from the back tees, Pine Barrens is truly a test for the good player and has already been used as a qualifying site for the US Open. Yet while the challenge from the back tees may be too much for many golfers, four additional sets allow players of all abilities to choose where their game is best suited for maximum enjoyment. While there are huge areas of natural wasteland to negotiate, the course also provides generous fairways and large greens nestled in between the pine trees and scrub oaks that cover the property. Each hole is truly separate in design and feel and challenges the player with a wide verity of shots leaving fewclubs untouched during the round.

www.PineBarrensMembership.com

Friendly & Active Membership

While our course speaks for itself it's our membership that truly makes Pine Barrens a special place. Our membership is comprised of successful professionals, entrepreneurs and athletes. All of whom share with you a deep passion for the game. You'll find them down to earth and always ready to welcome new players to their games. Whether it's the scratch group, the plus tens or ladies executive group, you'll find a perfect group for your interests and your skill.

Many of our members use our course as a sort of office away from work, and you'll quickly find that many of your business associates are eager to take you up on an offer to play Pine Barrens. Is there any better way to do business?

World-class Practice Facilities

Our practice facilities are no mere after thought and provide the perfect environment to work on your game before or after your round.

Our double ended grass driving range, chipping area and oversized practice green allow you to recreate any situation that you might find on the course. Your experience would not be complete if it were not for our dedicated team of service professionals always ready to help you get more enjoyment from the game.

The Clubhouse

Our impressive Adirondack-style clubhouse compliments the course. The subtle beauty of exposed timbers and the sweet smell of cedar is sure to soothe your senses after your round. While inside the clubhouse offers a restaurant, bar, full-service golf shop, and locker room facilities.

Knowledgeable, Friendly Staff

From the bag drop to the pro shop and the kitchen to the range, you will be always be delighted by the way you are treated as a member at Pine Barrens. Our team is dedicated to making your membership experience at the best golf experience of your life!

Call Now 1-877-574-2400 ext. 3

One side of a typical direct mail brochure. Notice all of the testimonials on the other side (on page 189).

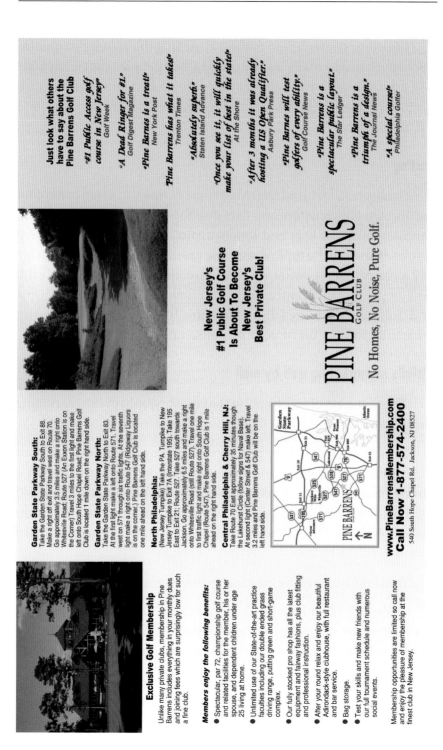

Just look what others have to say about the Pine Barrens Golf Club

"#1 Public Access golf course in New Jersey"
Golf Week

"A Dead Ringer for #1."
Golf Digest Magazine

"Pine Barrens is a treat!"
New York Post

"Pine Barrens has what it takes"
Trenton Times

"Absolutely superb."
Staten Island Advance

"Once you see it, it will quickly make your list of best in the state"
At the Shore

"After 3 months it was already hosting a US Open Qualifier."
Asbury Park Press

"Pine Barrens will test golfers of every ability."
Golf Course News

"Pine Barrens is a spectacular public layout."
The Star Ledger

"Pine Barrens is a triumph of a design."
The Journal News

"A special course"
Philadelphia Golfer

PINE BARRENS
GOLF CLUB

No Homes, No Noise, Pure Golf.

New Jersey's
#1 Public Golf Course
Is About To Become
New Jersey's
Best Private Club!

Exclusive Golf Membership

Unlike many private clubs, membership in Pine Barrens includes everything in your monthly dues and joining fees which are surprisingly low for such a fine club.

Members enjoy the following benefits:

- Spectacular, par 72, championship golf course and related facilities for the member, his or her spouse, and dependent children under age 25 living at home.

- Unlimited use of our State-of-the-art practice facilities including our double ended grass driving range, putting green and short-game complex.

- Our fully stocked pro shop has all the latest equipment and fairway fashions, plus club fitting and professional instruction.

- After your round relax and enjoy our beautiful Adirondack-style clubhouse, with full restaurant and bar service.

- Bag storage.

- Test your skills and make new friends with our full tournament schedule and numerous social events.

Membership opportunities are limited so call now and enjoy the pleasure of membership at the finest club in New Jersey.

Garden State Parkway South:
Take the Garden State Parkway South to Exit 88. Make a right off exit and travel west on Route 70. Go approximately 3.5 miles and make a right onto Whitesville Road; Route 527 (An Exxon Station is on the Corner) Travel 3 miles to the first light and make left onto South Hope Chapel Road; Pine Barrens Golf Club is located 1 mile down on the right hand side.

Garden State Parkway North:
Take the Garden State Parkway North to Exit 63. At the first light make a left onto Route 571. Travel west on 571 through six traffic lights. At the seventh light make a right onto Route 547 (Ridgeway Liquors is on the corner.) Pine Barrens Golf Club is located one mile ahead on the left hand side.

North Philadelphia:
(New Jersey Turnpike) Take the PA. Turnpike to New Jersey Turnpike to Exit 7A (Interstate 195). Take 195 East to Exit 21; Route 527. Take 527 south towards Jackson. Go approximately 6.5 miles and make a right onto Whitesville Road (still Route 527). Travel one mile to first traffic light and make right onto South Hope Chapel (Route 547), Pine Barrens Golf Club is 1 mile ahead on the right hand side.

Central Philadelphia & Cherry Hill, NJ:
Take Route 70 East approximately 35 minutes though the Lakehurst Circle (follow signs for Naval Base). At second light (Center Street & 547) make left. Travel 3.2 miles and Pine Barrens Golf Club will be on the left hand side.

www.PineBarrensMembership.com
Call Now 1-877-574-2400

540 South Hope Chapel Rd. Jackson, NJ 08527

The other strategy is to make it clear that the envelope contains a solicitation, and make it so appealing that people open it anyway! Use a graphic and teaser that gets people excited and eager to open it up. Promise a clear benefit like lower scores, a better deal, or a VIP invitation.

Testing

Finally, test, test, and test. Mail some to one list, some to another list and see which letters and lists pull the best. You'll find that you can use your best lists and letters again and again with excellent results. Some say the typical response rate for a direct mail campaign is 2 percent. Don't count on it! Figure closer to 0.5 percent until you've proven differently. Until you have a willing list of clients and followers, always figure on the low end. But follow-up telemarketing can boost your response rate much higher.

Pitfalls of marketing golf by mail

There is a lot of information that most people in the marketing business not only won't tell you, but often deny!

Let's say you decide to do a direct mail campaign to boost your membership. You write and design a wonderful package with a strong offer, print up 10,000 pieces and trust them to the good old US Postal Service. Then you sit back and wait for your 2 percent response because that's the number you have always heard thrown around!

Two hundred people rushing to the phones!

Sadly, this is fantasy because there is NO AVERAGE RESPONSE RATE. Response is driven by a multitude of factors and if you are going to guess what yours will be before it happens, start at 0.5 percent and you won't be too disappointed.

So you take my word for it and re-adjust your sights on getting 50 responses, but, sadly, my friend, you are still mistaken. You see, you are counting on a .5 percent response from the 10,000 pieces your think you mailed when the truth of the matter is you'll be lucky if 9000 of them ever make to the right mail box!

NO! You say, how can this be?

First, no list is perfect, most claim only 96 percent delivery which means do not be surprised if you get back a whopping 400 envelopes for every 10,000 pieces you send out!

And be prepared, no matter who you rent your list from: Some lady WILL call up and tell you her husband's been dead for seven years!!!

Some do a better job of updating their lists than others but even the real clean lists don't necessarily generate a better response, you just feel better that less mail came back.

So of the 10,000 thought you mailed, you are already down to 9,600.

I actually got ahead of myself because the "10,000 pieces mailed" assumes that your printer delivered all 10,000 pieces to the mailing house. Most printers work on a plus or minus 5 percent tolerance and all it takes is the press to jam for a few seconds and you're down another 300 or 400 pieces. (Ever spend a day in a print shop? I have!)

Then, of course, there is the mailing house itself, a massive, poorly lit warehouse, staffed mainly by illegal aliens with hundreds and hundreds of mail sacks just sitting on the floor. It is surprisingly common for mail to be sent to the entirely wrong list! (It's already happened to me once this year! After finally admitting their mistake six weeks later, the mailing house reprinted the mailing piece and mailed it at their expense.)

Then there are mailing houses that mail, say 10 percent less mail than they say they did. Just one sack, you understand, nothing that will be missed...but that sack of unstuffed, unmailed letters creates a tidy profit when you add the mythical postage!

And, as for that official looking U.S. Postal Service receipt, that's about as reliable as those blank ones you get from cab drivers. The mailing house brings in the forms saying that 10,000 pieces are being mailed and the USPS clerk signs a receipt for it. The postal clerks don't count the pieces. At some point, postal employees will estimate the size of the mailing by weight. For example, if one of your pieces weighs .8 ounces and the form that was presented at to the post office says you're mailing 10,000 pieces, then the total weight of your mail should be 500 pounds. If the mailing house only brought in 9,000 pieces, the weight will be less than 500 pounds, but you'll never hear about it as the postal service doesn't mind getting paid for more pieces than are actually getting mailed. The only time you'll hear about an error is if you've mailed more pieces than you've paid for.

With all those direct mail sacks and tubs lying around, one of your sacks could easily be missed by accident. But even the potential incompetence or larceny of your printer and mailing house pales in comparison to that of the U.S. Postal System.

Don't get me wrong. It's amazing that you can send a letter 3000 miles in a couple of days for less than 50 cents and, yes, there are lots of wonderful people who work in the postal service BUT...and it's a big BUT...I could fill a book with personal examples of incompetent morons as well. And I can vouch that several of them work at my local post office!

When you send bulk mail, it does not get treated like first class mail, it gets treated like NO class mail. If you're like me, you've received mailings sent via bulk mail whose offers are long expired. Bulk mail sits sometimes for days or even weeks until the people sorting it deem that they have the time to process it after getting all the regular mail on it's merry way. The longer it sits, the more chance it has of getting lost or dumped. (Whenever you do a bulk mailing, always make sure your name is on the list so you have some idea about when the pieces are delivered.)

Yes, dumping mail is a crime, but you can read about it every month in your local newspaper! It happens. Joe the postman is having a bad day, his wife is mad at him, the dog tore up the rug, his '88 Camero needs a valve job, and his back is aching. He's got a whole tray of JUNK MAIL to deliver, and who needs this stuff anyway? Why not just leave it in the van and do it tomorrow when he feels better; it's not like anyone is going to miss it. But tomorrow for this particular mail never comes and Joe eventually just disposes of it! Yep, that's right, he throws it away it and it happens often, far more often than you would believe! (People do not become government employees because of their incredible entrepreneurial zeal!)

Admittedly I get a lot of mail, but never does a week go by without me getting a piece addressed to someone else. I bet this happens to you too!

To say that 90 percent of the mail you thought you printed and mailed gets delivered to the right person is pushing it! Some people estimate as little as 70 percent of bulk mail gets through!

So with all these factors going against you, is it actually worth doing direct mail?

Absolutely! Done right, it is still the best, most responsive form of marketing money can buy! I just want you to be aware of the pitfalls, so you'll work harder on the key factors that can make your mailings successful.

SUMMARY

Direct mail is the purest form of advertising and can pay the greatest rewards, but only if you do it right. A great offer with dramatic headlines sent to a good list is a start. Then test and refine until your mailings pull predictable, repeatable responses.

Chapter Twelve

Building the Perfect Web Site for Your Club

WHY YOU <u>MUST</u> HAVE A WORLD-CLASS WEB SITE AND BUILD ALL OF YOUR MARKETING AROUND IT!

It's still tough to get some people to realize that your web site is the absolute foundation of all your marketing activities. It's better than print, radio, TV, billboards, and Yellow Pages. In fact, about the only marketing that gives the web a run for it's money is direct mail. Since that is about 100 times more expensive than a web site, it pays to focus your attention on the web first.

Think about your club's web site:

 ✔ It is the only employee you have who never calls in sick. It books tee times and answers questions 24 hours a day. (If your site doesn't do this and more, talk to us.)

 ✔ It's the only marketing you have that can send an instant and personalized response to prospective players or members at 3 AM on a Sunday morning by using pre-programmed auto responders and follow-up letters.

✔ It's the only marketing you have that can collect detailed information on outing, banquet, or wedding prospects while you sleep by using dynamic request forms.

✔ It's the only marketing you can do that incrementally lowers your future marketing costs with almost every visit to your web site.

There is no more important marketing tool at your club than your web site, yet most clubs are content to trade out to amateur designers, members, or the owner's son-in-law rather than make the commitment to a world-class web site. Even where clubs have made substantial investments with ad agencies or web design companies, they almost always miss the mark. While these vendors understand the technology and design aspects, they do NOT understand the marketing aspects of dynamic web sites. Nor do most understand the golf market, and those who do come at it from only an online perspective rather than integrating online marketing with their overall marketing efforts.

Your web site cannot just be pretty; it has to be a marketing machine to be an effective tool.
Ninety-eight percent are not!

In this chapter, you will discover:

✔ How your current site measures up

✔ How to design an effective web site

✔ What the most important features are

✔ Why you should automate as much as possible

Take this quick test to see how effective your current web site is as a marketing tool

	Yes	No

1. Do you have at least 5 different ways to collect data on your site? ☐ ☐

2. Can you make changes to your site anytime you want without calling anyone and without any computer experience necessary? ☐ ☐

3. Can you do e-mail blasts to drive play anytime you want with no computer experience needed? ☐ ☐

4. Can players book a tee time or buy products online at your site? ☐ ☐

5. Does your site have compelling copy that asks for action on every page? ☐ ☐

6. Can prospects make outing, meeting, and wedding requests online at your site and can you preprogram your site with sales letters to automatically follow up on all requests? ☐ ☐

7. Does your site update itself with new golf content automatically each month so there are always fresh articles, instruction, and humor to read? ☐ ☐

8. Does your site incorporate any features that promote viral marketing among players in your area (such as a free golf joke book or tips booklet they can download from your site)? ☐ ☐

9. Does you site offer a media section where the media can download high resolution pictures, logos, and fact sheets when they want instant information on your facility? ☐ ☐

10. Do you use a full-color electronic newsletter to stay in monthly contact with your players? ☐ ☐

If you answered "No" to more than two of these questions—you do not have a marketing machine—you have an average golf web site. **It looks pretty, but does little to help you!**

TYPES OF GOLF WEB SITES

There are basically three types of web sites for golf businesses.

✔ **A site to service your existing members** and perhaps attract some new ones. This site would include a lot of interactive features, like your schedules, news, events, and perhaps have a password-protected section that helps make the members feel special.

✔ **A pre-opening site** is mainly interested in getting local leads (which I call a direct sales site). There is nowhere to click, just a sales pitch to get you new business in the form of an e-mail address or phone call requesting information.

✔ **A retail site** would include daily fee courses, resorts, real estate developments, and golf schools, and all those looking to attract and retain ongoing play. These sites will often have an e-commerce feature so you can sell merchandise, tee times, or other items by credit card.

THE TWELVE MOST IMPORTANT FACTORS IN BUILDING THE PERFECT WEB SITE FOR YOUR CLUB

(For up-to-date real world examples of all the following features go to www.LegendaryVault.com.)

1 **Your web site must be a data collection machine.** The number one function of your web site is to collect information. Only when you have good information from your clients can you meet their needs correctly. This is every bit as true for a private club as a daily-fee club, resort, or real estate development. You must know your customers' wants, needs, and trends before you can fulfill them.

For this reason you need multiple data collection points incorporated into your site's design. If you just offer a single e-newsletter sign-up on your site, you are only collecting about 20 percent of your potential e-mail addresses. If you doubt me for a moment, look at your traffic and look at your sign-ups!

Some people are contest people; they respond to a chance to win! Some people are coupon people; they respond to discounts. Give *me* a chance to download information though (like 20 ways to hit it 20 yards further) and I will gladly give you my name, address, e-mail, and mother's maiden name!!! Everyone has a different motivation so the only way to get maximum response from your site is to build multiple data collection points into your site. (Our latest SmartSites have no fewer than 5 different ways to gather data. If your site doesn't, you are really missing the boat!!)

With the importance of data collection in mind, the key goal of your home page should be to collect data, either through surveys, contests, downloads, request forms, or online bookings. Other pages should also make a strong effort to collect data such as outing pages, weddings, banquets, meetings, and so forth. Feedback pages and member surveys work well at private clubs, as do monthly give-aways of dinner.

Detailed information must compel the visitor to ACTION! The second most important key to web success is to provide lots of information. One of the biggest complaints of web surfers is finding a site and then not finding the information they were looking for once they get there! Put as much information on your site as you can and let the visitors decide what's important to them. The more you make your web site the center of communication at your club, the more you will gain from it. Post news, schedules, specials, reminders, photos of members and guests, and so on. When visitors know that the site is updated regularly with the latest information, they will use it. When they show up several times and nothing has changed, they won't be back anytime soon.

Merely providing detailed information, content, and news—which few clubs do—is NOT enough. On your site's key pages—membership, outings, banquets, lessons, real estate, golf, and so on—the copy MUST SELL. Ninety-nine percent of all golf web sites ignore this vital truth. It's the *copy* that sells. Let me repeat—*it's the copy that sells!*

I was shocked recently to hear a so-called golf marketing expert speak to a seminar audience at the Golf Club Owners Convention and tell everyone that nobody reads so it doesn't really matter how good the copy is!!!!!!!!!!! I couldn't believe my ears. The number one reason people use the web is for information. If you present that information using Marketing 101 features and benefits you will get a thousand times more response than if you stick to a "just the facts ma'am" approach!

Each page should be a sales pitch for something

Each page must be a mini sales pitch to move the prospect to do something. Book a tee time, make a dinner reservation, take a lesson, or whatever eventual action you want them to take. It should be a complete sales pitch with a beginning, a middle, and an end; features, benefits, testimonials, and a call to action. Only if each page contains all these elements can it be deemed a great web page—and that's not just one page, it's every page you have that ultimately pushes for a sale. There is no such thing as too much good information, only too little information or information that is not relevant to making a decision.

(See the chapters on ads and direct mail for more details on writing great copy.)

3 **The site must be easy to navigate and easy to read!** A visitor to your site should be able to easily move from any page to any other page. Many golf sites I have looked at [thousands] break this rule. Use navigation menus that have a consistent look and location on

An easy-to-read, easy-to-navigate site with all the right data collection points.

every page at the top or left hand side—don't put any obstacles in your visitors' way.

Menu design 101

✔ Menus on the right don't work well. People naturally look left or up.

✔ Menus at the bottom of your site are often below eye level on many computers, meaning there is no menu at all as far as those users are concerned.

✔ Don't have more than about eight or nine choices in the main menu. You should use sub-menus from that point. Sites with twenty or more items in the menu are not user friendly. If you have that many, always used a left side menu

✔ Make the type style of your menus large enough to read. Many monitors (even today) have less than great resolution. Bigger is almost always better.

✔ White text on a black background is 33 percent harder for the human eye to read. Why make it harder?

✔ A small button on every page that links back to the home page also adds to the friendliness of your site.

4 **Your site must allow the visitor to complete a transaction.** There are few things as frustrating as investing time visiting a web site only to find once you have made a decision to act that your next step is to call between 9–5 to actually book a tee time or make an appointment. The web is open 24/7, 365 days a year, and a great majority of web surfing is done after normal business hours. You must have online reservations, a shopping cart, and the ability to request dates for outings and banquets without having to wait until the next day. If you do not, you will lose business. Web surfers will rarely, if ever, take the trouble to print out a form, fill it in, then mail or fax it to you. If you don't offer online booking for tee times, your web visitors are likely to go to one of your competitors who do, rather than wait to call you in the morning.

5 **The site must have automatic follow-up and content.** Perhaps the most radical difference between the Legendary Marketing systematic approach and other ad agencies and consultants is our commitment to relentless follow up. Nowhere is that better demonstrated than in the automatic tools we build into our SmartSites. These are the same tools you MUST build into your site if you are to get maximum results from your online investment.

Auto responders increase your response

An auto responder lets you pre-program sales letters, e-zines, and follow-up messages that respond immediately to any request generated from your site. For instance, when someone registers on your web site, you can immediately send them a message thanking them and providing your latest offers. For outing or membership leads, three or four follow ups can be programmed in. New clubs or real estate developments may follow up twenty times or more over the next year. Immediate, consistent follow up increases sales, branding and income! Best of all, it's automatic and does not rely on anyone at the club remembering to do it!

WARNING: DO NOT make your auto responses passionless John-Doe follow-ups that generate the excitement of the automatic train voice at the Atlanta airport! Write them like great ads, with compelling headlines, benefits, testimonials, and calls to action. "Thank you for contacting us," doesn't cut it!

Automatic content engine

Fresh content on your web site is critical. Yet most clubs seem to find it difficult to add new content on a consistent basis. If your web site does not have changing information people will not go back. While custom information from your club is always best, it rarely is produced consistently. For example out of one hundred pros who told me they would post monthly tips, three actually posted any and one only posted 12!

It is for this reason that we built a content engine into our Legendary SmartSite and I would highly recommend you do the same. Each month at the end of the month the content engine uploads 12 new golf articles to the site. These include golf instruction, golf book reviews, golf stories, golf jokes, quotes, architecture, golf history and more. If your pro has time to write custom golf articles, they can easily be used instead of the generic tips. These articles not only give visitors a variety of reasons to go back and browse, but also provide content for your newsletter.

Automatic newsletters save time and increase traffic every month

Your monthly electronic newsletter (e-zine) is another feature that you can automate with a huge savings in time, money, and postage (not to mention a large increase in traffic)! Our Legendary SmartSites are designed to automatically take clubs' posted news and specials from their web sites and add additional golf content from our content engine. The e-zine robot feature then creates and sends a full color e-zine newsletter with the club's header, headlines, and "shorts" from the various departments.

By sending out your monthly newsletter with brief samples of your content, you remind your recipients to go back to your site on a monthly basis for the full information and to view your offers and news.

So, to recap, the benfits of a good web site are little work, consistent marketing, increased traffic, and the "viral" pass-along effect of having your customers forward the humor, instruction, and other articles to friends, bringing others to your web site. It's like having a full-time web marketing person for about 50 cents an hour!! I highly recommend that you build this type of functionality into your site. It will save you around a hundred hours of work per year.

Campaign Manager does <u>all</u> your e-marketing for you!

Perhaps the most innovative and powerful feature you can use on your web site for marketing is an automatic marketing engine. For instance, our Campaign Manager feature can be preprogrammed with an almost unlimited number of promotional e-mail campaigns. You can decide to send a series of e-mail messages to each player, inquiry, local association, and so on. You can also have a series of e-mails developed to contact people based on their answers to any question you choose to ask on your SmartSite. This is true one-to-

In this month's edition

- The "Yes I Can" Attitude
- The Art of Golf Design
- Follow-Through
- Golf Quotes
- Golf Humor
- A 3-Step Routine that will Create the Consistency You are Looking For
- Online Proshop Specials

Latest Club News

- Overnights and Extended Stays
- YOUR COMPANY GOLF OUTING
- Improve your game in 2004!!

Anecdotes
The "Yes I Can" Attitude
"It's easy to play like Jack Nicklaus when you're Jack Nicklaus."
Jack Nicklaus
During the 1973 Ryder Cup, Jack Nicklaus was paired with Tom Weiskopf, who had won that year's British Open at Royal

Continue >>

Book Review
The Art of Golf Design
Michael Miller, who has the rare combination of being a golf professional and landscape artist (in oils), has captured the classic holes, from the 1920's and 1930's, that will make your mouth water with every new page...

Continue >>

Golf Tips
Follow-Through
Cutting your follow-through short can negatively effect distance, direction, and ball flight. The next time you're on the range, freeze your body after a full swing and take a look at your right foot.

Continue >>

Golf Quotes
Golf Quotes
"I play with friends, but we don't play friendly games." -Ben Hogan

"Golf is an ideal diversion, but a ruinous disease." -Bertie Forbes

"Putts get real difficult the day they hand out the money." -Lee Trevino

Continue >>

Golf Humor
Golf Humor
Three guys are playing golf earlSunday Golf Three guys are playing golf early on a Sunday morning. Ahead of them is a guy playing, and playing well, all by himself. As they all finished the round the threesome went to the single player and asked if

Continue >>

Instruction
A 3-Step Routine that will Create the Consistency You are Looking For
Most of us have had the experience of waking up and going through a normal morning, and as soon as you are ready to head out the door, you can't find your keys...

Continue >>

Online Pro Shop Specials
Coming Soon!

An ideal e-zine, full of news, offers, and golf content.

one marketing, automatically sending people offers on only the things that interest them the most.

For example, let's say you ask whether the player has any interest in Summer Junior Golf Camps. The person answers yes, but it's only January. Not to worry. Your Legendary Marketing Campaign Manager will AUTOMATICALLY follow up with an e-mail on May 15th letting ONLY the players who answered YES know the dates and details of the summer camps. It will follow up again June 1st with more information and a link so that they can go ahead and register their kids online! You do nothing! Campaign Manager sends a beautiful, four-color e-mail promotion out at exactly the right time for you, whether you happen to be in your office or vacationing in St. Andrews!

Here is another example: Let's say you carry Nike, Ashworth, and Fairway Blues clothing. The first person who fills in your survey says he likes Nike shirts the best. Campaign Manager will see this answer and send him follow-up campaigns with pictures and offers ONLY on Nike products. This connects with your customers at every level of your operation and drives incremental revenue for every department, from the pro shop to the dining room. Plus, of course, it makes your follow-up superior to every club in your marketplace. Best of all, it produces extra income for every single tournament, social, or pro shop event.

Think about your extra income potential if just four more people signed up for every single event at your club. That's four to the power of 100 different events, that's 400 people who, even at only $30 an event, represent an extra $12,000 in revenue. If it drove eight people, it would be $24,000. If the eight people paid $40 a head, it would be an extra $32,000. And remember, this is all automatic.

It takes us over 100 hours to design, write, and program all the campaigns but then they are done for the year. No worries about staff forgetting or calling in sick. No worries about staff leaving and

Campaign Manager

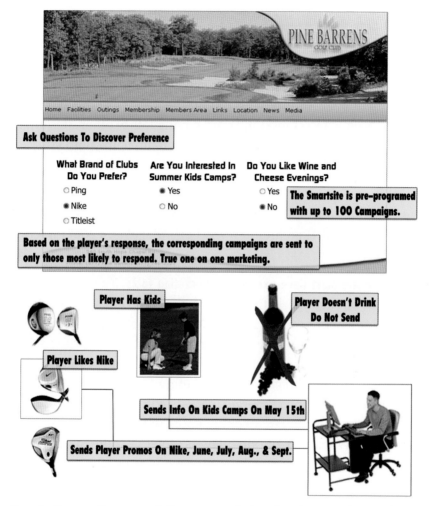

Campaign Manager allows you send offers automatically throughout the year to those poeple most likely to respond based on individuals' own preferences obtained through your SmartSite.

new staff needing to be re-trained; in fact, no worries at all, mate! Just beautifully consistent follow-up, on time, every time, without fail!

6. **If your site is expected to create business, you must take the search engine rules into account.** Search engine rules and tactics change weekly so writing a definitive piece that lasts is hard. But whatever the rules are when you build your site, you had better know them. Currently they include having 200–400 words of text on your home page, (which many clubs don't) and having lots of other sites linked to yours. It's also a good idea to have a domain name with your key word in it and name your title tags and pictures with keywords.

We keep up on the every-changing search engine rules and the new rules are constantly being programmed on our customers' web sites. See our article archive at www.LegendaryVault.com for recent updates.

7. **Your site must have excellent e-marketing tools.** This is where the gold lies in e-marketing. E-marketing is even more effective if you can segment your target markets and make specific offers to those most interested. Our new Superserver takes a traditional list server program to an entirely new level. Based on the contact points you choose in your Legendary Marketing SmartSite, you can sort and send e-mail to specific target markets with the touch of a button. For example, you can e-mail only people who have entered outing requests, only women, or only players who live more than 50 miles away. In fact, you can sort by any category you choose with the touch of a button. This allows you to promote "shrimp night" to the people most interested in dining, tournaments to those most interested in competition, and junior events only to people with teens. Because you target people's real interests, people receive what they are interested in and there are no spam problems. In other words, customers don't unsubscribe when you are sending them the information of most interest to them!

Is that how you do your current e-mail marketing? Can you see the advantages of doing it this way?

Your site must have excellent reporting tools. Your site's reporting tools are the mechanism that you will use to evaluate your site's performance and tweak your online offerings. There are four important areas you are going to want to generate reports from:

A. Web site traffic

Your site should record the following key traffic information and review it monthly—if not weekly.

- ✔ How many visitors did you get?
- ✔ How many pages did the visitor view?
- ✔ What specific pages did they view?
- ✔ How did they find your site?

B. E-mails results

When you want to track the success of your e-marketing, you need powerful reporting tools on your site for the elements that matter most to making good decisions about your future marketing. You can quickly and easily find out the statistics you need including:

- ✔ How many e-mails did you send?
- ✔ How many bounced?
- ✔ How many were opened?
- ✔ How many people clicked through to your site?
- ✔ How many people forwarded the e-mail?
- ✔ How many unsubscribed?

In other words, you can tell the results of your e-mails on almost any dimension, in any time frame after you send them. These reports should also be presented in various graphic formats for quick inspection. (See a sample SmartSite e-blast report on the following pages.)

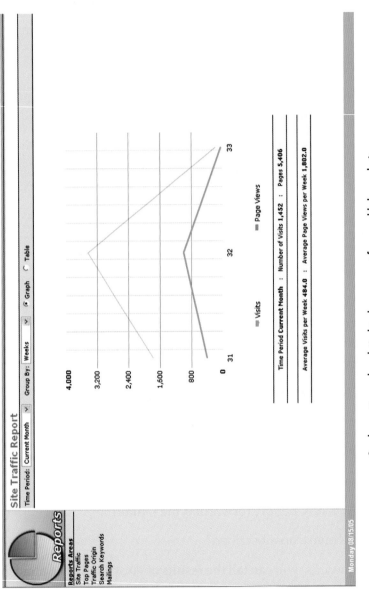

Good reporting and analytical tools are a must for a world-class web site.

Site Traffic Report

Time Period: Current Month   Group By: Weeks   ○ Graph ● Table

	Number of Visits	Avg Visits per Week	Pages	Avg Pages per Week
	1,452	484.0	5,406	1,802.0

Date			Visits	Page Views
31			408	1,783
32			995	3,432
33			49	191
Current Month			**1,452**	**5,406**

Reports

Reports Areas

Site Traffic
Top Pages
Traffic Origin
Search Keywords
Mailings

Traffic Origin Report

Time Period: Current Month   Origin: Summary   ● Graph ○ Report

Origin	%
Bookmarks / Direct A	78.03
Other Websites	16.19
Search Engines	5.78

Time Period Current Month

Reports

Reports Areas

Site Traffic
Top Pages
Traffic Origin
Search Keywords
Mailings

C. Contact point report

Since there are an unlimited number of questions you can ask in surveys or contact points, there are an unlimited number of reports you can run depending on what data are important to your operation. Common reports might include:

- ✔ Player frequency
- ✔ Player price points
- ✔ What other courses they frequent

D. Transaction reports

If you are running a shopping cart, your backend will log all the transactions and provide numerous reports on customer spending habits.

Your site must be easy to manage and update! This is a big deal because no one wants yesterday's news on the web; that's what newspapers are for! This is critical to your overall success because if your site is not easy to manage and update, your staff will never do it! Let me repeat that: *If your site is not easy to manage your staff won't do it!* Add to that a revolving door at most clubs for the position of *web site updater* and you have just washed your entire online investment down the drain. Ah, you say, but our web company updates our site for us.

Do they do it on weekends? Do they do it in the evenings? Do they do it immediately after receiving your request? In my experience probably not!

This is a feature we build into all of our web sites, so that even clients with very limited web experience can make simple additions to their sites *without* having to call us or *pay* someone else for changes. In fact, it's because of its ease of use that we called our product a SmartSite—the theory being that it is so easy and powerful to use that it makes everyone who uses it look smart! All a person has to do, in effect, is cut and paste whatever he wants to upload into a password-protected part of the site. Pick the page she wants to update, then paste—bingo!—it goes live. The edit and format features are designed to look like Word so control-C gets a headline centered and control-B gets it bolded. No code to learn, just a simple familiar interface! Legendary Marketing will of course update your site for you and, yes, we do work seven days a week. But even that does not deliver the personal satisfaction of waking up at 2 AM on a Sunday morning with an *ah-ha!* moment and being able to jump online and instantly add a special to your site or send an e-blast to your customers!

In less than five minutes we can train anyone at a club—and I mean anyone above the age of seven—how to update a SmartSite any time of the day or night. And, yes, I mean in FIVE minutes.

Make sure you have a feature like this built into your site, so that you are not held hostage to anyone and can quickly get news and information posted on your site to keep it fresh.

10 **The site must look good.** Notice how far down the list this rule came. On many people's lists, design comes first. The truth of the matter is that while look, feel, and design elements are important, they are a lot less important than the copy or what your site does on the back end. As long as you follow key guidelines about menus, make your type large enough to read, and have plenty of copy, there are almost an unlimited number of good designs you can come up with.

Here are a few key considerations:

✔ Be sure not to confuse the eye; people read from top to bottom and from left to right. Don't mess too much with that pattern.

✔ Highlight your four most important products at the very top of your site. For example Outings, Membership, Book a Tee Time, and Enter to Win!

Web sites should look attractive but must also follow several marketing rules.

✔ Avoid reverse type (white on black) it's 33 percent harder for the human eye to read.

✔ Make sure background colors or shading contrast enough that the text can be read. Can it be read if they print it out?

✔ Pictures work best at the top of the site with a headline underneath them, not above or over the top of them.

✔ Pictures in the body copy should always face in so the reader's eye moves towards the copy.

✔ The pictures should be big enough to actually see!

✔ Avoid overuse of bolded, capitalized, and colored letters. Use an easy-to-read font like Arial and understand that italicized words will slow down your reader. Have you ever come across a web site where the text stretches across the screen —and sometimes beyond? That is not the sign of a professional site. Generate a professional image by keeping your text in a narrow column—it makes for much easier reading.

✔ Make sure your site loads fast. Have you ever waited more than 30 seconds for a page to load? Probably not. And neither will your visitors. Compress all of your graphics for faster load times. Assume your web site is going to be viewed by the oldest browser on the slowest modem. You don't have complete control over this attribute, but what you can control, you should.

✔ Maintain a consistent look and feel. Be conscious of the rest of your course's printed material when you create your web pages. Be consistent in your graphics; use the same logo that appears on your letterhead and the same kind of color and style that's found on your other business material.

On a web site, you are not limited by the size of the paper as you are with printed materials. Make sure you tell the visitor everything you can about your property that helps sell it.

11 **The site must be built to grow with your club.** Web sites go out of date faster than computers; do you even remember the 286? It's for this reason that we designed the SmartSite in a modular form so we could constantly add new features and upgrades to the product. It's essential that you consider this when you build your site. Most clubs spend thousand of dollars only to find they have to spend thousands more and start from scratch two years down the line because their sites are dated and cannot integrate with newer technology.

12 **Be reliable; be protected.** Last, and by no means least, your site should be reliable. 24/7 is the colloquialism for expressing the expectation that the web, including your site, should be available twenty-four hours a day, seven days a week. If you are running your own server, it's advisable to have some degree of redundancy built into your system in order to meet this expectation. Having two servers (or more) is the best first step you can take to ensuring 24/7 capability. The day will come when your server will crash or you'll need to perform maintenance on it. You'd be surprised at the number of large companies that operate their sites on a single server. Most that do regret it at some point in time. If your hosting service is operating without some sort of backup, find a new provider. (We back up every one of our sites in two places every day, one on-site and one off-site.)

OTHER WEB-SITE FACTORS YOU SHOULD CONSIDER IN DESIGNING YOUR SITE

Think globally—the world can be your market

There's no shortage of consumers online. On the web your prospects are the entire world. In fact, nothing gives me a greater kick than signing up a new client in Sweden, or selling a set of clubs to a man in Pakistan! You'll experience the same euphoria when you start selling green fees, memberships, or products in places you don't even know how to find on a map.

Since most of your competitors will be focusing on their home markets, you can get the jump on the long-distance market. Visitors to your area often do web searches before they travel to look for attractions. For example, if you run a golf course in Orlando, why wait until golfers arrive from the UK or Canada and pick up a hotel guide. Help them find your web site ahead of time and offer an "out of towners" special. You can also run small ads or e-zine ads in other areas to get them to your web site before they even set foot on a plane. That's the type of marketing that makes millions (or even an extra round now and then!).

Add a media section to save time and money

Does you site offer a media section where the media can download high resolution pictures, logos and fact sheets when they want instant information on your facility? This is a simple example of using your web site to save time. By having a media section you increase your chances of getting your course free PR. You also don't have to spend time and money shipping out high resolution pictures or logos to people who want to design brochures and flyers for their outings or want to write articles on your club. Simply direct them to click on the picture of their choice and it instantly downloads a high-resolution image to their computer! Now that's instant gratification. Like most additions to our SmartSite product, we came up with this idea when I realized how much time and money we were wasting hunting around for clients' pictures or logos and overnighting them to various magazines or graphic designers.

Private club sites

Private clubs need specialized options to serve their members. Consider adding options to your site if you are a private club to increase members' communication and participation in your

An excellent example of a daily fee course that incorporates all of the
key elements into their web site.

activities. There are many member-only options you can offer
through password-protected gateways. These might include:

✔ **Photo gallery.** Special section to allow you to post club
photos that members can view, download, and e-mail to
friends or family.

✔ **Member directory.** Real-time updates of member
information to keep your directory current. Members will
always have contact information available to schedule
golf and social activities. Directories can also be printed
out in hard-copy format.

✔ **Reservations.** Offer convenient reservations to enable members (or others) to sign-up online for tournaments, dining, court times, and other events.

✔ **Calendar.** Post images and calendar messages to remind members of your tournaments, social events, and important dates. The calendar can be printed out for easy use with most day planners.

✔ **Online statements.** Allow members to access their monthly statements.

✔ **Menus.** Design and enter menus for your snack bar and dining facilities, and update special menu items daily, in seconds.

✔ **Meeting minutes, rules, and regulations.** Better distribution of business information that is for members' eyes only.

✔ **Custom member "dashboards."** Each member has a custom, personal area where they can keep a calendar of your events (and their entire personal schedules), fully password protected, of course.

✔ **Specialized member info.**
    ✔ Fitness info
    ✔ Tennis info
    ✔ Dining info
    ✔ Activities info

✔ **Specialized information.** Other info pages should also be customized to your membership's exact needs—for example, bridge info, ladies info, kids info.

✔ **Real-estate opportunities.** If you are selling homes or land, a real estate engine to display available property is also a good idea.

Members Only

Navigation	Club Calendar: August 2005						

<< Previous Month   Next Month >>

Navigation

- My Home Page
- Daily Tee Times
- Specials
- News
- Tournaments
- Private Club Calendar
- Directory
- Ladies Golf Association
- Player of the Year
- Links
- 2005 Tournament Schedule
- Member's Association

Printer Friendly Version

Sunday	Monday	Tuesday	Wednesday	Thursday	Friday	Saturday
	1	2 Ladies Day	3	4	5 Mixed Twilight	6
7	8	9 Ladies Day	10 Mixed Member Guest	11	12	13 Club Championship-Qualifier
14 Men's Club Championship	15	16 Ladies Day	17 Ladies Interclub Matches	18	19	20 Men's/Ladies Club Championship
21 Finals-Club Championship	22	23 Ladies Day	24	25	26	27
28	29	30 Ladies Day	31			

Latest News

- See All News Items

Club Calendar

August 2005

S	M	T	W	Th	F	S
	1	2	3	4	5	6
7	8	9	10	11	12	13
14	15	16	17	18	19	20
21	22	23	24	25	26	27
28	29	30	31			

My Information

,

Update My Information

<< Previous Month   Next Month >>

110 Pomona Road ~ Pomona, New York 10970 ~ Phone: 845- 362- 8200

This site is designed and maintained by **Legendary Marketing**

Keeping your members informed builds business.

As you can see, these are many factors that make up a great web site. Some publicize you to the outside world, others help you better serve your members or players. Your web site should be more than just a pretty brochure online. It should be the heart of your marketing.

SUMMARY

My discussion above of how to use the web comes from our experience doing hundreds of golf sites over the last few years. Legendary Marketing has built our SmartSite product from the ground up and enhanced it with feedback from several hundred clients. We heve designed our sites as more than just web sites, but as command and control centers for all a club's marketing efforts. Regardless of whether you choose to use our technology or go it alone, the items discussed above are the key elements you must build into your club's site if you are to use the web most effectively.

Chapter Thirteen

Building Your Club's Opt-In E-mail List

YOU CAN BUILD YOUR OPT-IN LIST TO 10,000 NAMES OR MORE IN 90 DAYS OR LESS

The last chapter showed you how important e-mail can be for your marketing. If you want to make money online, the key is to quickly build an opt-in e-mail list (where every member of your list has specifically requested to hear from you). This is directly opposite from those who choose to try to "spam" their way to riches. Spamming is when you send to e-mail lists of people who have not contacted you or have not registered to receive your offers. In addition to your own list, there are many e-mail lists of golfers who have indicated their interest in receiving golf offers (these golfers have "opted-in"). You can rent these lists. Then when people respond to your e-mail and sign in at your site, they become part of your own list.

In this chapter, you will discover:

✔ Why spam is evil

✔ Why opt-in lists are okay to send to

✔ 30 ways to build your opt-in list

E-MAIL SPAM

I know you get spammed. Everyone does. Personally, I receive around 50 or so a day. Of these e-mails, selling whatever products or services they have to offer, I delete most of them without opening them, yet they keep on coming. They are usually (though not always) poorly written and full of extremely hyped messages.

I get ads for dolls, cars, credit cards, merchant accounts, golf, vacations, and more. I won't even talk about the worst stuff which is sent out. One piece after another has to be deleted, and it just keeps coming.

Why so much spam e-mail?

If everyone is deleting it, then why do spammers keep sending it? It's simple. Although the response rates are extremely low, they still do get customers. Their financial cost in sending it is almost nothing, so it's looked upon as a good advertising vehicle. Some sales are better than nothing, right? Wrong. In all of the offers to send bulk e-mails for you, you never receive the full story.

What happens after you send bulk e-mail?

When you send bulk e-mail spam, you run big risks. If complaints are received—and they will be—your access to the web could be cut off. You are presumed guilty and must prove that the people who complain opted-in to your list. You could lose your local

Internet Service Provider, your web sites, your e-mail addresses, and more. Your server will cancel your account.

This doesn't even cover your reputation or the legal ramifications of sending unsolicited bulk e-mail. Currently, several states have laws on the books or in the works which can fine you $500 or more for each piece of bulk e-mail you send without a prior business relationship.

Bulk e-mail just isn't worth the problems. If you have considered using bulk e-mail, don't do it. There are so many other more effective ways to market your course on the Internet that it's not necessary to take the risks that go with spam.

What should you do?

I can tell you in one sentence what you should do instead of bulk e-mail. You should start building your own opt-in e-mail list today as covered in the previous chapter. E-mail marketing is effective. That's why so many people are using it. It can produce steady sales for your business.

BUILDING YOUR E-MAIL LIST—30 WAYS TO GET THOUSANDS OF SUBSCRIBERS FOR YOUR COURSE'S E-ZINE

Back in the 1700s in Holland, tulips became more valuable than gold. Today, the same can be said of e-mail names, with 1,000 really targeted names costing $350 for a single use.

Your goal should be to build an e-mail list of at least 10,000 potential players if you are in major market. If you are a resort or have more than 18 holes, 20,000 is your initial goal. Done right, this will slash your future marketing costs and keep your course full.

While no e-mail will be better than a TRUE opt-in at your club's own web site, here are some strategies we have used with various clients to build their e-mail lists. For each of these approaches, we invite the golfer to opt in and make it clear that we will stay in touch with them.

Contests. At one club's site we manage, you can enter a contest to win a free year of membership worth $6,000 when you sign up. We also do a monthly drawing for free golf and prizes, and send out an e-mail announcing that the winners have been posted on the site. This makes players go back to the site to see if they've won, giving us another opportunity to make an offer to them. Usually we get—listen to this—within 48 hours, a 100% response of

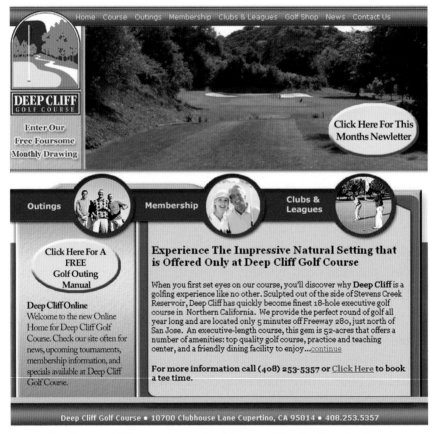

Note the several different techniques this club uses to collect data from its web site.

people checking to see if they have won within 48 hours. You can't beat that with a stick!

2   **Gift certificates.** At another club we offer a free $20 gift certificate for signing up. This is done automatically by sending the subscriber an e-mail with a code as soon as they sign up. We often do the same thing at GolfBooks.com. How about a green fee discount e-mailed to your prospect automatically when he signs up for your e-list?

3   **Free booklet downloads.** Some book sites give you the first chapter of the e-book version free of charge if you sign up. Can you offer a free booklet of golf tips or a free download of your yardage book? This is one of the most popular and best ways to gather e-mail addresses.

4   **Limited time offers.** Let your visitors know that the special offer and a subscription to your free e-zine is only available for a limited time.

5   **Free software.** Offer your visitors free software if they subscribe. We feature a golf stats program on some of our clients' sites that we developed as a "sticky" to make them re-visit the site again and again. It works, both in gathering e-mails and in getting them to come back.

6   **Exclusivity.** Offer your visitors access to a private members-only or VIP part of your web site if they subscribe. People like to feel special, on or off the web.

7   **Gifts.** You could offer your visitors a free tangible gift if they subscribe, like a free bag tag, golf ball, or cap.

8   **Access to content.** Tell your visitors, as I do, that they have the right to re-publish your articles in their own e-zines' content if they subscribe to yours. The key is they have to keep the resource box intact, so that anyone reading an article will be directed back to visit you at your site. This is great for golf pros, golf resorts, and golf schools.

9 **Teases.** You can tease visitors by letting them know what secrets or specials will be included in your future e-mails. Some courses offer special hot deals at their course by e-mail only.

10 **Free services.** You could offer your visitors a free service if they subscribe, such as a free 15-minute golf lesson. You can then up-sell them on a series. This is a very effective way of building your lesson business and is seldom used. Take advantage of ideas like this by employing the Nike principle: Just do it!

11 **Stated value.** Let your visitors know what the value of your e-zine is by placing a dollar price on it. "This information is worth $97, but it's yours free if you sign up now."

12 **Exclusive information.** Tell your visitors that you offer original content not found in any other place.

13 **Leads from e-mails.** When people e-mail you from your contact page or personal e-mail, in your response ask if you may place them on your mailing list.

14 **Pass-along subscriptions.** Include a direct message inviting existing subscribers to pass along your e-zine to someone else at the bottom of every publication. You'll be amazed at how many extra subscribers you can generate just by making this suggestion.

15 **Testimonials.** Publish testimonials about your e-zine throughout your web site, so people hear from others how great it is.

16 **Subscription numbers.** Let your visitors know how many people have already subscribed to your e-zine. This suggests credibility and value.

17 **Directory listings.** List your e-zine in all the free e-zine directories available online.

18 Ad trades. Swap ads with other e-zine publishers to drive traffic to each others' publications.

19 Buy subscribers. If all else fails, you can even buy subscribers for your e-zines. But be careful. There are a lot of junk lists out there and you need the opt-in names of people within driving distance of your course.

20 E-mail collection at check-in. Now, here's one of the best ideas, that's also one of the simplest, least-used ideas. Ask for customers' or players' e-mails at the counter when they check in. Make it simple for your counter people: "Hello, would you like to enter our contest to win a year's free play?"

21 Entry forms. Put entry forms and details of prizes on every cart that goes out. All it takes is a little effort. Ask the starter or cart attendants to remind the players to enter and win. Pay them $100 every month for the one who collects the most entries.

22 E-mail required. Require an e-mail for all tee times booked online. This is a no-brainer. If you use a tee service, ask them to send you your e-mails every month so you can add them to your list server.

23 Name trades. Trade names with other local web sites. In one state we got 3,000 opt-in names of people who wanted to hear when local clubs in the state have special offers for free rounds of golf. Now that's a bargain. (Make sure they opt-in to receive third-party offers.)

24 Signature file. Create a signature file with your e-zine ad included. You should have your e-mail software set to include a signature file on every e-mail message you send out. Your signature file should include an ad for your opt-in list along with your free bonus for subscribers. You will find it's easier to use an ad to get people to subscribe to your e-zine than it is to get them to purchase a product. Then, once they are on your list, you build a relationship with them and sell them more.

25 **A description that draws.** Write a good description for your e-zine.

✔ What will your subscribers get out of your e-zine? It has to benefit them, not just be a plug for you. Take the time to write good ad copy for this. Use bullets to describe the benefits people will be getting out of your newsletter. Don't just throw together a quick ad to get one out there. Write "killer" ad copy.

26 **E-book bonus.** Add an e-book bonus for subscribing. We first tested this strategy over a year ago and it doubled our daily subscribe rates from our site. It was proven years ago that your sales rates will increase if you add a bonus to a product or service you are selling.

27 **Free magazine.** Offer a free quarterly golf magazine in pdf format.

✔ When you add up the cost of running ads in local magazines you'll find that publishing an online magazine can be a real winner.

✔ One client averages 5000 downloads per month from a list of 11,000 people. That's almost a 50% response to the magazine, which of course is very biased towards our client's products.

28 **Easy access to subscription form.** Place a subscription form on every page of your web site.

✔ Your subscribers should start here. Make sure that every page on your site gives them the opportunity to sign up for your newsletter.

29 **Tee-time sign-up bonus.** Let them book tee-times an extra three days in advance if they give you their e-mails.

30 **Spread the word.** When you meet people, get their cards and ask if they'd like to be on your e-zine list. This can also happen online in a discussion group, or when you find a web site of interest to you.

SUMMARY

Whatever you do to acquire e-mail subscribers, treat them like the gold they are. Having the power to distribute your message to a large number of people with the touch of a button is marketing power you can't afford to miss. Remember he with the biggest database wins!

Chapter Fourteen

E-Marketing
The Secret Weapon of Golf Course Marketing

Done right, e-mail marketing is low cost, generates high returns, and provides instant gratification. Done wrong, you'll spend weeks trying to clean up the mess you leave behind, with irate customers who may never return.

On one campaign we worked on this year, we were able to sell two and a half weeks of tee times from a single e-mail. In another case, we were able to increase revenues by $1500 per weekend with a simple, last-minute e-mail to sell prime tee times that had been cancelled. A Florida resort we work with sent a blast to Canadian golfers just as a winter storm hit. This perfect timing (we waited for bad weather) generated $28,000 in room nights plus the same again in golf for an investment of just $1500.

In another case we had a blast ready for when the airlines started a price war in the Northeast. It hit e-mail in-boxes within an hour of Delta's announcement of $99 flights from all New York airports to all of its Florida destinations. A good e-mail marketing strategy is power at your finger tips.

In this chapter, you will discover:

✔ How to connect with your customers using e-mail

✔ 10 ways to avoid spam filters

✔ The four ways to use e-marketing effectively

✔ The power of creating your own e-zine

✔ How to segment your lists for greater response

✔ How to personalize your messages for greater response

✔ How often to mail your list

CONNECTING WITH YOUR CUSTOMERS USING E-MAIL

Many people in the golf business, while acknowledging the tremendous impact the web has had on marketing, somehow think that the rules don't apply to them. They think that Internet marketing is just for big companies, or that it's just not applicable to a more local business that draws the majority of its customers from a 30–50 mile radius.

The truth is far different. The Internet is a wonderful way to market your course locally, nationally, and even internationally. There are several great reasons to use e-mail to market your business. The first is retention, the second is referrals, and the third is profits. It's a fact that the more often you connect in a meaningful way with your customers the longer they will stay with you and the stronger your brand awareness will be in the community. This in turn leads to more play, more referrals, and more profits.

E-mail can also give you the benefit of "viral" marketing. If your material is interesting or valuable enough, your readers will forward it to their friends who can then register themselves to receive your material regularly.

List servers

Before you send out an e-zine or any type of content to a large group of players and prospective players you will need a list server.

The technology for list servers changes. But basically list servers allow you to send any number of e-mails to your own list. They also automatically accept new subscribers and take out duplicate subscribers.

In other words, you don't have to handle your e-mails manually. If you use a list server for your e-zine, all you need to do is place it's e-mail address and subscription information in your ads or on your web page and it will take care of all the technical aspects of recording new names for your list.

One-touch list purge avoids duplication

Any time lists are added to your SmartSite master list of addresses and e-mails, duplicates are eliminated to keep your list clean and avoid annoying your recipients. Make sure your solution does the same.

Auto unsubscribe—keeps your opt-in list in compliance

Your list will be an "opt-in" list. That means people ask to be on it and can remove themselves at any time. Any time someone asks to be removed from your list, it is done automatically by your program. In addition, the names are kept in a file to be re-excluded if they are later added to your database from another list. This keeps your system fully opt-in and avoids many spam complaints.

10 WAYS LEGITIMATE E-MAILERS CAN AVOID SPAM FILTERS

Recently several subscribers informed me that their spam filters were not letting their copy of **Golf Club Marketing Strategies** through. I decided to check and, sure enough, several factors were causing my own e-zine to get rejected. It's a sad fact that because of the massive amount of spam perhaps as much as 20%–30% of legitimate e-mail does not get through to its intended recipient. Various spam filters such as Spam Assassin block some legitimate e-mails in addition to spam. That's bad news for golf clubs looking to use their lists to attract players. The good news is that by paying attention to some key factors you can still get most of your messages through!

Spam filters these days are much more sophisticated than the typical e-mail filters of the past. The new ones can be made to delete an e-mail message that contains a number of "bad" words. Filters such as Spam Assassin look for patterns and add or delete points for certain factors. If your total score reaches a predetermined level, the message is flagged as spam. By looking at what adds points (bad) and subtracts points (good), you can learn to construct e-mails that will do better with the filters, if not escape them entirely.

1   **Avoid suspect spam phrases.** There are hundreds to avoid if you want your e-mails read, but here are a few key ones.

- ✔ Free

- ✔ You won

- ✔ Amazing

- ✔ Special offer

- ✔ Promotion

2   **Be careful with your subject lines.** Spam Assassin is particularly interested in subject lines. Here are a few subject line no-no's to learn from:

✔ Contains "FREE" in all caps

✔ Starts with "Free"

✔ GUARANTEED

✔ Starts with dollar amount

✔ Subject is all in capitals

✔ Subject talks about savings

3 **Use capitalization carefully.** Capital letters are seen as "yelling" and spam-like. Excess capital letters cost you points.

4 **Use color judiciously and keep html simple; highly stylized formats can hurt your score.** Realize that high art is likely to cost you something. A font color tag that isn't formatted quite right can cost you points and if you are using special font colors that aren't in the palette of 217 web-safe colors, you are dinged big time.

5 **Let readers know it's a newsletter.** Fortunately, being a legitimate newsletter lowers your spam score so make sure you tout being a newsletter in your headers.

6 **Message size of 20k to 40k helps.** Since so many spam messages are short and under 20K, Spam Assassin gives you credit for a message size between 20K and 40K

7 **Use a signature.** You're helped if your e-mail contains an e-mail signature—since so many spam messages don't.

8 **Don't mention spam law compliance.** It's unwise to claim that you observe all the spam laws. Only spammers say that!

9 **Carefully word your unsubscribe system.** It seems ironic that legitimate opt-in e-mailers are penalized for having information on how to unsubscribe. But since so many spammers have bogus systems, it is apparently a spam indicator. You need to include ways to unsubscribe, of course, but avoid the phrase "click here to..." and substitute something like "use this link to..."

10 **Use a spam checker to test your message.** We're now seeing some services and software you can use to test the spam quotient of your e-zines and e-mail offers before sending them out.

By using all of the above tips, more of your e-mail will reach the intended recipients. Or call the professionals at Legendary Marketing and we will help you! Since this information can change often visit www.legendarymarketing.com for up-to-date tips and info.

YOUR E-MAIL NEWSLETTER

Your e-mail newsletter will be your most powerful tool. Communications to members or regular customers will bring your best results. E-mail will also be useful for lead generation and special offers to your list.

What is an e-zine?

An e-zine is simply a newsletter which you send out to your subscribers by e-mail. Your can publish monthly, weekly, or irregularly.

Start your own e-zine

Most success online can all be credited to one thing, e-mail marketing. I created my own weekly e-zine early on in my Internet career. I quickly noticed two interesting aspects to my online income. First, every time I sent an e-zine, my income grew. Second, every time my newsletter list grew, so did my income. You could actually look at my income growing online and see a direct relationship at all times to the size of my list and the frequency of my e-zines.

What happened to me is not an isolated case. Course managers I have spoken to have experienced this as well. When they build e-mail lists of players and prospects and then provide high-quality content and personalized offers to them on a regular basis, their play and income grow with their lists.

THE "SECRETS" OF A SUCCESSFUL E-ZINE

The first thing you need to understand is that a big e-zine is not the goal you are reaching for. It is a means to the goal. Your business goal probably isn't to build a 10,000 plus player e-zine list. Your goal is to make money at your course. Building the list is just the vehicle which will take you there. This isn't just semantics. Having the right focus and position for your e-zine is all-important online. If you don't understand why you are running an e-zine, then I guarantee you won't get maximum value out of it. I have been teaching golf pros and managers about the importance of e-mail follow-up, multi-responders, and e-zines for well over seven years now and I see many people who have fallen into some major misconceptions on this subject.

Say this out loud with me: *"The goal of my e-zine is to build relationships with golfers and turn them into regular customers."*

You probably didn't get it the first time, so please say the sentence out loud once again: "The goal of my e-zine is to build relationships with golfers and turn them into regular customers." If you are building a large e-zine list just to fill this weekend's tee sheets, then you are missing out on the primary income stream it can provide. Your e-zine is the gateway to selling more of your tee times, products, and lessons. In fact, your e-zine should become the source of multiple streams of income.

Give your e-zine a personality

One of the biggest mistakes I see being made by e-zine owners is not inserting their own personalities into their e-zines. Part of the advantage to having a small business is that you are a real person. Readers can contact you, agree, disagree, and so forth. All of your articles could be from other people. The key is to add some of yourself to your content. What you need to do is add in a few paragraphs you wrote yourself at the top of the e-zine. Do an editorial section, just like in magazines to talk about what's going on at your club. Tell your readers how you feel about your course, how it was built, what the design philosophy was, its history, and so on. Talk about current events, politics, or what you love about golf. Be personal. You may be so afraid of making mistakes in this area that you don't do anything. So make some mistakes; we all do. It's part of being human.

What you say may offend some people and they may unsubscribe from your e-zine. So what? They weren't planning on buying from you anyway. I'm not telling you to purposely offend anyone, just letting you know it's going to happen. Use spell checkers and have someone edit your writing for you. But guess what? There are still going to be mistakes people will let you know about.

People always ask me how I have gotten my name published all over the web. Here's the secret...

Be a real person.

It's not what you were expecting, is it? It's not exciting or highly technical. It's just the truth. People online are looking for people who are real, who have opinions, and who make mistakes. One of my most popular articles being published around the web mentions my dog Winston. Some people won't like you mentioning "daily-life" items such as this. Let them unsubscribe. The ones who stay on your list will buy more once they know you. Personality is one of the most underused tools in the e-zine publisher's arsenal (and for all marketing).

Right alongside personality is good content

You won't be able to produce a growing e-zine without good quality content. If you don't feel you can write good content for your newsletter, then use other people's articles. Just keep in mind your primary goal: to build relationships with prospects and turn them into customers. (We have lots of content available for you if you need it. Golf book reviews, instruction and tips, golf stories, history and even golf jokes.)

Come up with some good content for your newsletter, then get started doing it. You can't afford not to.

(Take a look back at page 205 to see what a decent e-zine looks like.)

OTHER "SEND-OUTS"

Besides e-zines, there are other types of opt-in lists that are very successful, such as "of-the-Day" lists. The most popular of these that I know of is "Golf Joke of the Day." There's "Golf Tip of the Day" and more. What idea could you come up with in this area?

What about a free online golf class? You could develop a 6-, 12-, or 24-lesson class and have them receive the next issue every week, every two weeks, or once a month. Then, once they complete that class, you can offer advanced classes. You could also put them on an update lists for new information. How could you use any of these ideas in a new way? Don't limit yourself.

To sum up, your list needs to be opt-in and you need to build a relationship with your subscribers. You can do this by letting your personality shine through and providing good content every month, every week, or every day. Your subscribers will soon start getting to know you. Then they'll trust you enough to visit your course and buy from you.

PERSONALIZED MESSAGES PRODUCE BETTER RESULTS

You will always get better results when you target specific groups with custom offers. You personalize your offers. The more you know about people's interests, the better you can tempt them with a powerful offer tailored for them.

Once you've segmented your list into more specific groups, we can provide sample e-mail templates that you fill in quickly.

Most good list servers allow the addition of fields such as a player's name so the offers you send are more personalized. One-to-one personalization is a proven key to building long-term customer value and higher response rates. We use our Campaign Manager product to implement a true one-to-one marketing solution. Personalize your mailings to the people who have already indicated their interest in specific offers. It's all automatic!

MANY USES FOR E-MAIL

Connect with your customers more often, in a meaningful way

E-zines are just one method to reach your customers. E-mail allows targeted offers to go out to specific players or for a specific date only.

This helps fill up the course and maximize tee times, but you have to be careful so as not to pollute your list with offers and drive your customers to unsubscribe. For this reason you should either use such offers sparingly or you should develop two lists, one list for your regular e-zine that goes out once per month and another list for people who want to hear from your every time you have a special offer.

Reselling cancelled tee times

Many courses have caught on to reselling last minute tee times using their e-mail lists. Many more have not. The idea is simple and so effective that, as mentioned earlier, one of our clients is making an extra $1500 a weekend using this strategy alone. Simply check your tee sheet at 6 PM on Friday for the weekend and note your cancelled tee times. Then e-mail your list, letting them know what prime spots are available and that it's first-come-first-served. Stand by the phone or let your web site do the booking for you, but you'll be amazed at just how effective this strategy is in filling up holes on your tee sheet.

Plugging rainy days

Assuming that your course handles the rain just fine, you can boost play on rainy days by offering a rainy-day reduction in your green fees if the weather is bad. E-mail gets the word out fast.

Segmenting your market

By sorting your e-mail list and dividing it into segments (you can do this by the information you ask when they book a tee time or register at your web site) you can really target market your players.

You might try:

- ✔ A members-only list
- ✔ A men-only list
- ✔ A women-only list
- ✔ A junior-only list
- ✔ A scratch (low handicap) list

✔ A hacker (high handicap) list

✔ A local residents (by zip code) list

✔ A traveler's list

Our Superserver takes a traditional list server program to an entirely new level. Based on the contact points you choose in your Legendary Marketing SmartSite, you can, for example, e-mail only people who have entered outing requests, only women, only players who live more than 50 miles away, and so on. In fact, you can sort by any category you choose with the touch of a button.

Targeted messages and offers can be designed for each group so that you can maximize your success. As with everything, the more targeted your groups and the more specific your offer is to meeting that group's needs, the more effective your marketing efforts will be. While it may sound like a lot of work, it's really just a couple of hours spent on programming. The computer will take care of the rest.

Extend your club into your customers' daily lives

One of the challenges we all face is how to turn a once-a-month player into a once-a-week player, a twice-a-week player, or even to make your course part of their daily life.

✔ Recently, at one course we started to e-mail students after a lesson with a follow-up tip as an extension of their range activities.

✔ At another, we started a student's day off on the right foot with a motivational golf quote.

✔ To some, a daily golf joke is a way to stay in touch.

These have all proven to be very powerful ways for us to connect with our clubs' clients and increase their level of personal service. As the old saying goes, people don't care how much you know until they know how much you care!

Invite your customers to e-mail their questions and problems to you

This is an excellent way to get your players and potential players interacting with you. It not only gives you the opportunity to provide service, but also to gain new business. Our "ask the expert" option at personalquest.com has resulted in several pieces of business, where total strangers send in questions about how to market their businesses. You can also provide a forum for your golfers to interact with each other.

You can turn this idea to your advantage, as well by using questions to help promote your course, your golf schools, tournaments, and other services. Just make sure that when they ask, you answer.

Open 24 hours with an e-mail auto responder

By installing auto responder software on your web site, you can, in effect, be in business 24 hours a day. This option lets you preload a series of letters, answers to questions, tips, or any other printed material, and then e-mail the specific information about your business back to the customer on demand. It's like the old fax-on-demand but quicker, faster, and in clear print.

Check your e-mail often

Speed is king on the Internet. Customers don't expect to wait until tomorrow for an answer. Check your e-mail and respond throughout the day, not just at the end of the day. Many courses we talked with don't even do it every day.

Using these strategies will allow you to connect more often, provide better service, and acquire and keep more happy customers.

HOW FREQUENTLY SHOULD YOU SEND E-MAIL TO YOUR DATABASE

In general I don't advise doing mailings to your list more than once a week unless it's an "of the day" type mailing. If you mail to your list more than once a week, you'll just end up irritating your readers and more of them will start asking to be removed from your list.

Even doing a mailing once a week might be too often for a particular list if you aren't telling your readers anything exciting or newsworthy. In this case, you may need to keep your mailings down to twice a month, or in the case of newsletter once a month.

The more exciting and informative your e-mails are to your readers, the more often you can get away with mailing to them. You can also avoid unnecessary unsubscribes by offering customers the choice of monthly, weekly or, in the case of specials, even daily updates.

HOW QUICK WILL YOUR RESPONSE BE?

For most e-mails, 80 percent or more of responses take place within 48 hours of the time the e-mail is sent out. A great 'viral' e-mail will last for weeks, but e-mails good enough to be forwarded to others are few and far between.

SUMMARY

E-mail is a powerful tool for golf marketing. With its speed, low cost, and ease of customization, it should be your favorite tool. Using what you learned in the this and the previous chapters, you should now be ready to ramp up your e-mail marketing.

Chapter Fifteen

Legendary Sales
Getting Ready to Maximize Sales

Recently I had a call from a major resort asking what one idea I could give them to instantly improve revenue. The answer was easy and would have been the same had the caller wanted to sell more memberships, more banquets, more real estate, or even more tee times.

Train your people how to sell!

Nowhere in this entire book will you get faster results in terms of pure income than in this and the following chapter on how to sell.

Few people in the golf club business genuinely love selling. Fewer still are good at it! (Read the bonus chapter for some horror stories.) In many ways, it's not surprising that most people don't like to sell. Selling not only has a bad image in many people's minds, *it often deserves it!* Telemarketing calls at dinner time, pushy salespeople who won't take no for an answer, and products and services that don't live up to the sales claims. These have all contributed to the bad image that sales has today.

In defense of sales, almost everyone sells in their everyday lives. Teachers need to sell students on the benefits of paying attention. Spouses sell their ideas to each other. Children sell their parents on staying up for that special TV show, and so on. Practice will bring comfort if you have the right attitude.

Increasing your sales skills by even a few increments can dramatically increase your club's income. Imagine if you closed two out of ten leads instead of one—you have just doubled sales at NO cost! Even small improvements in how you answer the phone, handle objections, and close can have a massive impact on your club's bottom line. Yet few, if any, clubs engage in meaningful sales training.

Before you can sell, there are several things you will need to understand in more detail. First you must understand the fears that hold most people back from maximizing their sales potential. Next you must learn about bonding with prospects and developing rapport. Finally you will discover secrets for quickly qualifying your prospects so you focus more of your time on those people most likely to buy.

In this chapter, you will discover:

- ✔ How to overcome typical sales fear
- ✔ How to develop instant rapport
- ✔ How to separate suspects from prospects
- ✔ How to qualify prospects

GETTING MENTALLY READY TO SELL

It is not the mountain we conquer, but ourselves.
—Sir Edmund Hillary, first man to
stand atop Mt. Everest

Sincerity sells

If you believe in what you are selling, your sincere attitude will communicate itself to your prospective customers. But you must have a positive attitude about the sales situation as well. If you feel uncomfortable selling, your prospect will feel uncomfortable buying from you. I'll use membership sales as my major example here, but the concepts apply to selling lessons, real estate, or clothing in the pro shop!

CONQUERING THE THREE GREAT FEARS

Before you can set off in pursuit of your quest for sales excellence, you must overcome the three great fears that hold back mere ordinary mortals. These fears exist in almost everyone, even great salespeople to a degree. They are:

- ✔ Fear of money
- ✔ Fear of responsibility
- ✔ Fear of failure

Until you have confronted these fears and put them behind you forever, you will not achieve your true sales potential.

FEAR OF MONEY

Believe it or not, many salespeople are afraid to ask for money. I was giving a seminar in South Carolina when I realized that the membership directors I was dealing with were victims of this dreaded affliction. I devised a simple little exercise where they paired off, and each of them said to the other, "Our memberships are $50,000."

I had trouble deciding if the results were tragic or hilarious! The first few times we did it, three of the membership directors actually couldn't get the words out of their mouths. We practiced for half an hour, going up and down in various increments until they could say "$100,000" just as easily as "ten bucks." By the membership directors participating in this exercise, and then my explaining the reasons for their reluctance to ask for large sums of money, they were able to conquer this long-held fear.

Why should membership salespeople be afraid to ask for money?

Salespeople may be afraid to ask for large sums of money because they don't have enough money to buy the memberships they are selling. The fact that they are selling a club they themselves cannot afford may lead them to believe, at least subconsciously, that other people can't afford it either. Membership directors too often place a mental barrier on themselves and, in doing so, thwart their own efforts to obtain the success they deserve.

In my work with the PGA I have found that despite the fact that golf professionals are working with some of the most affluent individuals in the country, many of them are desperately afraid of asking for money. In this case, it's not because they don't make decent money themselves but because they don't want to be thought of as salespeople. What they don't seem to appreciate is that 90 percent of the people they deal with are businessmen or former businessmen who aren't offended by being asked for money. They expect it!

Overcoming your fear of money

It's okay to make money selling memberships or anything else! The more people you help to enjoy the benefits of what you offer, the more money you deserve to make. Whether or not *you* can afford to join your club does not mean that others can't. Whether or not you think it's expensive doesn't matter at all. Put your personal thoughts and prejudices away. Let your prospects decide whether or not they will spend their money. It's your job to give them the opportunity.

FEAR OF RESPONSIBILITY

The "demented mole" syndrome: Time management

A key factor in accepting responsibility is how you manage your time. Since every salesperson in the world starts the day with the same amount of time, it's the way you use that time that ultimately determines your success.

Treat your work time like gold so you can enjoy maximum results in a shorter period of time (a strategy that will provide you with greater free time). Follow a carefully scheduled plan of appointments and follow ups, and never fall victim to the dreaded demented mole syndrome that has struck down so many potential salespeople in their primes.

I first witnessed the effects of the demented mole syndrome at my local golf club when I was a teenager. I was helping a friend who had secured the contract to rebuild the 16th green. At one point during the afternoon, we were waiting for the arrival of some gravel trucks. I watched a workman fill up a wheelbarrow with soil, then move it to the other side of the green and dump it. This was a distance of approximately thirty-five yards. After wandering around for a few minutes doing nothing, he filled up the wheelbarrow again and moved the soil back to its original position!

There were, of course, a million and one other more productive things he could have been doing, but this worker chose instead to focus on waiting for the gravel. In his mind, there was absolutely nothing else of importance except looking busy and waiting for the gravel trucks.

> *99% of failures come from people who*
> *have a habit of making excuses.*
> —George Washington Carver

There are always papers to be shuffled, mail to be read, reports to write, and desks to clear. There are always things that can take your attention and time—the economy, the weather, the time of day. The trained eye can easily spot the afflicted. They plan extensively. Despite always looking busy, they never actually accomplish anything! I'll bet if you look around your club, you'll find someone already displaying advanced symptoms.

Get a day planner, a laptop computer, a contact program, and a cellular phone. You don't need anything else. *You are now armed and dangerous!*

> **Take responsibility for you own actions,**
> **time management, and results.**

FEAR OF FAILURE OR REJECTION

> *One of the reasons mature people stop learning is they*
> *become less and less willing to risk failure.*
> —John Gardner

Sometimes the problem that holds salespeople back is fear of failure or rejection. If membership directors had real faith in their clubs, they wouldn't feel rejected when prospects say no, but would sympathize with the prospects for not having the wisdom or money to take advantage of the opportunity they are being offered.

A young up-and-coming executive with IBM approached the company president, Thomas Watson, Sr., and asked him the key to success. The older man turned to the younger and announced, "Fail twice as fast." The young man, perplexed, asked the question again. "But, Mr. Watson, I really, really want badly to make it. Please tell me what should I do?" "In that case," replied Watson, "fail three times as fast."

Sound advice, indeed, from one of the smartest salespeople who ever lived. Watson had learned that rather than fear failure, you must embrace it in order to become a Legendary Salesperson.

What the younger man failed to understand is that the quicker you get the inevitable failures behind you, the sooner you will reach success. If you double the number of phone calls you make in a day, it will probably double your failure rate. But it will almost certainly double your sales at the same time.

What's the worst that can happen?

When you make a phone call, greet an appointment, or welcome a "walk-in," what is the worst thing that can occur? I mean, after you have introduced yourself, made a presentation, and asked them to join, what's the absolute worst thing that can happen to you?

The prospect can hang up, walk out, call your mother names, or say no. That's it! Those are the worst things that can possibly happen. Compared to the millions of people who are dying every day, rejection is pretty minor! Great! Now let's move on.

There is one small problem we didn't mention—**EGO!**Our fragile human egos are such that when a person rejects our proposition, we take it as a personal affront. We feel humiliated, embarrassed, or even belittled. Rejection attacks our self-confidence and self-esteem.

ıeι ıſ we can let it go for what it is—a rejection of a sales proposition—we will have jumped a hurdle that many never cross.

Sales is a numbers game

You know that when people don't buy a membership they are *not* rejecting you! You know that when people can't afford a membership they're *not* rejecting you. You know that when people are looking for a free round of golf, they're *not* rejecting you. How could it be personal when they don't even know *you*?

Yes, it can *feel* like rejection; but come on, it's not!

Membership sales is a numbers game. Depending on the quality of your leads, only 1 in 20 or 1 in 30 of the people you see has any interest in buying a membership. So when most people say no, they're *not* rejecting you.

Yes, many people will say no to you if you're doing your job. But every no gets you closer to the person who wants to join. And even the people who say no can give you referrals to friends who are more serious about membership.

So even if you *feel* like you're being rejected, you're NOT. You can't get over your feelings immediately, but you can begin. Take control of your feelings and move on to successful membership sales.

> *Our greatest glory is not in never falling, but in rising every time we fall.*
> —Confucius

The power of persistence: The five reasons you must persist

Persistence is a virtue that many salespeople overlook. There are five key reasons why you must be persistent if you are to join the ranks of Legendary Salespeople. Knowing them will benefit both you and your members.

1. **The customer doesn't always know what's in his best interest at first.** You may have new information for him. You have to persist and educate him.

2. **Prospects are almost always reluctant to change.** You must persist and help them realize what the cost will be if they don't change.

3. **Your prospects often have difficulty comparing different products and services and become confused.** Confused people are afraid of making a mistake so instead of buying they procrastinate on making a decision. You must persist in your attempts to minimize the confusion and provide them with a clear path to enjoying the benefits of your club membership!

4. **Prospects have many different priorities.** You must persist and help them arrange their priorities in such a way that your club moves up the list and helps them achieve their goals.

5. **Some prospects are just not ready to buy right now.** They might, however, buy next month or next year. You must persist to make sure you are still in the forefronts of their minds when they eventually do!

BUILDING RAPPORT

Rapport is the ability to bond with another person as you would with a friend, and, for a Legendary Salesperson, it is the most sought after of all conditions. Good rapport puts other people at their ease. They treat you as a *person* they are comfortable with, *not* a *sales*person.

You start most sales relationships with one strike against you. People assume that you have *your* interests at heart rather than theirs. Thus, they naturally don't trust you until you can demonstrate that you are interested in them and can be helpful to them. Because of this negative conditioning, it is essential that you go the extra mile to be courteous, friendly, and professional as you start building rapport.

Calming your prospects' fears

When people walk into your club to explore membership options, it is very probable that they do so with some degree of trepidation. They are unsure of what to expect. Maybe you'll put a lot of pressure on them and it will be unpleasant. Maybe they won't be able to justify the purchase to their wives. Maybe they won't feel that they fit in.

One way to make most people more comfortable is to immediately tell them what will happen. For instance, you could say something like:

> Here's what I was planning to do in our time together:
> Ask you a few questions about your golfing interests,
> tell you about our club, show you around, and answer
> your questions. Does that sound reasonable? Is there
> anything you want to know before we get started?

Your foremost task in the initial sales contact is to make your prospect feel comfortable with you. Until this happens, it will be impossible for the prospect to make a buying decision. Use the first few minutes to remove the prospect's fear and help him or her to relax.

If you don't sell yourself first, you won't sell anything

> *Men in general judge far more from appearances than*
> *from reality. All men have eyes, but few*
> *have the gift of penetration.*
> —Niccolo Machiavelli

If prospects don't like you, they will not buy from you! That's pretty simple, isn't it? Consider for a moment. Do you buy products and services from people you don't like? No? Neither do most other people. Above all else, selling requires *selling yourself* to the prospect. If you don't do that, no sales technique in the world is going to save you.

The first few seconds of your contact with a prospect can determine your success in any sales interview. First impressions are lasting impressions and are usually the right impressions, at least as far as your prospect is concerned.

Your appearance

The way you dress is very important in selling. Always be careful to strike a happy medium between *over*dressing and *under*dressing. Smartly attired people have an air of success about them. Without overpowering the audience you will be selling to, make an effort to improve your image by improving the quality of your clothing and tailoring. In the words of Henry Ward Beecher, "Clothes and manner do not make the man; but, when he is made, they greatly improve his appearance."

Is your office destroying rapport?

If you are selling from your own office or sales area, take heed. The way your office looks and feels can cost you sales. Be sure to avoid displaying anything that could create a negative response in a prospect or customer. The power of one negative image is almost ten times stronger than the power of one positive image. Your ultimate sales skill is to create in your prospect a powerful mental image of enjoying the benefits you offer.

Making your office sales friendly

Make your office the image of what you want to accomplish. If you want to sell memberships, decorate your office to inspire the prospect to want to join your club. Try hanging beautiful pictures of your best holes. Add pictures of celebrities playing at your club, big social events, and so on. Impress them with the quality of your club. Testimonial letters from current members are never out of place!

The best sales organizations in the world set up their offices in a very carefully thought-out way to inspire trust and positive feelings. They remove clutter and distraction so that the prospect's focus remains on the sales process.

Develop winning personal traits

When asked what great secret he had found to influence people to his way of thinking, Abraham Lincoln replied, "If you would win a man over to your cause, first convince him that you are his sincere friend." To a great extent, the way people react to you depends on the little things—like smiling. When you are introduced to someone, always respond with a warm and friendly smile. Shake hands firmly because there are few things that turn people off quicker than a limp handshake. Stand up straight with your shoulders back and chest forward. Make good eye contact and generally let the other person know by your body language that you are a successful, professional, friendly, and confident individual who is genuinely glad to meet them.

How do you sound?

Next to your appearance, the tone of your voice and the way you deliver your words are the most important parts of making a good impression on the prospect. Make your conversation enthusiastic, friendly, and professional. If the prospect talks in a loud voice, raise yours slightly above its normal level. If the prospect speaks quietly, lower your voice a couple of decibels. Mirror your prospect's speech patterns by speaking a little slower or a little faster as appropriate. Remember, people establish the highest levels of rapport with others who are just like them! Your voice can indicate to prospects that you are indeed like them.

Body language

The value of matching your prospect is equally true of basic body language. If the person you are dealing with has a military bearing and stands straight and tall, rather than lounging or slumping, it will definitely pay you to do the same. In your office, if the prospect leans forward, so should you. In short, mirroring your prospect's largely unconscious physical demeanor is one of the most effective ways to rapidly establish rapport. Be sure to use this technique in conjunction with the others mentioned in this chapter.

Compliments

Giving genuine compliments about your prospect or his possessions will almost certainly bring a favorable response. However, use caution in this area. Prospects easily detect insincerity. If you are insincere, you will lose their confidence, never to regain it. There are ways to make sure this never happens to you. Never make a compliment you do not mean, and add a qualifying statement to all your compliments for added weight.

Qualifiers prove your sincerity. Your compliment is made more meaningful and personal if you add a brief remark to prove you mean what you say. For example, you might say to a women who walks into your place of business, "That's a beautiful sweater." Then immediately add a qualifier. "I gave one just like that to my wife, last Christmas." You have demonstrated your sincerity. Why would you buy a sweater for your wife if you didn't find it attractive?

What's in a name?

One of the surest ways to develop rapport is to remember a person's name. In his classic book, *How to Win friends and Influence People*, Dale Carnegie stated, "The sound of a person's name said correctly is one of the nicest sounds in the world, at least to them." Using someone's name is indeed one of the sincerest compliments you can pay a person. It builds self-esteem and lets him know you think he is important.

How to open a rapport-building conversation

In order to build rapport beyond the superficial stages, you have to get the prospect to talk to you. The best way to accomplish this is to ask open-ended questions. Open-ended questions are questions that can't be answered with a simple yes or no. They demand a more detailed response. Not only does this method build rapport, since you allow the customer to respond without interruption or contradiction, but it also provides you with valuable data for use in the sales presentation. After you exchange names, it's time to start questioning as discussed in the next chapter. This time, however, we will be using the responses not just for data, but also to develop future questions.

> Where are you from, Jack? [In states with rapidly expanding populations, like California, Florida, Arizona and Nevada, this is a good question, since the majority of people were born elsewhere.]
>
> What line of work are you in?

Move smoothly from basic questions to more specific lines of inquiry.

> How long have you lived here?
>
> That's an interesting occupation. How did you get into it?

The more others talk about themselves, the more rapport you will be building, especially if you use active listening techniques.

Developing active listening techniques to increase rapport

Active listening means showing the prospect that you are not only listening to what he has to say, but you are interested in what he is saying. Here are some of the ways you can do this:

✔ By holding eye contact and not looking around at anything else

✔ By nodding your head at appropriate points

✔ By raising an eyebrow (like Mr. Spock in Star Trek!) to express surprise

✔ By laughing, smiling, and making occasional comments like, "Yes," "Uh-huh," or "I see" to show you are an active participant in the conversation, even though you aren't doing the talking

You will find that such active listening will draw people out and they will consider you an interesting person.

How people process information affects rapport

After all, when you come right down to it, how many
people speak the same language, even when
they speak the same language?
—Russell Hoban

Essentially, people process information in one of three main ways—visually, aurally, and kinesthetically. Knowing which of these applies to a particular person can give you a much better chance of getting your point across.

If a prospect asks to *see* the course or comments on the view, he is almost certainly visual (and the majority of people fall into this category.) If he wants to *try* it for himself or comments on the *smell* of the trees, he is probably kinesthetic. If he asks you to *tell* him about your course, or *explain* membership benefits, then he is probably auditory. In cases where someone displays a combination of two, or even all three of these forms, you can use multiple approaches, but one of them will usually be dominant. Understanding this human characteristic can be invaluable to your presentation by helping you to communicate better and faster with your prospect.

Asking a kinesthetic prospect to look at something is not nearly as valuable as having him do it himself. If you prevent a kinesthetic person from "feeling" things, you risk losing the sale. In the same way, if you simply talk to a visually oriented person you will soon lose his interest.

If you can't tell which method your prospect uses to process his information, try to use all three in your speech patterns. (It takes a little practice!) You will either find out what you need to know or at least will be sure that you have covered all the bases.

QUALIFYING YOUR PROSPECTS

Once rapport has been achieved, the next step in the sales process is to qualify your prospects.

One of the biggest complaints by salespeople is that they are receiving "unqualified leads." The corresponding complaint from managers is that their salespeople can't close sales from the "great leads" they are given. To have success in any sales, you need to set up a system and then measure the results to demonstrate its effectiveness. You need to produce qualified leads, train your salespeople well, and measure performance.

What is a qualified prospect?

Traditionally, a qualified prospect is someone who has a need for your product or service and the means to pay for it. If you are a golf course selling daily rounds, any regular golfer in your area—or even visiting—would be technically qualified. With golf, you're usually talking about a "want" rather than an actual "need."

If you are a club selling memberships or a golf realty development, you will want further qualifications, such as high income. And you will need further information about their "means."

You need to help them justify the purchase. You need to find out how they would pay for it and if financing will be involved. And you need to find out how they will measure the value they receive for their investment.

Some prospects are more equal than others!

If you look at your prospects as a whole, you will get a very wide range of people—from those chomping at the bit to sign up to those with no intention of ever buying. Think of them as A, B, C, and D prospects.

The success of membership programs is based on generating the total number of leads needed to reach your goals. Successful programs recognize that leads come in various qualities even with qualifiers in place:

- ✔ "A" leads include referrals, golfers moving to the area, members of other clubs unhappy with their current clubs, and social climbers.

- ✔ "B" leads include daily fee players with no permanent home who can afford what you offer if they are shown the service and value they expect.

- ✔ "C" leads might be prospects or might not. They could be a source of future members and should be kept on a tickler program.

- ✔ "D" leads are simply not real prospects.

Referrals and people new to your area are often the best prospects. Direct mail leads offer the next best prospects since they can be prequalified by income, zip code, and other demographics. Telemarketing produces a wide range of leads but most tend to do better than average simply based on the professions that are targeted such as doctor, lawyers, and so forth.

Web inquiries and telephone inquiries from newspaper or magazine ads tend to be far less qualified unless the ad was specifically written to discourage people from calling, which is an art in itself. (For instance, an ad might mention the financial qualifications needed to buy.)

The bottom line is that all leads should be counted and standards created for the conversion of each kind. Referrals might sell at the rate of 1 in 2 or 3, while web leads might sell 1 in 20 or 30. You should measure an average return from each source.

Questions to ask

You need to develop a series of questions that not only qualifies people but goes further to expand their thinking about their needs and your offer. For instance, confirming that prospects play golf and fit your income category isn't enough. You need to cover frequency of play, specific reasons they don't play more often, social influences, and so on. Prospects need to see you as helping them satisfy their needs, not selling to them to meet yours! Your questions need to be interesting to them. They need to enjoy the conversation.

The key qualifying questions you ask will depend on the nature of your club, your offer, and your location.

Here are some examples:

- ✔ How often do you play?
- ✔ What's your handicap?
- ✔ Where do you play now? [If you know your market well, you should know if the answer is public or private, high-end or low-end, is the prospect looking to move up or down?]
- ✔ What three things do you enjoy most about playing?
- ✔ Does your spouse play?

✔ Do you have children? Do they play?

✔ What type of other activities does your family enjoy besides golf? (swimming, tennis, etc.)

✔ What type of work do you do?

✔ How often will you be visiting the area? (second memberships)

✔ Do you entertain clients on the course?

✔ What are the most important aspects of club membership for you? (get a game, great layout, convenient, etc.)

Casually work the three or four most important questions you need into your initial conversation.

Qualified is not motivated!

The key flaw in most sales systems is that they don't acknowledge that *most technically qualified prospects are not motivated to act now.* For outings, weddings, and banquets, motivation is usually not a problem. That is, those prospects need to contract with a facility in a specific time frame, so they are motivated.

For lessons, golf real estate, and club memberships, motivation can become a problem. Prospects may have an interest in making a purchase, but they have no urgency. The decision can be put off forever. Selling daily rounds falls in between. A regular golfer doesn't have to play at any particular time, but they are likely to want to play fairly soon.

Another reason people will delay acting is because they don't feel a connection to you. There is no relationship. They have no reason to trust you. They have no desire to please you. This is where long-term qualifying can come into play. If you approach prospects realizing that many will take a year to commit to action or make up their minds, you will design a sales system that allows you to keep in touch and build the relationship in addition to finding the short-term sales.

Qualifying prospects out?

There are cases when finding prospects is very expensive for you, but they are also worth a lot, for instance, when you are selling golf real estate or memberships in an expensive club. In these cases you have to decide how much a prospect is really worth to you and how "hard" you want to qualify them.

Each case is different depending on your prospecting and closing systems. To decide what is right for you, you'll need to test.

Let's take a typical case we've worked with in selling memberships for various clubs. Say the membership is $100,000, excluding any special offers, rebates, and so on. And let's say that most of the club is built or is a conversion. We call wealthy people in the area of the club and invite them to a free round of golf, and a presentation on club membership that usually includes breakfast. We might organize these events for groups of 20 prospects.

It could take a month or two to produce 400 membership prospects. All prospects are qualified in the sense that they say they play golf, are interested in playing the course, can afford the membership fee, and know that they will be subject to a sales presentation. Here is where further qualifying and screening begins. Some people don't show up for the presentations. During the tour and golf, salespeople talk to the prospects. Perhaps only three have any serious interest in membership. After the presentation, these are the ones you focus on, as well as any other prospects who put themselves forward.

This level of qualifying means that most of your money is spent on people who aren't good prospects. With a well-designed sales approach, this still pays off handsomely in sales. However, you could take a harder line. By requiring people to take an action step, you are qualifying them further. For instance, you can require them to send you something, to meet with you, or to give you further information.

A simple way to screen out people who are only interested in a free round of golf but don't care enough to work for it is to require prospects to sign up for your presentation at your club's web site. You direct them to the proper page and they have to answer some qualifying questions there. In our experience, this cuts out about half of your "prospects."

You have to track your results to decide what screening and qualifying approach is best for you. Is it better to have 20 prospects of whom three are serious, or 10 of whom one to two are serious?

The answer is not simple. Some people end up buying when they didn't plan to. This can be the case with memberships or real estate. People may come for the free golf and become more interested when they see your offer.

As we said earlier, the only way you can see how your sales skills match up best with your prospect pool is to test different approaches and see which one is most cost effective for you. We generally like to get more prospects there, even if they are weaker. People can't judge your club until they've seen it. And more people seeing it creates more word-of-mouth and referral possibilities.

Why qualified prospects don't raise their hands

One complication in qualifying people is that sometimes your best prospects won't say that they want what you have to offer and can afford it. Why do people deny being good prospects?

They do it for a many reasons that vary from wanting to stay in control of the situation to wanting to make you jump through a few hoops. Some reasons can work for you; others create problems.

Perhaps the most common reason that the wealthy "hide" themselves is that they don't want to be bothered. Many of the well-to-do are approached every day with a new offer. Many companies go to great lengths to identify the wealthiest one percent of the country who can buy almost anything. (The same goes for the top 5–10 percent as well.)

Another reason for sales resistance is the desire to see how good you are—how persistent and how skilled. These people are sophisticated in business. They are familiar with most sales approaches. If they have time, they may entertain themselves watching how you sell to them. They may also use resistance as a way to test your sincerity. They throw up obstacles but expect you to overcome them. They reason that if you're willing to put a lot of effort into signing them up, you may be more likely to put effort into making them happy once they buy.

False prospects

On the other hand, there are people who will lie about their interest. These people may be retired and miss the action of business. Or they may simply like whatever freebies you offer. Some prospects are even fantasizing. By pretending that they will buy, they get some fantasy pleasure at little cost.

Interestingly enough, there are situations where people who have no intention of buying end up doing so. Timeshare vacation rentals are a prime example. Almost no one who goes to a presentation intends to buy, but enough do to keep the hard-sell sales practices going. So you'll have to make your best guess on how hard to qualify prospects, and then test to develop a better profile of actual buyers.

If you're selling something like memberships where you're willing to spend some money on prospects, you can use credit checks as one way to screen out false leads. You will also find that people who are referred to you are much more serious than people who respond to ads. And the more freebies you offer, the more "Looky Lous" you'll get.

SUMMARY

To maximize your sales potential you must understand and overcome the common fears that hold back most people in sales—fear of money, fear of responsibility, and fear of rejection. In sales, success is up to you. Manage your time well and realize that the more noes you get the more sales you will make.

Learn how to quickly build rapport with your prospects by asking open-ended questions, demonstrating active listing techniques, and being aware of your body language. Once rapport is established, probe to qualify the prospect. There is no point in spending time selling to people who don't want to buy. By setting up a qualifying system, you will improve your results, make prospects happier, and have more fun selling. Design your system for both short- and long-term sales. While you harvest the "low hanging fruit," you will be building relationships for long-term sales. Even prospects who never buy may become sources of referrals and positive word of mouth when they are treated professionally and respectfully.

Chapter Sixteen

Legendary Sales
Presentations, Objections, and Closing

Once a prospect has been greeted, bonded with, and qualified, it's time to get to the meat of the presentation, handle objections, and close the sale. All presentations should be scripted and orchestrated for optimum results. If you do not approach presentations in a scripted systematic manner, your approach and results will differ from day to day and person to person—but you won't know what is causing the variation!

To get the most from your sales, you must follow a system and be prepared with perfect answers to any question. Since you can double your profits by doubling your sales results, it will pay you to keep track of what you're doing and what works!

Objections are a natural part of the membership sales process. While you might prefer that people come in with their checks in hand, already all made out to your club, it's natural for people to have questions or concerns just as *you* would in any major purchasing decision. These concerns are generally expressed as objections. An objection is nothing more than a question in the mind of the buyer that has to be defined and answered. It gives you the chance to clarify or improve your presentation. A prospect who does not raise objections is not engaged in thinking about your presentation.

Most sales are lost simply by not asking for the sale! Close early and close often. Find the closing techniques that best suit your style and audience and use them!

In this chapter, you will discover:

- ✔ How to build a perfect presentation
- ✔ How to uncover and isolate objections
- ✔ The five-step process to deal with objections
- ✔ The *feel, felt, found* way to deal with objections
- ✔ Exactly what to say to specific objections
- ✔ How to spot closing signals
- ✔ How to close

> *I never learn anything just by talking. I only learn things when I ask questions.*
> —Lou Holtz

MAKING AN EFFECTIVE PRESENTATION

Because each presentation is different, this book can only give you pieces to use and an approach to put "standard" pieces together with your own custom material. (On a consulting basis, Legendary Marketing can develop custom presentations for you, as well as train your staff.)

As you design your presentation, start by assuming that everyone who has qualified as a prospect wants to buy and buy *now*. This may eventually prove to be incorrect, but assume it anyway. Many people who are on the "edge" will make the decision to buy without your having to make a great deal of extra effort simply because you are so confident they want what you have to offer and today is the day they should buy.

Getting the audience involved in the action

The more senses you can bring into play during the presentation, the better your chances of making a sale! Clearly with golf you have many senses involved: the visual, the feel of the club, the smell of the cut grass, the sounds of players, and so on.

Using questions for involvement

Questions can be an important part of your presentation by getting the prospects *involved* with your points. Prospects can't just sit back and pretend to listen when you ask them questions. And often, even if they wanted to remain detached, good questions will "hook" them into considering your club more seriously. Open-ended questions—questions that can't be answered yes or no—are best. Ask questions that get them talking about things that relate to features or benefits of your club, such as how they find business contacts now or what their wife likes to do.

The points you need to cover

Many people think that giving a great presentation requires a gift of gab or a certain type of personality. Not so! There are many ways to give a winning presentation, the best of which is to write a script and practice it until you can deliver a legendary performance.

A good presentation script will read a lot like a good direct mail letter. It will be full of features and benefits. While features are more objective, your emphasis should be on the benefits. There are usually more benefits than you think, and many of them are several levels deep. For instance, playing golf may be relaxing. That's a benefit for your prospect. Being relaxed may mean your prospect is more cheerful with his wife. That's a benefit for her. And when spouses treat each other better, it improves their relationship. The kids are less stressed by their parents fighting. That's a benefit. (And more kids may be on the way, which we won't talk about!)

You see the point. You can spend a long time listing multiple benefits, which may be subtle but more important than the obvious benefits. Another example: Most people like more money, yet your club costs money. But they'll make contacts that can lead to better jobs, more business, and so on. And when you have more money, you can afford to relax more, like at a club! So you'll be able to relax *and* make more money to pay for your membership. Instead of having to wait to relax, you can relax while you're investing in your future. Not simple, but workable.

List the features of your club that you want to cover in your presentation. They should include features such as:

✔ History

✔ Regional points of interest (for recent movers)

✔ Types of members

✔ Social activities

✔ The club house

✔ The course(s)

✔ Tournaments

✔ Other facilities

✔ Membership costs and financing programs

Now list the benefits that come from your features. (You may skip many features and go straight to benefits in your presentation.)

✔ Family recreation and togetherness

✔ Safe place for the kids

✔ Relaxation

✔ New friends

✔ More social life

✔ Exercise

✔ Business contacts

✔ Status

✔ Meeting the "right" type of people

✔ A place to take customers

✔ Money saved on vacations and entertainment

When you simply spell out each benefit you want to convey, you have your basic presentation. Add a few member testimonials and you're well on your way.

Quitting while you're ahead

One thing that epitomizes Legendary Selling is knowing exactly when to stop presenting and start closing. The key to selling golf is getting the prospect excited about your offer. Once that has been accomplished, you must provide him with logical reasons why he must buy *today*. Then you must close. Continuing to talk after the prospect is ready to buy is overkill and often leads to lost sales rather than successful closing.

Anticipating objections

When Abraham Lincoln was a lawyer, he always summed up his opponent's arguments before he gave his side. That way the jury saw him as a fair man and he got to "frame" his opponent's points the way he wanted to. If you *know* that certain concerns will be in the prospect's mind during your presentation, you are usually better off dealing with them as part of the presentation. Otherwise, prospects will tend to not listen to *your* points as they think about the problems on their own. For instance, price is often a concern, so acknowledge it and show how the value your club delivers outweighs the cost. Another example is competitive clubs. You need to know how they compare to your club on all important dimensions. When people are looking at other clubs, you need to deal with them briefly in your presentation. Never "bad-mouth" other clubs. Say something like you hear they are very nice, then cover your relative advantages.

How to present to a couple

As a general rule of thumb, sell to the person of the same sex. If you are a man, direct your main attention to the man, and vice versa. However, you'll need to use eye contact and body language to make sure the second person is not excluded. Most wives are used to the husband receiving more sales attention for golf-related activities. They won't be offended if you direct things to their spouses. Just make sure that you keep in visual touch with them to let them know nonverbally that they are not being excluded. Husbands are often a little more sensitive about *not* being the center of attention.

Too many choices

Complexity is your enemy. It only confuses prospects. Design your presentation to offer no more than three options. If you have to present more than three options, do it in stages. For example, if you have nine options, offer three groups of three. Help your prospect to reach a decision on which group of options appears to be most suitable, then concentrate on those three options in detail. When you give people too many choices, they become confused. When they are confused, they become scared, and when they are scared, they rarely make a buying decision.

Reduce risk, build trust

Another thing you can do is use guarantees to reduce people's perceived risk. Make their choosing you a safe choice so that they can reap your benefits for themselves and their families. Written testimonials can produce some trust effect, especially if the testimonials are from people similar to them.

The to-the-point sales presentation

The entire sale process should, in most cases, take no longer than fifteen minutes from contact to close, unless you play a round with them! If you take too much time, your prospect will probably become bored or confused as the presentation drags on, and you will be frustrated as a result. Tighten up your presentation. Be fast, fluid, and professional. Act as if completing the sale is second nature to you, and you do it every hour of the day, week in and week out. After all, selling *should* become second nature to you!

Use emotion backed up by logic

You want to use emotion: the excitement the prospect experiences as a result of his perception of the benefits your club will bring him. Your prospect should feel that this pleasurable sensation is real and waiting for him and him alone.

Once prospects have decided to buy, they use logic to come up with good reasons to justify their decisions. Back up their reasons with your own supporting evidence. Indicate features and benefits that they may not have considered and you will make the sale. Help them to see that their emotional reasons are also logical ones. Reinforce the buying decision by complimenting them on their choice and assuring them, sincerely, that you know they will get satisfaction and pleasure from their membership.

What's in it for me?

A basic motivating force that drives nearly everybody is "What's in it for me?" Some membership directors are so busy selling that they can't see the forest for the trees. Few, if any, potential members will be initially interested in the *quality* of the service you offer them.

That may come later. Initially, they will be much more concerned about what the club, and *you*, will do to make them better people — to improve their lives. You must understand that their decisions are often exercises in positive selfishness.

While your prospect *is* concerned about himself, there are multiple ways you can approach this. For instance, even if he is motivated by playing golf with "the boys," he may respond to looking good with his family by providing them with swimming or other activities. So you could show how he can justify the purchase to his wife (and himself) with family benefits. For instance, kids who play golf can get college golf scholarships. The kids will make better lifelong social contacts at the club. The family will save money on vacations, and so on. The more wants you can satisfy, the more problems you can solve, the more needs you can meet, the more that's in it for them, the more likely your sale. And the more personalized and reliable your service is, the more successful you will be!

Write it down

You should address all the above points and actually type up a script for selling memberships, outings, banquets, and anything else you sell. This should include diagrams of the very best places to stand as you deliver your lines and point at something of interest! It takes time, but once you have done it you will reap big dividends and the script will always be there for training as staff come and go. (Legendary Marketing also offers custom sales manuals and follow-up training for everything from real estate sales to membership sales for those not wishing to tackle the project themselves.)

OVERCOMING OBJECTIONS

Objections are a necessary part of the membership sales process. Learn to deal with them and you will close a much higher percentage of the prospects you meet. Unfortunately, many salespeople take objections personally and their ability to complete the sale is adversely influenced by this negativity.

It's not personal. They are turning down buying, not turning down you!

Think of objections not as rejections but as steps toward your final goal. Rather than fearing objections, you need to ask good questions to bring them out. An objection is not the *end* of the sales process, it is the beginning! Many objections mask a real or perceived problem. For instance, if the prospect doesn't know anyone at your club, they will hesitate to join but may not bring up their "shyness" as a reason. You should anticipate this issue and others such as cost, and deal with them early by asking them if they have friends at your club, assuring them that there are other people like them, and so on.

Hidden objections are often associated with money. They will not want to admit that they are not qualified or don't have decision authority.

Overcoming objections is usually taught in a one-step sales approach, and it *is* one step for smaller items such as one lesson. But for memberships or real estate you can't expect everyone to make a fast decision. As long as you have permission to keep in touch with the prospect, you are in the game. Keep in touch for the short term when they're in the decision-making mode. And if necessary, keep in touch for the long term if they either don't decide or join another club. Some objections will dissipate over time—"I'm happy with the course I play now." Either their course will make a "mistake," or you will use the repeated sales contacts to better build value. When you keep in touch with them, you build your credibility and sincerity. Put them on your SmartSite e-mail newsletter list and they will see all the activities they are missing! That gives you something to build on to resell them on membership.

Sometimes, you have to break out of the sales–sales-resistance cycle that can be created between you and a prospect. You have to step back and say "George, I've talked to you several times about membership here and we don't seem to be making any progress. I don't want to keep bothering you—should I just leave you alone?" This will often turn the situation around—they'll start to sell you on why you should keep in touch! And they'll often tell you their true objection. The key is for them to talk to you person to person, *not* prospect to salesperson!

Some objections arise as the result of nothing more serious than a lack of understanding. Your presentation didn't come across. In these cases, it is necessary to further define and explain the benefits of your membership in clear and simple language. Use your membership kit as the excellent business tool it should be. Put it in front of the prospect and check off the listed benefits, giving a short explanation of each benefit as you go. When features and benefits are there in black and white, any misunderstandings should soon vanish.

Anticipate the objection

As mentioned earlier, many objections can be dealt with in the sales presentation by bringing them up before the prospect does and taking away the objection before it is even voiced. Those that can't be dealt with during the presentation should have already been anticipated and a perfect answer scripted out as the response.

In a system, there can only be one
perfect answer to any objection.

The answer to each objection should be carefully crafted to be the best answer possible, then should be learned and used by everyone on staff exactly as scripted. This is the type of approach used by Disney, Ritz Carlton, and other world-renowned companies for a simple reason—it works!

This may sound very rigid, but, if you really think about it, it's true at least 95 percent of the time that a scripted answer works best. Sure, intuition and experience can come into play 5 percent of the time, but 95 percent of the time a well-orchestrated response will produce better results. That's why movies have scripts. That's why comedians have scripts and practice them so they don't sound like scripts. Remember, 95 percent of the jokes you ever heard from Jim Carrey were scripted, rehearsed, practiced, and timed to be delivered as if they were a natural and spontaneous. Let me give you an example.

Suppose the prospect asks: "How long does it typically take to play a round?"

Now let's look at how three different people could choose to answer that simple but *deadly* question.

That question could be answered in several ways:

- ✔ It takes about 4 hours and 45 minutes.

- ✔ It depends on what day you play; sometimes it's fast, sometimes it's slow.

- ✔ We are committed to a pace-of-play policy that insures maximum enjoyment for all of our members.

Now all of these are possible answers to the question but only one is actually the very best answer. I am sure you know it is the last one. The best answer will produce better results for you than an off-the-cuff answer every time. And not just for you, for everyone on the property.

There are five important things to remember when you are dealing with objections:

1. **Listen carefully to the objection.** Resist the temptation to jump in before you have heard the full objection. Sometimes the prospect will talk himself out of it before you say a word.

The first thing you should do after an objection is thank them! This changes the tone of your interaction from adversarial to cooperative. It shows that you're not defensive or trying to avoid the objection. For instance, after you listen to an objection you could say, "I'm glad you brought that up." Or "Thanks for asking that question. It gives me the chance to explain…"

 Never argue with a prospect. Remain calm and pleasant. They may just want you to listen to them.

If the objection is unclear, as in, "Well, I have to think about it," then ask more questions to isolate the real objection.

When you have the information you need, you can deal with the root of the objection.

Convert objections to benefits

Remember, objections are not a surprise for you. And they should not lure you into an argumentative situation. After some study of this chapter, and consideration of your club's situation, you will know the issues that people will raise. Each concern they bring up gives you a chance to clarify a point and build further rapport.

OTHER WAYS TO DEAL WITH OBJECTIONS

"Fast forward" your prospects to help them understand the benefits

In order to overcome an objection, it's very helpful to involve your prospect emotionally in how his future will improve from the moment he agrees to join your club. This is particularly true when dealing with money issues. By "fast forwarding" your prospect into the future, you can help him see how different his life will be if he joins your club.

I understand your hesitation about the investment Mr.
Miller. Lots of our new members felt the same way.
Even when they could easily afford it, they didn't want
to make a mistake. For instance, George had his doubts,
but found that he actually made a *profit* on his
membership because of the new business he did. Plus,
he and his wife made many new friends and are
enjoying life much more. And, by the way, the value of
his membership has gone up as well.

> *The biggest problem in the world could have*
> *been solved when it was small.*
> —Witter Bynner

Feel, felt, found

In the fast-forward process above, we used a *feel, felt, found*
method that can be adapted to handle many types of objections.
When the prospect raise an objection, you sound agreeable by using
three steps:

(1) I understand how you *feel*. [This avoids being
argumentative and takes their objection seriously.]

(2) Many of our members *felt* that way before they joined. For
instance, Mr. Miller is in your business/church/age
group, and so forth. He worried about that but...

(3) He *found* that _____ [answer] plus his family enjoyed
the club facilities, the contacts were valuable to his
business, and so on.

The Feel-Felt-Found approach has been proven for over 50 years
as a good way to respond to an objection and create a little story
about someone with whom the prospect can identify. You can adapt
it to almost any objection you encounter.

Testimonials

Just as examples about another member are important in dealing with objections, written testimonials can be invaluable. Gather a portfolio of letters from your satisfied members. Together they should address all the objections that your prospects will have.

The easiest way to obtain a range of testimonials covering different issues is to ask satisfied members to address particular issues. Your portfolio of testimonials will be impressive by itself. It can even be given to prospects while they wait. By organizing it according to type of objection, you can also use it when specific objections are raised. For instance, after you answer a couple of objections, as a change of pace, you might say "Instead of me answering that question, why don't I let one of our members do it for you," and bring out the relevant testimonial.

Isolating objections

There are two times when you need to isolate objections. When people make vague objections like "I need to think it over," "I'm not sure," or "I need to talk it over with _____," you don't have much to work with. In the specific objections dealt with later, we show you how to ask for the real objection. These approaches acknowledge prospects' need to think it over and then ask them what they need to think over.

The second time you need to isolate an objection is to find out if this is THE KEY objection. When there are several objections on the table, many times most of them are minor. Don't be distracted with secondary objections. Focus on finding the major wants and the major objection. For instance, if there is an objection that you know you can answer, don't just say yes. Say something like "If I can arrange flexible payments for you, are you ready to join today."

By isolating the objections that really matter to the prospect, you can answer them and move to close the sale.

What will others think?

A key decision blocker that is often overlooked is how others' feelings and views may affect the buying decision of your prospect. Where most membership purchases are concerned, the question is, "What will my wife think about the buying decision?" (This is even more important if you sell family memberships.) Sometimes, but by no means always, this question is verbalized as an objection. However, a man's ego may not allow him to tell you that he must consult with his wife before making a buying decision.

Any time a third person is brought into the sales decision, your presentation must take them into account. You need to give your prospect the ammunition they need to "sell" the spouse.

Business to business

If you sell corporate memberships, the other significant party to the deal tends to be the boss or department head. You must make sure your benefits work at the corporate level.

"I'm not sure head office is going to like it" is often heard from a corporate buyer. Try this solution. "That's why I suggest we get everyone involved in the decision. In my experience, when your executive officers participate, they'll have complete confidence in your decision." If you don't have all the decision makers present for your membership presentation, you may not have qualified the prospect properly.

Answering objections is NOT solving every concern

While I can give you a *lot* of ammunition here to answer objections, some can't be eliminated. For instance, your club doesn't have a tennis court, a pool, or whatever. You can't change that. You can only suggest that it is not crucial. (You may also be able to create a reciprocal arrangement with a non-golf club for use of their facilities.)

You'll add to your rapport and credibility by being frank about things you can't change. At the end of answering objections, you or the prospect might agree that there are a couple of points that are not perfect. But that can still compare very favorably to other clubs, or them not joining anywhere. Nothing is perfect. Help your prospects make a decision anyway.

COMMON CONCERNS, OBJECTIONS, AND STALLS

In our 40-hour, five-day sales training course, we cover over 60 objections in detail. Here are eight examples of scripted responses to common questions and concerns.

I would prefer a course that does not have houses all around it—something a little further out of town.

I can certainly understand what you mean. Other members have said the same thing before they joined. The upside is that because the course is so close to the major highways and the places people live and work, they get a lot more use and value from their membership.

There are rumors the club is in serious financial straits.

I'm glad you brought that up since we want you to have every confidence about that issue. We have the certified financial statements of the club available. The owners have deep pockets and have committed $XYZ to demonstrate their commitment.

- or -

Interestingly, those rumors are being spread by a few unprofessional salespeople who are selling for competitive clubs and find that they can't match our benefits.

The price is too high!

I understand. Prices today are certainly higher than they used to be in the past and will no doubt keep rising. This of course may work to your advantage for your investment.

- or -

Too high compared to what Mr. Miller? After all, this is the only top-100 golf course community in Chicago and it's certainly the only 45-hole Fazio community in the area. What other community would you say was comparable to the Legendary Country Club?

I can't play enough rounds to justify joining.

The value of joining a club is a lot more than just multiplying your golf games by a green fee! Looking at it the other way around, many people in businesses like yours say that the business contacts pay for their membership and the golf is free! For example, there are great networking opportunities for businessmen like yourself that some members would consider priceless. And of course that's exactly the value of the many new friends you will meet at the club as you socialize with other members and their families.

I don't see anyone my age [like me] around. [Or why are there so many kids, seniors, and so on?]

We have lots of members like you and part of my job as membership director is to make introductions. Not only can I think of X people right now who are in your occupation, but we have tons of people with handicaps like yours. And we can line up games for you with just a little notice. We also have a number of members who would probably like to hear more about your business since they buy services like your regularly. [Name sample names here and get back to them with more.]

I hear not all the members are happy.

As Lincoln so aptly said, "You can please some of the people all the time and all of the people some of the time." I suppose there will always be people who are unhappy about something, sometime. Our member surveys show satisfaction levels as high or higher than any other club around here, and we're always trying to further improve our service.

Do members have a voice in how Legendary Country Club is managed?

For Legendary to be successful, the members must be involved.

   A. Because we are a member-owned club, you have a direct say in everything through your board of directors.

   B. Our professional management is always open to input from the membership. We conduct membership satisfaction surveys on a regular basis. A Membership Advisory Committee advises management and acts as a liaison between the membership and management. If you'd like to volunteer to serve on the Committee, I'll pass your name along to them.

I want to think it over. [This is your classic objection. Expect it often. You must pin them down to a more specific objection in order to deal with the true objection.]

I agree that a decision such as this should be thought about carefully. May I ask, is it the location or the price that you are thinking about the most? [Probe and close on the issue that is causing the procrastination.]

LEGENDARY CLOSING

Well done is better than well said.
—Benjamin Franklin

Closing a sale is the key step in the sales process and the first step to starting a series of lessons, welcoming people to membership in your club, or handing them the keys to a new home. You've spent time and money to generate leads, given free rounds and tours, and answered questions. Now you need to communicate your enthusiasm for your club to the prospect and sign him up. Just as in a golf game, a great drive and approach shot become almost meaningless if you take five putts to get the ball in the hole!

All the money, time, sweat, and skill you've put into your sales effort mean nothing if you can't get the prospect to buy. Many membership directors get so caught up in their sales pitches that they fail to observe that the prospect is radiating all kinds of buying signals. The prospect is ready to buy, but the salesperson doesn't know when to be quiet and go for the close.

In fact, studies show that an astonishing 63 percent of all sales presentations are given without the salesperson actually asking the prospect to buy!

Close early and often

As you probably know by now, "closing" a sale means that your prospect has agreed to purchase. To be even more specific, they need to have signed the contract and given you a check (that clears the bank!).

Closing is *the purpose* of the sales process. Many people are uncomfortable actually asking for the sale. As mentioned in the last chapter, most of us have a bad image of sales and don't want to seem "pushy." That's one reason people don't close enough. Another is that they think closing should come only *after* all the other steps in the sales process. In fact, sometimes the prospect is ready to be closed early. You won't know this unless you try.

The prospect may be ready to buy when he walks in the door. You will make more sales if you ask for the sale early and often. Another benefit of trying to close early in the presentation is that it will get you over your discomfort about asking for the sale in general.

Early attempts to close the sale are called "trial closes." You don't necessarily expect them to work, but they sometimes do.

Here are a few examples:

When Mr. Miller walks in your office for your appointment, you might say:

> Welcome to Legendary Country Club Mr. Miller. Are
> you ready to join today or do you have some questions?

A similar but more extreme approach can be used with people who are in professional sales, such as car dealers or realtors—and also with people who act impatient. With the salespeople you could say:

> Welcome to Legendary Country Club. You're in
> professional sales yourself, so you can probably help me
> do my job for you by telling me what I could cover that
> would let you make a decision to join today.

While immediately asking for the sale is an unusual approach, you'd be surprised how often it can work. And you can see how it gives you more information, flatters the prospect, and focuses the interaction on the sale.

In response to the first question, Mr. Miller might say yes, no, or maybe. Exactly what he says, and *how* he says it will give you information to better direct your sales presentation. For instance if he says "I might be interested if you can show me XYZ benefit," then you know what you need to start with.

Another point where you might try a trial close is when the person looks bored or distracted. You might say:

> You look as bored as my husband does when I'm telling him what he needs to do around the house. Is there something else you'd like me to cover, or are you ready to join now?

If you don't feel comfortable using a humorous approach, you could say:

> It looks like you may not need more information on this point. Is there something else you'd like me to cover, or are you ready to join now?

The exact words you say for these trial closes can vary. You need to adapt your script to your circumstances and personality. By asking early, you'll get more information about the prospect and his interests. You'll have a chance to better focus your presentation on what he wants to hear.

Asking early and often makes closing a natural part of your presentation—not something you put off until the end when it may be too late to make adjustments. So ask—you never know when you'll get a pleasant yes.

SPOTTING CLOSING SIGNALS

Let's look at some common closing signals that will alert you to when your prospect is ready to buy.

Verbal closing signals

Often you can tell that a prospect's level of interest has risen by the type of questions he starts to ask. These questions suggest that the prospect is now thinking like a Member.

- ✔ Do you have other doctors who are members?

- ✔ Can I pay my initiation fee in three payments?

- ✔ Will my wife and children be able to play on my membership?

- ✔ How often may I bring guests?

- ✔ Can you prorate my dues for the rest of the season?

- ✔ What month is _____ [a specific event]?

Stay focused on closing

When the prospect asks questions like the ones just mentioned, try another trial close. Answer each question quickly and professionally in accordance with the answers in your presentation and objections scripts and then go directly for the close. Ask for the sale.

Note: Do not allow yourself to become distracted from selling by answering a series of questions that do not lead to the close. Always draw your prospect's attention back to closing (or your presentation if necessary). If the prospect persists in a series of distracting questions, excuse yourself and leave the room for a moment. This will help you regain control of the conversation. When you return, sit down and get right back into your closing sequence or structured presentation. Lead and remain in charge, but never be "pushy."

Just because someone asks a question doesn't mean you have to answer it immediately, or even at all. For instance, you could say, "I'll be getting to that point a bit later." You are in charge of the situation. It's up to you to dictate the pace and control the interaction. When a prospect asks if he can pay his initiation fee in three parts, don't say yes. Instead, say, "Are you ready to join if I can arrange a three-part payment?" The answer will tell you if it was an idle question (or one trying to distract you), or if the prospect is ready to go.

Sometimes questions that indicate a readiness to buy aren't as clear as the previous example.

"What month is the member-guest championship?" This question is a subtle indication that a prospect is identifying with members. If you give a quick answer with the month, you will miss a closing opportunity. Instead say something like, "Do you have a guest you'd want to bring to this event?" If they say yes, try closing them immediately. While they may bring up other questions—like the financing one—they may also be ready to buy.

Nonverbal closing signals

You must not only listen to what your prospect *says*, but watch his body language as well. The majority of communication is *not* based on *what* your prospect says. Below are some of the clues you may observe that will help you pick the right moment to close.

- ✔ Nodding in agreement
- ✔ Making more frequent eye contact
- ✔ Leaning towards you
- ✔ Picking up your sales literature and intently studying it

Be alert for such signals. When you observe any of them, bring your presentation to a pause point and try a trial close. You will find your sales volume increases significantly when you raise your level of alertness to nonverbal signals.

GETTING TO THE CLOSE

In order to ask for the sale smoothly, you need to set it up in advance. The way to do this is with your trial closes. As just mentioned, usually you'll attempt a trial close after the prospect has shown buying signals. If the close works, great! If not, follow the procedures in the objections section to isolate and answer any concerns and then float another trial close.

SAMPLE CLOSES

The professional salesperson knows that every prospect has a close that fits him or her—one that appeals to him on a most personal level. The secret is to find out which one will resonate most deeply with your prospect, so you can obtain a favorable response and make the sale.

There are several closes below that have been successful for decades in selling golf. Although you might know them by other names, anyone who has been in sales for even a short period of time will recognize many of them. Others may be new to you. Some of them you might like; others you might hate. It's important to be completely comfortable with the closes that work best for your style and personality. As you go through the following closes, adapt them to match your style and selling situation. Whichever closes you choose to adopt, practice them, role play them, and perfect them. The more you practice, the more they will flow naturally. The one thing that is certain is that if you don't ask prospects to buy, they won't!

The straightforward close

> Mr. Miller, based on what you have seen, do you think
> that Legendary Country Club is the type of club in
> which you would like to become a member?

The assumptive close

Always assume that the prospect is going to buy. The assumptive close handles the sales interaction as if you were certain that the prospect would buy.

> Mr. Miller, based on our conversation it seems like
> Legendary Country Club meets most of your criteria.
> Would you like to start your membership at once before
> the initiation increase?

The alternative close

The alternative close is perhaps the best known of all closing techniques and has many variations, depending on the exact circumstances. Another common name for it is the "either-or" close. This close gives the prospect the choice between buying and buying, between yes and yes.

> Are you interested in a corporate membership or single
> membership?

> - or -

> Would you prefer the $500 pro shop credit or twenty
> free green fees for your friends as your welcome gift?

When your prospect is on the verge of making a buying decision, the most direct way of closing the sale is to ask how he intends to pay for it. This approach can best be used when a prospect has made the decision to buy, but is asking unrelated questions—the kind that prevent him from giving you the order! At this point, "Will you be using a credit card or check?" is the best way to take control of the sale and complete it. Each one of the previous alternative closes offers the prospect a choice. No matter which one they choose, they will feel committed to buy once they have made the choice.

The action close

In the action close you ask the prospect to *do* something to accelerate the process and help them make a positive decision.

> Mr. Miller, would you like to go to the locker room now and pick out your locker?

- or -

> Mr. Miller, I've gone ahead and filled out most of the membership application for you. If you would like to go ahead and approve it, I can get your application processed at once.

Hand the prospect a pen and casually slide the membership agreement across the desk.

Or, end your presentation in the pro shop:

> Mr. Miller, every new member gets a welcome gift of a new logo shirt. Would you like to pick yours out right now?

Once the prospect accepts whatever action you have asked him to take, he has already mentally signed up for membership.

The Ben Franklin close

The Ben Franklin close is ideal for prospects who are considering additional clubs or who are very detail oriented. It is so named because it was the method employed by the legendary statesman to help him and others make a decision. It is an excellent way to summarize your benefits and the positive response you have received from the prospect during the sale presentation about various features the club has to offer. When written down in black and white, the impact of the words is greater than the spoken word.

Start with a blank sheet of paper and draw a large "T" on the page. At the top, write on either side of the line Pro/Con. Look at the prospect and say:

> Mr. Miller, when Ben Franklin had an important decision to make, he'd make a list of the pros and cons and make a decision based on them. I always think it helps in any important decision to write things down on paper. Would you like to give it a try?

Now give them the paper and pencil and ask them to start with the "pros."

> Why don't you start with the things you liked that we offer here at Legendary Country Club?

One of the keys to this close is that your prospect states the pros and cons, and that you give him lots of help with the pros.

> You agreed that this is one of the finest courses in the area, right?

> You liked the fact that, unlike most clubs, we have no food minimum and offer exceptional dining. And as a member you enjoy a 20 percent discount on pro shop items.

> You liked the fact that there are no assessments ever, so you know exactly what your investment in membership will be.

> You mentioned that you enjoy working on your game and you saw we have excellent range and short game practice areas.

> You mentioned that our location is convenient to your office so you will be able to enjoy the range at lunch time or fit a quick nine in after work.

Prompt the prospect to contribute additional positive benefits to his list.

Then tell your prospect to write down the negatives. Because he's done the positives first, his mind will have a harder time changing gears to come up with negatives. And you don't help! This is one reason it's important to have the prospect do the writing (unlike some ways this close is taught). You might even say, "Now that you've got the hang of it, list all the negatives you can think of and I'll be right back."

When the prospect is done he will typically have ten or more items in the positive column and no more than three items in the negative column. This alone gives you a psychological advantage in closing. You may be able to say "It looks like the positives far outweigh the negatives. I guess that's it," and go into final closing mode. For instance:

> Mr. Miller, it certainly looks like the benefits of membership at The Legendary country Club are in favor of you joining our club. What do you say we go ahead and complete the paperwork?

If there any important negatives, you now have the chance to deal with the objection and close. It's the hidden objections that create problems. [See the Objections section for more details.]

The making-a-life close

> John and Sally, one of our new members said the other day, "I spend so much time making a living that I ignore making a life." It seems to me that many people are in the same position today, wouldn't you agree?

> One of the reasons people join Legendary Country Club is because it helps them to get their priorities in better order by putting their money into something that will

be a positive lifestyle investment. Lots of people say they want to spend more time on the golf course or with their friends, but they never get around to it. Life is short. What good does it do a person to work hard and not spend money to enjoy life?

Can you see how becoming a member at Legendary Country Club would give you a great deal of personal enjoyment?

The minutes or cents close

If you have a prospect who is stuck on price, the way to handle it is to break it down to ridiculous proportions. This is how life insurance has been sold for decades, but this type of close works just as well selling memberships, especially to value-oriented prospects. When you show people how little your club will cost them on a daily basis, it makes it much easier for them to justify, or rationalize, the purchase.

Mr. Miller when you think about it, membership at Legendary Country Club works out to be less than $15 a day. Wouldn't you agree that's an amazing value for a world-class club?

When all else fails there are three more closes you can try to get a positive outcome.

The reverse close

Occasionally, someone will come in and announce up front that he is not going to sign up for membership right now or that he is just looking around at the clubs in the area. This is a classic "shield" or defensive technique designed to give the prospect a clean way out if he doesn't hear exactly what he wants to hear. Now is the time for reverse psychology.

Thank him for coming in and offer to put his name on a waiting list for membership tours. Explain to him that you have so many people who are interested in joining right now that you can't possibly spend time with someone who is not ready to make a decision. Be polite but be firm; ask the prospect to pick a date for his tour a month from now. For example:

> I'm sorry, Mr. Miller, but I have so many people scheduled for membership tours this month who are ready to decide that I will have to make an appointment for you next month. Tell me what's a good date for you and I'll be happy to add you to the list.

This never fails to change the prospect's mind. The moment he hears he *can't* take a tour, you have dissolved his shield. Suddenly he wants the membership. An interesting turn of events occurs at this point. Now the prospect is actually trying to sell you on letting him buy! A side effect of this close is that it automatically builds value and credibility into your club. What kind of restaurants have waiting lists? Good ones!

The Columbo close

Over the last thirty years, there have been hundreds of cop shows on television. Few TV detectives have been less glamorous in appearance than the seemingly bumbling Columbo. After interviewing a suspect, when he reached the door he would always turn back and ask if the suspect could just help him go over the details one more time so he could understand.

> **Membership:** Mr. Miller, I understand that you're not joining the Club but wonder if you would do me a favor?

> **Prospect:** Sure! [At this point they will drop their sales defenses because you have acknowledged that they said

no. They are now more willing to help you to cushion the blow of them turning you down.]

Membership: You see, I truly believe that Legendary Country Club has the most incredible membership program that I have ever seen...I feel so great about what I do that I just don't understand why I fail to get others as excited about membership as I am. I would really appreciate it if you would tell me why I didn't communicate that same feeling to you so it will help me in the future. Can you tell me where I went wrong?

At this point Mr. Miller will do one of two things. He will either tell you exactly why you didn't convince him, or he will reveal his hidden reason for inaction. In either case, this gives you an opportunity to provide him with additional information and ask him for a response on the new and improved proposition. In the process, it doesn't hurt that you have stroked Mr. Miller's ego and self-esteem by asking for his advice.

The puppy dog close

This close is often used when a prospect is hesitant to purchase because of price. The "giveaway" close, or puppy dog close as it is often called, allows the prospect to enjoy membership (or a set of clubs) without a final commitment for a period of time before making a final decision on whether to buy. Once the prospect has experienced membership in a risk-free way, made new friends, and been treated well by your staff, he will almost always buy! He'd almost be embarrassed not to.

Let me do this, Mr. Miller. I am so sure you will enjoy membership at Legendary Country Club that I am prepared to offer you a very special deal. Give me a credit card on which to bill your monthly dues and member charges and try us out as a member for 90 days.

Meet the other members, play in some events, and experience exactly what it's like to belong to our club. At the end of 90 days you can make your decision on whether or not this is the right club for you. How does that sound?

If your prospect doesn't respond to this offer, you probably haven't uncovered his real objections, or he is not financially qualified.

SUMMARY

Your sales presentation should be carefully scripted. However, you don't need any special gift of gab to be a Legendary Salesperson. You just need to involve your propsect and explain your benefits in a credible way.

Overcoming objections to your presentations is one of the most challenging parts of the sales process. Yet if you believe in your value, you will be helping people to see the benefits more clearly. As you learn to deal better with objections, you will also improve your qualifying and presenting. The sales system works together to make you more effective. Just remember, your benefits can overcome any objections for the right prospects. Look for them, find them, and help them see how your offer meets their needs.

There are almost an unlimited number of ways to close a sale and I've covered the most successful ones here. Try them out, say them out loud, and role play them with your staff. Find the ones that seem most natural for you and put them into action at once!

Chapter Seventeen

Building a Referral Machine for Your Club

Ask any good golf club how they generate most of their membership or real estate sales and they will instantly and enthusiastically tell you they do it through referrals. However, if you ask them to explain their referral system to you, you are very likely to get a blank stare or a shrug.

I recently asked the vice president of a major golf real estate development and the president of a high-end country club what type of referral systems they had in place. Both had the same answer; they didn't; referrals just happened. So does death, but it doesn't mean you should wait around for it!

Referrals are the best way to bring in new customers for three simple reasons. First, other people are doing the marketing for you, usually at no cost to you. Second, when other people promote you, they are seen as more objective and credible. Third, referrals are generally made in order to help prospects improve their quality of life. A prospect who comes to you referred by his family, friends, or neighbors is already leaning towards a purchase decision.

Referrals are the life-blood of any good golf club or golf real estate development. There is simply no quicker and less expensive way to build your customer base and increase your income than to double or triple your referral rate. It doesn't matter what type of business you are in, referral business makes you more money than any other type of new business (not surprising as referrals cost little or nothing to get).

While some referrals will happen by accident, you cannot build a reliable marketing system on accidental events. You have to plan, measure, and implement a referral system that ensures two or three referrals from every single person with whom you come into contact.

In this chapter, you will discover:

✔ The difference between word of mouth and referrals

✔ How to measure referral success

✔ The psychology of referrals

✔ The best time to ask

✔ How to ask

✔ Who to ask

✔ Seven ways to get referrals

✔ Setting up an ambassador program

YOU ALWAYS GET WORD OF MOUTH, BUT IS IT GOOD OR BAD?

Perhaps you hadn't thought about it, but you are always getting word of mouth, whether you ask for it or not. While the terms "word of mouth" and "referrals" are frequently used interchangeably, there is a difference. Referrals are specific attempts to help someone— either the person you refer to a business, or the business you refer to an individual, or both. Word of mouth can include a referral, but it can also include general comments. For instance, someone might say "I would have made par my last time out, but the green was all torn up." Or "I hear that they've made some improvements on that course." Or "I hear that the scenery is great there."

You get the point. People talking is word of mouth. Sometimes it helps you and sometimes it doesn't. By combining a strong USP, a program to communicate to all your staff and players, and a system for driving referrals, you can generate more and better word of mouth *and* more referrals.

REFERRAL GOALS

The age-old business adage that what gets measured gets done is just as true for referrals as for any other part of your business. Referrals are far too important a part of your marketing strategy to leave them to mere chance as most clubs do. They must instead be sought from every customer, every client, every contact, and every supplier that does business with your club. Furthermore, they must be sought out from all your personal relationships from your accountant to your dry cleaner!

The only way you can see whether your referral program is working is to set goals in each category and measure your progress against them monthly!

Depending on your facility, you should set monthly goals for referrals in the appropriate following areas:

- ✔ Family memberships
- ✔ Corporate memberships
- ✔ Social memberships
- ✔ Sports memberships (tennis, swim, and so forth)

✔ Outings

✔ Banquets

✔ Weddings

✔ Lessons

✔ Special events (tournaments or theme nights, for instance)

✔ Real estate

✔ Room nights

THE PSYCHOLOGY OF REFERRALS

Start building your referral machine by first understanding the psychology of referrals. Giving referrals involves two contrary impulses. First, people like to give referrals because it allows them to help others at low cost to themselves. It makes them feel good about themselves and be a "hero" to others. Second, people worry about giving referrals because if something goes wrong they get the blame. Yet, if things go right, the thanks they get is usually small. Because of this ambivalence, it's easy to get some people to give referrals and hard to get others to. The same people may change their attitudes over time, or be more comfortable giving referrals to some types of people than others.

Clearly, your job is to encourage referrals and also make it *safe* to give referrals to your course. One way to tilt the odds in your favor is to provide a reward for referrals.

People like to give referrals for three important reasons

1. **Ego.** When someone buys a new home, membership, car, or investment, he wants his friends and neighbors to be impressed. He wants them to know what a great deal he got. When was the last time someone who bought a new car told you what a

schmuck he was for buying it? It simply doesn't happen, at least not in the first few weeks!

2. **Most people like to feel important; they like to be the center of attention or information.** When the opportunity to take center stage arises by giving a referral, they are more than ready to step up to the plate.

3. **Birds of a feather flock together.** People like their friends and neighbors to share and experience the same things they do! There are two parts of this equation. The first is that people want their friends to share in the joy of the same experience. The second, and less talked about motivation, is that people want their friends to share the risk. A person who has spent big money to join the Country Club wants a friend to join as well so if it turns out not to have been such a great idea at least they are in it together. Few people talk about this side but it exists nonetheless—the "I'll do it if you do it" syndrome!

There are many other reasons for giving referrals, from trying to help people, to hoping for referrals in return.

WHEN IS THE BEST TIME TO ASK FOR A REFERRAL?

The short answer is anytime; ask often. Early in the relationship can be the best time. Asking for a referral is a good habit to get into when you talk with people. The second best time to ask for a referral is as soon as you have developed a rapport with the prospect. He may not buy and you may never see him again so you should never let the prospect leave without asking for a referral. After someone has told you no is also a good time. Oftentimes a person who has just turned you down feels bad about having done so and will give you a referral to compensate.

The very best time to ask for a referral is right after you have completed a sale with a new customer. People who have just purchased from you are very open to helping you. Over 80 percent of all referrals happen within six to eight weeks of selling a prospect. This is the time when excitement and anticipation are always at the highest level. After that period, people tend to fall into their regular routines, they join cliques and tend to be more reluctant to bring others into their new world.

A similar scenario happened at the country club I used to belong to in California. When it first opened, we all promoted the club at every opportunity because we wanted new people to play golf with. A few years later, the club was fully established and we long-time members remembered the days when we could play whenever we wanted and didn't even need to book a tee time. When I resigned my membership, there were 900 members and you could hardly get on the course at all. None of the golfers in my group wanted more members. On the contrary— they wanted fewer. Consequently, they didn't refer anyone. New members, on the other hand, who didn't know what a paradise it had been ten years prior, put up with abysmally slow play and encouraged their friends to join.

HOW TO ASK FOR REFERRALS

Many people are bashful or just downright scared of asking for a referral. They don't want to seem pushy, desperate, or—heaven forbid—both. While I assure you that most people really do like giving referrals, you can make the process even more painless by reframing the way you ask for a referral. Plan your referral requests in advance so they flow smoothly and effortlessly from your mouth.

As mentioned earlier, *how* you ask for referrals can make a big difference. The most important point is that you have to develop a method that works for you, remembering that it takes a little practice before you'll feel completely comfortable asking for referrals.

There are many ways to ask for referrals. The way you ask will depend on your club's specific offer, positioning, and your personality. Some people just **come right out and ask,** business-person to business-person like this:

> Joe, just as you probably do in your business, we find we get most of our new members from referrals by other satisfied members. Who else do you know who plays golf regularly?

Notice that we asked "who else," assuming that they know people who play golf rather than "Do you know anyone?" This subtle difference creates very different results!

Or you might ask Joe if his customers, rather than his peers, could benefit:

> Joe, which of your clients want to get their games in shape this year and who might enjoy some golf lessons?

If the answer is affirmative, get a name and phone number. If the prospect doesn't know, or is reluctant to give you this information, try to recruit him to your team. Ask if he would convey one of your brochures, or at least a business card, to any potential prospect. If you have established any degree of rapport during the sales process, your customer should at least be willing to do that.

Another type of appeal is a **personal appeal:**

> George, it would really help me if you could suggest two or three other people I could talk to about the wonderful membership programs we offer here at Legendary Country Club.

Notice that we set an expectation by asking for two or three other people.

You can use a **personal favor** approach:

> George, I wonder if you could do me a favor. I'm looking for a few new students and I'd appreciate it if

you could suggest some people who might be
appropriate for me to approach.

If they give you names, ask if you can use their name as the referral
source when approaching the new people.

You can offer **rewards:**

You may not know that we have a program here that
provides a $50 gift certificate for every qualified referral
you provide the club who makes an appointment for a
membership tour. And should they join, we give both
you and the person a $200 certificate.

Notice that we reward both the tour and the sale. It costs money to
get leads—usually far more than $50 a lead so why not spend some
of your ad budget in the place most likely to pay off by rewarding
your members for leads? Notice that you're asking for *qualified* leads?
You set the qualifications.

You can provide tools to **make it easy** to give referrals:

George, here are five bag tags (etc.) to give out to your
friends. There is an offer on them to play the course.

Here are some other examples of ways to ask for referrals. You
should pick or develop ways that fit your own style and your club's
position in the marketplace.

George, we're trying to build up our outings business
here at the course on Mondays. It would really help me
if you could suggest a few groups you're a member of
who might hold a golf event, or a local company. Are
you in Rotary or any other group that might hold a
tournament for charity?

If the first answer is "No." try a few probes with specific
examples. For instance:

✔ Are you a member of the local Chamber of Commerce?

✔ Do you have any kids in schools that have fund raisers?

✔ Do you work with any charities that raise money?

If this doesn't work, try for the names of other people who are better leads.

✔ Can you suggest someone else I can ask about group events?

✔ Who do you know that is a member of a local association?

✔ Who do you know who knows the most people? Who do you ask for a referral when you need a new contact?

If you were looking for members, your questions would be similar:

✔ We're always looking for good new members. Who do you know that you'd like to have in the club?

✔ As a new member we want you to be comfortable here right away. Here are three free guest passes if you want to fill out your own foursome. Whose names should we put on them?

✔ Who do you know who plays golf the most often?

✔ Who do you know who might be dissatisfied with conditions at their current club?

WHOM TO ASK FOR REFERRALS

The short answer is, ask everyone you know or do business with for referrals.

Did you ask the UPS truck driver to buy today? I did. When I say everyone, I mean everyone. I include the mailman, the fire inspector, and the plumber. Hey, you won't know if you don't ask and everyone has friends who can afford to buy or is affiliated with a group that holds a golf outing!

SEVEN GREAT WAYS TO GET REFERRALS

There are seven key groups from whom you can gain referrals

1. **Ask new clients to buy again.** The reason we get referrals is so that we can sell more, right? Well, the first thing to consider before we ever work on the referrals to others is self-referrals: Can we sell anything else to the new golfer in front of us right now? Can they upgrade their membership to a multi-year membership? Can they buy a corporate membership and get their employees and partners involved at the club? Can they book an outing or give us the name of a cause they support that raises money though a golf event? Can they book a wedding or a birthday party at the club? Can you develop new things to sell them?

2. **Ask new clients who else might benefit.** Even if your most recent customer doesn't want to buy something else from you, it's almost certain that he knows someone in his line of work or situation who has similar needs. Everyone is an opinion leader—at least to a few people. A special few are opinion leaders to hundreds, or perhaps even thousands, of people. (See Chapter 19 on Customer Loyalty.)

3. **Ask non-customers for referrals.** Even when a sales presentation has not been successful, there is absolutely no reason why you should not ask the prospect for the name of a person who might benefit from what you have to offer.

The landscaper who did my yard dropped by recently to see if I could refer him to any potential new customers. He told me that he had contracted to do two new jobs in my area in the last month.

Each was worth almost $50,000, and both had come as a result of asking for a referral from homeowners who had turned his bids down because of the cost.

Simply say to the prospect:

> I'm sorry I don't seem to be able to meet your needs today. Who else do you know who might be interested in looking at Legendary Country Club?

4 **Ask ex-customers.** Just because a golfer is an ex-customer doesn't mean he or she can't or won't refer your business, especially if you parted on good terms. Make it a point to stay in contact with ex-members at least a couple of times a year and let them know you are still in business. I frequently get referrals from ex-customers who have since moved on to other things but still have friends or contacts in golf. And as a bonus, often ex-customers come back because you bothered to keep in touch.

5 **Ask business suppliers for referrals.** Remember, you and your club make purchases. You buy goods and services from others. You are a good customer to someone. That *someone* should be glad to give you referrals as a reward for the business you give him. At the least, suppliers should keep you up on industry happenings, but they also know people who golf. They may belong to groups that have outings or charity events. In sales, just as in other areas of your life, you won't receive if you don't ask, so be sure to remind your suppliers that you are always in the market for new leads.

Don't forget personal suppliers

You bought a car locally, a home locally, and have relationships with dry cleaners, gardeners, and a host of other personal service companies. They have *your* business; have you asked them to help your business?

Get everyone on staff involved

Make it a clear policy at your club that SALES is *everyone's* job! Remind employees that "Nothing happens until a sale is made" and that the club's success and their PAYCHECKS depend on a constant stream of new business! You can also reward them for each referral or sale.

What about your club manager, golf professional, super– intendent, and chef? Have they leveraged their personal relation- ships by asking for referrals?

How about bartenders and wait staff? They come into contact with hundreds of people a week and often have jobs at more than one place. They can be a huge source of referral business. The more people on your staff you get involved at a grass-roots level, the quicker your referrals will grow exponentially.

60 **Catch bees with honey: Get referrals from your competitors.** Most business owners would be surprised to learn that your competitors can often be a good source of referrals. Before you think that I'm a couple clubs short of a full set, think about it! Sometimes you get a request for an outing on a date you're full. Or you and the prospect simply don't hit it off! She's from Venus, you're from Mars, he wants a club closer to home, or whatever. In these cases, instead of letting the prospect bounce around to three or four more people, take the proactive approach and refer them to someone who can help them at once. Then call that person in advance to let him know what you can about the prospect. When you give referrals, others should return them out of courtesy.

You can also set up a formal alliance whereby it's agreed in advance that all extra business gets referred. In one case, two of our clients in Orlando have this arrangement and give each other a 30 percent commission for the referral. THINK ABOUT that; a day when your course is full and you generate more than 100 percent of revenue!

7 **Give referrals to your members.** Getting referrals is your goal, but you have to *give* referrals to get them. That's often the best way to generate referrals—and if they don't reciprocate, find someone else to refer to! (Good referrals also reward your members, thus making their memberships more valuable, and thus more likely to be renewed.)

It may be hard for a golf course to give referrals to some people. In that case, there are at least two things you can do. First, you can talk up your contacts. For instance, you can plug the local Chamber, banker, or housing development. Second, you can facilitate business among your members. When you learn that a new member is in a business that might be of use to one of your other members, immediately ask for that person's business card. Ask for several cards, so that you can pass them on to your clients. It will make your member feel good and it will build your list of resources.

There are many ways you can facilitate contacts among members. Maybe you can plug new members in your newsletter, host networking events, or provide a bulletin board for business cards. You should make yourself a central source of information in the networking among members. Then they'll keep you in mind.

For instance, one club makes their meeting room available to nonprofit groups for free. Since meeting rooms are scarce in town, many opinion leaders appreciate the facility. And, of course, it's easy for members to arrange the room for their favorite groups. That makes them look good with their groups, exposes new people to the club, and gains the club publicity in the group newsletters and the local newspaper's event calendar.

BUILDING YOUR REFERRAL MACHINE

With all your tools in hand, it's time to commit to the development of a referral habit that will pay untold dividends over the course of your business career. (Even if you're not in sales or marketing, the ability to generate business—to be a rainmaker—makes you more valuable in any position.)

The first thing you must do to build a referral machine is to make a serious commitment to gathering referrals and following them up. You can often double or triple your referrals by simply asking for them. Not sometimes, not when you feel like it, not when you are having a good day, not if you feel the prospect likes you, but every single time in as many different ways as you can until you get what you need. In the book *Marketing Your Services: For People Who Hate to Sell*, the author (Rick Crandall) says that most people have a "prayer" referral system—they simply *hope* that someone will give them a referral! They say it takes 28 days of constant

---

Be specific when asking for referrals

Once you are given a referral, make every effort possible to get a little background on the person you will be dealing with. When I was selling my consulting services for golf courses a few years ago, I asked each client to provide me with three referrals. One client in Mississippi faxed me right back with the names of three people.

The first was mildly interested.

The second told me that if this client was using me, then he certainly wouldn't.

The third started shouting at me on the phone at the mere mention of the client, and went on to tell me what he would do with the "son of a #@!#@" if he ever got hold of him.

I was completely confused and called the client back to ask him what was going on. He said he had simply referred people to me whom he knew needed my services. He didn't know they had to like him!

Whenever you get a referral, try to find the connection between the person referring and the referral. Ask how Joe knows Harry. Ask how long Sally has been friends with Chelsea. Ask what line of work the prospect is in. The more information you have about the referral, and the clearer you are about the referree's relationship with the referrer, the better are your chances of a successful outcome.

repetition to develop a habit, so give yourself more than a prayer of a chance for referrals—get started today!

CULTIVATE REFERRAL SOURCES

Some people don't give referrals no matter what you do. Some people like to give referrals. It might be a manager of a sporting goods shop, a realtor, or the Chamber of Commerce that is a good referral source. When you find one, look for more that are similar. Most important, when you find a person who gives referrals, build the relationship. Keep in touch. Give them referrals back. Put them on your newsletter list. Find out what they like. Treat them or their family and friends as special people.

Show your gratitude

Once you have received a referral, whether it works out to your advantage or not, make sure that you thank people. When a customer gives you a referral that results in a sale, make a big production out of the event. At the very least, you should send him a "thank you" note. If the amount of money involved in closing the sale is substantial, consider sending the customer who gave you the referral a suitable gift for his assistance. A book on a subject that interests him or a bottle of his favorite wine will go a long way towards ensuring that this particular person will continue to refer good prospects to you.

Reward with money?

Many clubs offer a financial inducement to encourage referrals, but they do not always work. Studies show that a large percentage of people feel uneasy about being paid for referring their friends unless their friends benefit equally in the process. For instance, they get a $500 credit and so does the new member. They get a staff bag and so does the new member. They get a cruise and so does the new member. You get the idea. Coming up with a reward whereby both parties benefit is by far the most effective way to say thank you for a referral and encourage more.

Ask again for referrals

Every time you thank a customer for a referral, you have the opportunity to repeat the cycle by asking for another referral. Always end each thank-you communication, whether it's a letter or a phone call, by asking if the customer knows of anyone similar who might benefit from what you have to offer. Remember, the best time to get a referral is right after a sale. Strike while the iron is hot and ask for more names at once.

Make it easy to give referrals

The easier you make it for other people to promote you and your club, the more they will do it. Provide free postcards or discount passes for visitors at the pro shop, restaurant, or front gate. At a seminar with over two hundred people in Las Vegas, I distributed 200 postcards and asked the audience members to write down the three most important things they had learned and send the postcard to a friend who could then remind them to take action on these items. At the next break I announced that if everyone would drop the postcards up front, my secretary had a bunch of postcard stamps and would take care of mailing them. Ninety percent of the people dropped them off for mailing! 180 referrals in the mail at very little cost! Now, to me, a program like that makes a lot of sense.

The law of large numbers

The more people you know, the more referrals you get! Now that's a pretty simple concept, but far too many people fail to take advantage of this simple fact! Join the club or association in your town that will bring you into contact with the largest number of prospective contacts!

Okay, so there are already ten people in your field involved in the Chamber who are more established than you are, so now what? Well, before you take the next step, consider this: More than half of them never go to a meeting anyway. Of the half that go, they only go once a year or spend their time in aimless socializing rather than building relationships. As Woody Allen said, "Ninety percent of success is just showing up." If you still feel there is too much competition in the local chapters of whatever organizations you have considered, try a jump to left field and change the game. Join a related organization rather than the most obvious. Join the Chamber in the next town over, or instead of the realtors' association join the builders' association or the mortgage association.

Word of mouth is the life blood of any golf course. And you receive good words a whole lot more predictably and effectively when you develop and follow a system so that good leads don't just slip through the cracks.

LOOK FOR OPINION LEADERS; THEY ARE EVERYWHERE

In Joe Girard's remarkable book, *How to Sell Anything to Anyone,* he talks about the "250 rule." Basically, this states that everyone knows at least 250 people, and each of them knows another 250. Get the idea?

I know many more than 250 people, and I conduct seminars and give lectures to thousands across the country. What if the person to whom you are selling something is in the same position as I am, coming into contact with thousands of new people every year? What appears to be an individual, isolated sale could turn into hundreds of sales. Ask questions after each sale to find out what you can about your customer's sphere of influence. (Also see Chapter 19 for more information on building Customer Loyalty.)

SALES CYCLE LEADS

Certain products have sales cycles. On average, people buy a new home every seven years. When golfers in the Northern states hit their late forties or early fifties they start looking for a home in the SUN! Being aware of your product's life cycle gives you the edge in knowing when a previous customer will be ready for another purchase. Keep an active file in your computer's database that lets you know a couple of months in advance when these previous customers will be at their hottest to replace the golf course membership or house. But let me give you an even simpler example. Everyone has a birthday. Do you approach a member's spouse a month in advance and suggest a party at the club? Perhaps even a surprise party? If you're not sure of the timing, follow the first rule of referrals, ask early and often!

SETTING UP AN AMBASSADOR PROGRAM

Why take care of all referrals yourself when you can enlist the help of others? Develop your own Ambassador program.

In short, your goal is to have a group of your members dedicated to reaching out to the community on your behalf to find new members. Look for people who want to have an official role in your success. Maybe they are retired and have time. Maybe they are in fields like insurance where they want a reason to meet more people. They are likely to be naturally outgoing.

These will be the people who will play with, introduce, and bond with prospective members. Having a friendly person show a prospective member around the club and introduce them to the various groups is a very strong way to create a positive impression. We often forget that a great part of the golf experience is social interaction, not just the quality of the course. Members can be assigned by age, geographic background, and skill so that similar people get to play together.

A formal rewards program should be set up to thank ambassadors based on their success in attracting new members.

SUMMARY

There is no quicker or less expensive way to increase your business than to build a referral system rather than leave it to chance as most clubs do. Your system must be structured and measured. Then your staff must be trained and rewarded for following it. No less important is the recognition and rewarding of those who are doing the referring.

Chapter Eighteen

Free Publicity

Publicity is free mass media exposure. Historically, "media" meant TV, radio, newspapers, and magazines. Today the Internet gives you many more places to obtain free publicity. Publicity can vary from a mention of your club tournament in a newspaper calendar listing to a major feature story with color pictures of your course in a national or regional publication. A big story about you can create a surge of immediate business and build your visibility and image for the long term.

The simplest way to think of publicity is as free advertising—although it almost always will cost you time and effort to get it. For instance, you might pay for an ad in a travel magazine, but that same magazine might do a story about your course for free. Or you might spend money for a staff person or outside consultant to write a press release about your new club house and get it sent out to editors.

Publicity can be worth ten times what an ad of the same size would cost you. Publicity is worth more than advertising because it is an implied endorsement by the media. People pay attention to media-produced stories while they ignore the ads and have a healthy skepticism of claims made in advertisements.

This chapter will show you how to package stories for the media, how to deal with the media, and how to make your publicity even more valuable *after* it comes out than when it first appeared.

After you read this chapter, you will know more than 99 percent of your competitors about how to get publicity. If you put in the time and effort, you'll dominate the golf publicity in your market.

In this chapter, you will discover:

- ✔ 7 major ways to get publicity yourself
- ✔ How to hire PR professionals
- ✔ How to approach journalists
- ✔ What journalists *don't* like
- ✔ How to use press releases properly
- ✔ How to use publicity *after* it comes out
- ✔ How to obtain online publicity

While publicity can be very cost effective, like any tool it has to be used correctly for best effect.

PUBLICITY IS A TWO-STAGE SALE

It takes a two-step process to reap the benefits of publicity. You first have to sell the media on using your story and then, when it appears, the story helps sell you to your ultimate customers. As discussed later, journalists are a difficult group to sell to, so it pays to know what you're doing. Because publicity is free, lots of people are competing with you for it. In order to stand out, you have to work to develop what journalists call your "hooks." These are concepts to "hang" a story on (somewhat similar to USPs as discussed in Chapter 7). Fortunately, getting the media's attention in the golf area is not terribly difficult. You just have to make the effort and be persistent.

One big advantage you have in getting free publicity is that few golf businesses do a good job of working with the media. For most, a few feeble press releases are about the best effort they make—and few enough of those. There are also some media that *want* your story and will be much more receptive to it. These "easy touches" can give you a constant trickle of publicity while you work to get the bigger exposure.

LONG-TERM VALUE

One *great* publicity item about you can add dozens of players to your course. Regular articles by you can build your credibility and a steady flow of business.

Publicity is one of your best long-term marketing tools. However, because its effects are seldom immediate, publicity is most valuable when used consistently. The best way to get ongoing publicity is to set up a regular schedule for contacting the media.

Any mention of your course, personnel, or any visibility you achieve, will help you in the long run. There is a saying that there is no such thing as bad publicity. However, if investigative journalists like those from the *60 Minutes* TV show come calling, I would think twice about granting an interview!

You can't rely on the media to find you. If you host a big tournament or charity event, some sports media may seek you out. However, up to 90 percent of what you read, see, or hear in the media about golf comes from people and companies contacting the media, rather then the media finding them. So *you'll* have to make the effort to go to the media if you want regular publicity.

Now, let's get right down to the details of getting publicity for you and your course.

MAJOR WAYS TO GET PUBLICITY

I'll cover seven major approaches to getting publicity, plus many details and examples of how to do it. Some of them are guaranteed. If you apply them regularly, you will get coverage that you didn't have before. Others depend on the response of the media people you contact.

Different media present different degrees of difficulty to you. The bigger the newspaper, web site, magazine, television station, or radio station, the more people want publicity from them, and the harder it will be for you to get placements. So start with the smaller units. The easiest ones are your local weekly newspapers, smaller web sites, and association newsletters.

1 **Tie to current news or a trend.** If something is happening in the news today, like a politician commenting about physical fitness, the media is open to you commenting on how it would apply to local golfers. For instance, when doctors say that people need to walk an hour a day, you could talk about the exercise involved in golf if you allow walking. This hook can also be tied to events like National Heart Week.

"Trends" where you can take your time

There are also hundreds of trends or events you can tie to that are predictable long in advance. For instance, every year brings Thanksgiving, Easter, Christmas, Mother's Day, Father's Day, tax deadlines, and so on. Many of the minor holidays were, in fact, created by groups simply to get free publicity (or even by Hallmark

Cards!). And the media doesn't mind since they like to tie stories to events. They're there, so why not use them?

If the existing "golf months" don't work for you, you can create your own. For instance, San Diego declares February as golf month when the PGA comes to town. The Three Rivers Park District in Minnesota declares July as "family golf month" and offers many family specials at their courses.

Your "trend" doesn't have to be linked to a date. Issues like fitness and the environment are always in season. Numerous clubs we deal with are Audubon Society sanctioned clubs, offering endless possibilities for additional PR on that angle alone.

As a lifelong outdoor recreation activity, golf has good "hooks" with exercise, the elderly, the importance of leisure, and the value of nature. There are even publicity angles with the "lost" balls on your course. For instance, you could get publicity if you let the local high school golf team come out to the course once a month to pick up balls from the rough for their team to use. I've even seen artists who made mosaics out of different colored golf tees they picked up on the course. That could get you publicity in the artistic community. (Jumping ahead to another section, you could even sponsor a contest for artists and display the best efforts in the clubhouse.)

In today's media-driven culture, tying publicity to a movie works nicely. You can get advance information on when new movies are coming out in order to prepare ahead of time, or wait until you see the movie and react quickly. For instance, think of the stories you could have gotten related to *Bagger Vance*, *Tin Cup*, *Bobby Jones*, or even *Happy Gilmore*.

Other possible news hooks

✔ Was your club designed by a famous architect?

✔ Get local landscapers to comment on features from your course that could be used in home landscaping.

✔ Did you redesign your course, or a few holes?

✔ New head pro? Lady greenkeeper? Famous owner?

✔ Did the golf team that plays at your course just win a big event?

✔ Is your club champion very young or old? A veteran, fireman, local school teacher? This gives you a new angle every year.

Getting PR is not mission impossible

"Your job, should you choose to accept it," is to prepare yourself now for New Year's, Mother's Day, Father's Day, Grandparents' Day, the British Open, and other predictable events.

Think about this: The media needs your help. Take the Masters. It happens every year and the media hasn't been very creative about doing stories other than how people are scoring (unless there's a boycott about women playing). National media are dying for a new angle and your local media would welcome a local tie-in. Has your pro played Augusta, or coached one of the current players in the field? Have players now at the Masters played your course? Did Bobby Jones ever visit your course?

The key is to consistently look for hooks, call your media contacts, type up your news, and send it in!

2 **Create your own news.** By creating something that didn't exist before, you are automatically newsworthy. When you offer this to your local papers, they will generally publish it.

This can be as simple as a one-page sheet of tips from your pro for a better golf game. Or tips on how to have a better lawn from your greenkeeper. Or a series of lectures at your clubhouse on golf-related topics.

How about giving an award?

Another way to make your own news is to present an award or create a list. These can be locally or nationally oriented. It could be golfer of the year, or golf journalist of the year. Or you could get creative and present an award for lawn of the year, judged by your staff.

You're already familiar with some nationally publicized lists of "best dressed," "worst dressed," and so on. Any awards give you publicity. And they give you a great reason to call people—to ask for nominees, or to tell them they are potential candidates.

If you don't think that your giving an award will be credible, get a charity or trade group to sponsor the presentation with you. If you offer to do most of the work, they have little to lose. After all, they need publicity too! Similarly, when you sponsor one major charity event a year, both you and the charity get publicity.

Local-best lists

If you don't want to create your own award or list, there may be the chance to exploit existing ones. Many local newspapers, often weeklies, do readers' polls of the "Best of Your Town." Usually, these have to do with shopping, restaurants, entertainment, and so on.

Be like the all-star voters in every city with a major league baseball team: Ask your fans to vote for you. Actively "stuff" the ballot box to be rated "the best golf course" in town!

Stunts. In the old days, to get publicity, you would set up some sort of stunt: sitting on flagpoles, holding a race, swallowing goldfish, cramming into a phone booth, and so on. That's a pretty old-fashioned approach to publicity, but surprisingly enough, it still works. When the Russian MIR space station crashed to earth, Taco Bell put out a target where it was expected and promised everyone a free taco if MIR hit it.

The bottom line is that if you're willing to do something dramatic or silly, the media is willing to help you make a fool of yourself! Of course, your stunt could be for charity as well, which makes you look like someone with a sense of humor. Even the oldest stunts could be recycled for your club. How many golf balls would it take to fill a phone booth (instead of college kids)?

- ✔ Have a Halloween Monster Day tournament where you lengthen your course to 8,000 yards.

- ✔ On a Monday, put in holes the size of buckets and see what your players could really shoot if the hole were "only a little bit bigger!"

- ✔ Have the whole club hit balls on the same par three to see how many holes in one you can produce in a day.

- ✔ Have a Night Lite Championship as discussed in the Promotions chapter.

Photos

Getting publicity for many stunts depends on good photos. Unusual pictures are a kind of visual "stunt." The Associated Press carries a novel picture almost every day. It might be 10,000 golf balls photographed from above. It is always an unusual view, something you don't normally see.

Use your imagination to stage a great photo (or use your computer special effects). What about the world's biggest golf club, or ball? (You might make the Guinness Book of Records.) Including a little fun in your image can add a dimension for your customers, attract attention, and create publicity. Even the most dignified professional may find a little clowning inspirational for the staff in a skit at the staff meeting.

4 **Giving talks.** Another way to get publicity is to give talks. In most trade publications and local papers, there are calendars

of meetings and seminars you can check. If you're a member of the local Rotary, that's a place to start. And there are probably several other chapters near you. Put together some topics, from how to do business on the links, to lawn maintenance, to putting tips. Your audience will want to come to your course if they feel a connection to you. And if you offer a special coupon, they'll be even more likely to visit your course.

If your golf professional, greenkeeper, or manager start giving talks to any group that will have them, you will get additional business for your club. (Start them off at the service clubs, or at Toastmasters if they're shy.) People like meeting someone from a business, including yours. But whether or not you get immediate business, you can polish your image, gain referrals, and get names for follow-up with your free golf e-zine. Eventually, you'll see results. As mentioned elsewhere, I give numerous talks to PGA Sections and owners' organizations across North America, and it always results in new business.

When you give the talks, you want to be sure to have a press release for the local calendar—just a few brief lines giving the time, place, and sponsor, and saying how people can attend.

Get referrals and more publicity

Talks can bring you referrals as easily as business. At the end of her speeches to business groups, one speaker offers to write an article on her topic for their trade magazines or internal newsletters. About 20 percent of the audience gives her their cards. This gives you the chance for more publicity, for ongoing columns, and a reason to keep in touch with these people or put them on your e-zine list. If your talk includes a PowerPoint presentation, offer to e-mail it to your audience (a great way to add to your mailing list) or give them a printed copy *after* your speech. Be sure your name, club, and contact information is prominently displayed on the handout.

5 Be a "columnist." It's hard to become a regular golf correspondent for your local paper, or radio or TV station, but it's worth shooting for. And today, you can have your column or "blog" on your web site if no one else will publish you.

Let's say you start with your own e-zine sent out to your e-mail list and posted on your web site. Make sure to add local newspaper, regional golf publications, radio, and TV people to your distribution list. If you're interesting, they'll start to quote you and it will pave the way for them publishing you directly.

Your biggest opportunity to do columns will come from newsletters published by organizations (volunteer editors are usually short of material), or with smaller web sites and e-zines. If you can be counted on to produce something of interest on time, you often will earn their gratitude and have a constant outlet for your thoughts. That goes for your weekly newspaper as well—they always need local material.

If you want to appear in a specific place at a specific time, you can always pay for advertising, but produce the ads as if they were columns (or radio/TV spots). This looks more professional and is more effective than a simple ad.

Your own TV show

You can even become part of the media yourself. Most local cable systems are required to offer a "cable access" channel. This means that after taking a brief course to qualify yourself as a producer, you can use their equipment free to host your own talk show, shoot pictures of a tournament at your course, or give lessons. Of course, not many people look at this channel, but some do. Why not become the golf guru? Talk about how to play better golf, get clips of famous matches, answer questions, and so on. Call your local cable operator and ask about FREE PUBLIC ACCESS.

Would it help your outing business to tell people that a highlight tape of their outing would be aired on the local TV channel? (Or you can give them the tape if they don't want publicity.) Any charity event would appreciate being interviewed before the event to draw more entries or donations. In addition to your small audience, you can use copies of your best tapes to promote yourself as a guest to "real" TV shows. And you can offer guest spots to your best referral sources and clients.

6 **Publicity from donations.** Working with charities for publicity has already been mentioned in passing. The media is willing to give you extra attention when you're donating your time and expertise to a charity or other worthy cause. When you have a big event, working with a charity sponsor will help you. But you can also donate memberships, rounds, scholarships, and gift certificates to worthy causes. Gift certificates not only give you publicity, but allow you to prove the value of your course. If you're lucky, the people who bid for them paid enough that they actually have an interest in golf and may become a regular with you.

Most local school districts have auctions, as well as PBS TV stations. You'll get some publicity for your donations and, if they're big ones, you may get special attention (on the list of big donors, invitations, and other perks).

Your charity can even be one that serves your interests. How about starting a junior golf foundation to help youth play golf. Every inner-city student could be the next Tiger Woods, and when you help them get college golf scholarships, you'll be a hero.

7 **Use your golfers.** What you want are feature stories about how wonderful your course and staff are. But that will happen only occasionally. So, what do you do? You use your golfers or members!

The media will only do one story a year about most aspects of your course and business (not counting special events and other news you create). But your golfers can make interesting stories to tie to. For instance, your golfers may include the principles of a local film production company, a skydiver, and many other interesting people. Now, you have many possible stories by linking yourself to your interesting clients. The film producers talk about how they come up with new ideas on the links. The skydiver uses golf to relax. Of course, to get these items placed, you use the other techniques discussed in this chapter. (For instance, your members can be guests on your TV show.)

Every member is a possible story. And somewhere in that story, the member will mention the tie to your club because you wrote the story! So, talk to your members about getting them some publicity. For them, it's an unexpected bonus, and they should be incredibly grateful if you're successful. Even if you are not successful, they should be flattered that you thought they were worth publicity and pleased that you were willing to make the effort for them for free. (If you can't place the story in the media, you can always use it in your e-zine or club newsletter.)

IF YOU'RE TOO DIGNIFIED FOR SOME TYPES OF PUBLICITY...

For some of you, publicity won't seem dignified or in keeping with your "image." If your club is that distinguished, you should have a waiting list for membership and your publicity can center on your charity events.

Go for the kind of publicity that fits your style. If your pro wants more students, he can write articles that show his expertise. That's dignified enough. But remember that it's nice to have a sense of humor, so an occasional "stunt" may fit you fine.

You never know where extra visibility will lead you. Sometimes a short blurb that you support the local high school volleyball team will be just the thing to build a connection to a corporate chief who played volleyball in college or whose daughter plays high school volleyball now.

HIRING PR HELP

If you want to hire a professional public relations firm, look for referrals from people you know, just as you would when hiring any professional firm. They will generally cost you from $5,000 to $10,000 a month and want a several-month commitment because it takes time for stories to appear.

The first sign of a good PR firm, like any marketing company, is that before they start they will first interview you closely and observe your business. They will look for hooks to tie a story to—anything the media would find interesting, novel, or newsworthy. (They'll want to know your USP, positioning, or uniqueness.) Ask them what kind of results they expect to produce within what time frame. While they won't guarantee results, they will at least have some goals. A great PR firm will work harder when they don't get placements so you should see some results.

In today's world, consumers are changing and your public relations effort needs to change as well. There are many more opportunities for PR programs. The power of PR lies in what others say about you rather than what you say about yourself. That's why publicity in general is more powerful than advertising. Your PR firm should have solid media contacts, provide creative ideas and strategic thinking, and have industry insight. (Legendary Marketing offers PR consulting services and can be of assistance to you.)

APPEALING TO JOURNALISTS

One of the best ways to obtain publicity for yourself is to do as much of the work as possible for the media to which you're appealing. Journalists usually feel overworked and underpaid. They know their stories can be valuable for you. Combined with the facts that they see "pitches" every day and have done hundreds of stories, they are a very difficult, cynical audience to sell yourself to. They have seen it all, so why should they give you the benefit of their coverage?

The short answer is that you have to offer value to them AND their audiences. First, for the journalists, you provide value by laying out the story for them and doing most of the work. Second, the media is willing to trade publicity for you for benefits to their audience. That might be a simple as "10 Tips" credited to you that help readers. But if your efforts help a charity, the media will be even more helpful.

Write like a journalist

Journalists need to decide what's newsworthy or interesting about your story (the "hook"). The best thing you can do, particularly for smaller media, is to figure it out for them and write the story the way they would write it.

Now, for your lesson in writing like a journalist.

One thing most journalists have in common is that they know the Rudyard Kipling rhyme about the basis of journalism.

> "I keep six honest serving men.
> They taught me all I knew.
> Their names are What and Where and When,
> And How and Why and Who."

Give journalists what they need to look good

Put less poetically, journalists are taught to put these six components (what, where, when, how, why, and who) very early in every article. Many journalists are overwhelmed with press releases to sort through and don't have the time to hunt for your message. (Or they may be lazy.) So, when they're looking at your press release, they want to see who it is and what it's about—immediately—right there in the first paragraph. Putting in all the facts of the story early was originally developed to allow editors to cut stories more easily. When studies are done of what readers actually prefer, they do not particularly like this "inverted-pyramid style," but it is the accepted standard.

What editors want

There is another side to the process of getting a press release used. I participate in studies of editors, and what we like or dislike about press releases.

Most editors are remarkably open to press releases. (Remember the estimates that 90 percent of what you see, hear, and read comes from video, audio, and printed PR.) What editors *don't* like are press releases that are not appropriate for their audience or publication.

This means you need to identify your release as relevant to editors very quickly.

If you say that you're a local club, it lets your local paper know that it's relevant to them. If you're going for a national trade publication, you should identify yourself as part of that industry.

COMBINING APPROACHES: AN EXAMPLE

Let's take the earlier idea of tying to a trend, and I'll give an example of how you would take a journalistic approach to writing up the story.

Every year we know that there is the first day of spring, the first day of summer, the first PGA tournament, and so on.

How would a reporter write it?

Let's use the first day of spring as an example. If you were a journalist, to do the story right you would interview people with different points of view. One might be a college professor in a Recreation Department or the head of the local Park Department. One might be a doctor who advocates exercise and fresh air. Another would be a passionate golfer. And, as a change of pace, you might interview a "golf widow."

Your story would talk about how golf provided life-long exercise and social contact and would contain quotes from your different experts. You'd have statistics about how many golfers there were, and how many local courses. You'd have quotes from golfers about how they celebrated spring with their first golf game of the season. And the doctor would say how healthy it was for people to stay active.

The pictures for the story would be taken on your course. And you'd be quoted as saying that you loved running a golf course because it makes people happy to get away from their routines for a few hours and play a round with friends.

That's the way a journalist would write it. And you would write a sophisticated "press release" with all those elements already in place. Likewise, for TV, it would be a video press release.

If you're good enough at it, some of your weekly papers will publish the article exactly as it is, putting their own name on it. But bigger media, which are harder to crack, will at least feel comfortable with it because it's written the way they would write it. (Of course, you've also done their work for them.)

As mentioned in the Web Site chapter, you should have a press section on your web site with quotes, pictures, and story material all ready for any journalist to download and use as is. When they see that, journalists will know that you understand their needs for "instant" material.

CAN YOU MAKE OTHER SECTIONS?

When trying to get publicity, don't overlook the personal things about yourself that may be newsworthy in the Features or Lifestyles sections, rather than just Sports. This could be a collection or hobby, your charity work, background, skills, or education.

In many local and trade papers, there are columns specifically for brief business items. Here, in just a few lines, they'll note hiring, firing, moving, seminars, and the like.

HOW TO APPROACH JOURNALISTS

Don't use press releases for local items

If you're appealing to the same outlets regularly, like local media, I recommend that you call them. Until you've established a relationship with journalists, they won't pay as much attention to your press releases.

Press releases are rather impersonal. Most media people get dozens of them every day, sometimes hundreds. If you have to contact dozens of places, you have to use a press release. But it's much better to call key places personally.

Placing stories is just like selling anything else. The more personal the approach, the better your odds. Remember that you may be able to obtain later publicity if you build relationships now.

The absolutely best way to build a relationship for the future is to invite a journalist out to lunch at your club if you have a good story, or just to get acquainted. (Real media are not open to bribes, but free meals are an exception to that rule. Most golf writers I know won't turn down a complimentary round of golf either.) The next best is to visit them by appointment, next best is on the phone, and next is a personal letter.

Call some of the local media; tell them that you were told that something you are doing might be of interest to them and you thought you'd call to find out. Then, briefly describe the point of the story or item. Of course, despite my advice, they'll usually say, "Can you send us a press release?" But now they've invited it so you can use a personal letter with the facts.

Get journalists to "find" you

Journalists are funny creatures. They know that people want to get publicity, so they worry about being exploited. But, at the same time, they depend on people who come to them because they don't spend much time out in the community looking for stories, especially about golf! And it's expensive to do so. No media has enough staff to cover their local area well.

This creates a paradox. Journalists like to discover you and they like to not have the feeling that you are simply contacting them to get publicity. So what do you do?

Playing a bit dumb can help. Try acting modest and say, "I don't really know if this is of any use to you, but a friend of mine suggested that I call you," then let them draw it out of you. When they say, "Can you send a press release?" you can say something like, "I can write it up in a couple of pages and send you a note." They'll say that's fine.

When you write, send them a personal letter saying, "As we discussed on the phone, here's the information. Thank you for any help you can give me. I'd be interested to see if you think this is anything worthwhile."

Get a referral

If you take these observations that reporters are too busy or lazy, like to discover things for themselves, and resent being exploited into account, the absolutely best way to contact them is through a referral.

Someone who knows them says, "By the way, I met an interesting person at a group last night; you might be able to get a good story out of it." Now, they haven't had to do much work and can still feel like they found you. They become more eager to do the story.

It's likely that some of your members or golfers know people in the media. Enlist their help for referrals when you have a story idea to sell. You'll also occasionally see local media giving talks that you can attend (for the purpose of introducing yourself).

Press releases

While not your most effective tool, the classic way to reach the media is to send a press release or a press kit. And, as already mentioned, you should have this material on your web page in a "press" section.

In one survey of editors, 45 percent of editors said they get more than 30 press releases a day. E-mail has caused the number to go up tremendously. With some national publications, press releases can number in the hundreds every day! When you talk to important journalists who you will want to contact repeatedly, ask them how they prefer to receive material; they'll tell you and will appreciate your consideration. About 20 percent said they read more than half of the releases and a third said they scan them all. In other words, they do actually look at them. However, 42 percent said only 10 percent or less were actually useful. Remember, editors are looking for something very early on that indicates that it's appropriate for their audience.

Editors suggest that you know their needs and send in custom-tailored information. Be sure to keep your mailing list up-to-date so your release doesn't go to someone who's no longer there. Editors I've spoken to recently advise against sending e-mail releases as a word document attachment that they have to open because the download takes time and they are rightfully leery of computer viruses. They prefer your news release in the body of the e-mail itself.

Interestingly, editors are not being deluged by phone calls. Sixty-two percent of the editors said they receive five or fewer phone suggestions for articles each week. While most of the suggestions they receive aren't useful, calling is a good way to find out what they want. Don't sell your idea, ask them what they need and adapt your idea.

If you're not doing anything that the media would want to cover, start doing more activities and events that are publicity worthy. As you start doing things to benefit your image, you'll also end up helping your community—so everyone gains.

Anytime you have an anniversary, expansion, hiring, or other change at your club, send in the brief items for these columns and you'll often get good results. For instance, for one of my businesses, we had a notice published about our one-year-anniversary open house. It generated four or five calls, and one of the callers became a client.

Most media have a plan for future coverage called an editorial calendar. For features, find out what is planned in future issues and discuss possible coverage with the editor. This allows you to slant your offerings to fit their themes. Don't be discouraged if they're not receptive. I know one case where many editors told a golf pro that they were unlikely to use his articles. But when he sent in a collection on disk, they used many of them. Not only were they well written, but there's nothing more attractive than having prewritten material when a deadline is looming. (Editors can be lazy, too!)

Press Release Basics

Angle each press releases to suit the needs of your particular target audience. If you are a golf pro and your audience is the general public, focus on the benefits of your teaching, your location, and special features unique to you.

A golf magazine would want more detailed information than a general newspaper, which will want features having high consumer appeal. If your audience is comprised of fellow golfers and peers, then you should slant your release towards providing more information about your particular techniques or method of teaching. Send readers a message that makes them want to find out what special advantage you have to offer them.

A proper press release contains a date, headline ("Golf Pro Doug Maddock to Give Free Swing Evaluations to Senior Golfers," for example), lead paragraph, and body copy.

Here are six elements of a professional release:

1. Date the release by day, month, or season, and name the authority or spokesperson making the announcement.

2. Compose a positive headline of twelve words or less.

3. Define the subject of the release and mention no less than three specific elements that make your service or method a trendsetter.

4. Touch on your unique benefits and describe tactfully how you stand apart from the competition.

5. Include the date and location where a specific activity will occur. It could be scheduled at your facility or at a recreation center, for example.

6. Give the name and phone number where queries and any possible sales leads may be directed.

Send your press release (unfolded) in a 9 ×12 inch manila envelope. Attach a short note stating your reasons for submitting the release and include an offer to send a more detailed media kit on request. Editors tend to favor press releases that are printed double-spaced on stationery with your business logo. Professionally written releases save the editors time and expense. That means they have a greater chance of getting printed.

Publicists often submit bulky media kits crammed with press releases in a 'shotgun' approach. Editors will immediately dump these kits into the waste basket. They don't have the file space or the inclination to become experts on your operation. If it survives at all, your kit will most likely end up in the publication's advertising department as a sales lead. If the editor needs a media kit, he'll contact you and request one. Or you can have it on your web site where the editor can pick and choose what he wants.

(continued)

Focus on the facts. Publicity editors are generalists. Don't expect them to rewrite weak copy, or know the details that make your business a winner. Most readers skim the first four to six lines of text before they either lose or gain interest. It's important to put your stronger points first. Editors tend to edit text from the bottom on the assumption that you opened with your main points of interest.

Remember to take the time gap for actual publication into consideration when you submit your press release.

How NOT to Get Your Press Release Read

1. Send a press release about your golf business to a magazine dealing in restaurant supplies.

2. Bog down your tight, incisive copy with a detailed and verbose history, or long-winded quotes from a spokesperson with nothing valuable to say.

3. Submit a coffee-stained press release typed in red ink, over two pages long, single-spaced, and typed on onionskin paper.

4. Send press releases on a dozen different activities with an abrasive cover letter demanding an "immediate release."

5. Tell a Publicity Editor that if they don't use the release, they're either "...stupid or crazy...or both!"

6. Fail to provide your phone number or the number of the PR agent who wrote the release.

7. Demand that a magazine hold your release "for publication at a later date."

8. Use flowery language and technical jargon.

9. Miss the submission deadline by a week...then ask them to "fit me in."

10. Congratulate yourself on the 'Super!' new method of instruction you have personally created. The intent is to promote your service. You should promote yourself only if name recognition is certain to help your business.

Multiple media contacts

Most media have multiple staff. For example, in newspapers there are a number of columnists and sections in each paper that select their own material. For example, the Business, Feature, and Lifestyle sections all might take a story on "women who golf." By seeing what individual journalists write about over time, you can design your press releases to appeal to each one.

Look for individual names on stories in the sections that interest you. For instance, in the Sports section, there are usually several sports reporters. If you send in a general release, the sports editor may or may not like it and assign it to an individual. Trying individuals first gives you more chances of getting published.

Keep clippings and names of journalists who write golf-related stories. The individual names will give you multiple chances to gain exposure. By having names, you can call each individual reporter directly. It doesn't hurt to start your call or e-mail with, "I read your golf story and really enjoyed it. I was wondering if..."

USING PUBLICITY AFTER THE FACT

There's a much overlooked fact about publicity alluded to earlier. Publicity is worth much more to you *after* it appears than immediately.

When your publicity comes out, some people will see your columns, the stories about you, and the stories in which you are quoted. You can get some calls, business, or recognition from these (as well as people trying to sell you various products and services!). But publicity actually has a much bigger impact *after* the fact when it's no longer fresh. That's because you should clip (or record) the item. Then, put it on your web site, distribute it in your press kits, or pass it out to people you're talking to about your club.

Keep good printed items in your office or on the wall of the clubhouse. Be like restaurants that keep their last good review in the window until another one comes out! When you send past clippings to the media, rather than hurting your chances of a new story, past publicity will help you. The media "borrow" from each other all the time. Save radio and TV interviews as well, and online provide links to items about you.

Clippings give you a credential. People feel that if the media have covered you, they must have screened you in some way, that you must be trustworthy and your club superior. Of course, none of this is true. But it at least shows that you have been around a while and were smart enough to read this book and keep your clippings!

ONLINE PUBLICITY

Online publicity has already been mentioned in other sections because it follows the same general rules. The best thing about online publicity is that there are many more places to get it. You are almost guaranteed that someone will publish anything you send them or write yourself.

Start with local discussion groups or web sites. Most areas have places where local businesses are featured. When in doubt, do a search on google.com and yahoo.com. Then ask your local reference librarian. Any place that you can advertise may also have possibilities for free online publicity. For instance, various travel guides may have online newsletters or discussion groups as well.

There are many directories of newsletters and e-zines online. Search them out on google. This will give you a list of places to submit articles to. Many of them have audiences of thousands.

It's also important to note that your searches online are an important type of marketing in other ways. While searches are often for specific research on an article you're writing, they can serve other important purposes. When you find items of interest that don't go in your newsletter, you might forward some of them to individuals to show that you are thinking of them. You will also run across web sites and people you will want to build relationships with. For instance, some journalists put out calls for information when they are writing articles. Or you may see an article you like and add that journalist to your database. You'll also see outing planners and charity groups that might use your club, equipment manufacturers who can demo equipment at your club, and new suppliers. The possibilities are endless online if you keep your eyes and mind open.

When people who plan to visit your area search for golf courses, your site should come up. While your relevant content is a starting

---

More Publicity Tips

In time, you will be able to assemble an information kit filled with a credible collection of press clippings that will come in handy as collateral information when someone decides to do a new story on you.

Don't be afraid to offer your services as an expert on the subject of golf. It could lead to you being quoted by a reporter or feature writer doing a story in a widely read local publication on the booming increase in golf in the area, how to solve problems with the speed of play, how to select a new set of clubs, and so forth.

Don't stop with print.

Mail your materials to local radio and TV stations in care of their public service community affairs representative or program manager. Regional broadcast TV channels maintain county bureaus and assignment editors are always on the lookout for stories with interesting angles. Remember that all TV stations have a weekday and weekend assignment editor, so get to know both of them. And they are always on the lookout for an upbeat story to end their newscasts. Pitch them on a warm and fuzzy human-interest story at your club like a junior golf event, charity fundraising tournament, or celebrity who's at your course that day.

Don't be discouraged if you don't get coverage when you submit a story idea. News changes fast and assignment editors need to react quickly to breaking news. Just be persistent—not pushy.

point to being found, you can enhance this with links to your site from others and links from your newsletters that are republished on other sites.

SUMMARY

Free publicity is available for you in your local media, in travel media, and online. Knowing how to approach journalists, you will help them achieve their ends so you can achieve yours. Then you can save and reuse most of your publicity for greater impact later. To optimize your publicity, you will have to change some of your habits, build relationships with the media, and try new events that will get you more attention. Knowing more, you'll also be better at hiring good help. Long range, publicity will support all of your other marketing efforts and give you higher credibility.

Chapter Nineteen

Developing Legendary Service

One of the most overlooked parts of marketing at any club is service! While a reputation can be built, enhanced, and even achieved with marketing, at some point your reputation is going to be put to the test. You may be the fastest gun in the West on all the wanted posters, but when the other guy staring you down draws, reputation doesn't count for much unless you really are fast! When you can back up your reputation with legendary service, you immediately vault yourself to the top echelon in your field. Great service drives repeat business, referrals, and long-term relationships with members and guests.

There is a lot of talk about providing great service in the golf business, about making your members and guests feel special. We all want it yet so few places deliver it! In fact, when you ask the managers at most clubs what good service is, you won't get a very straight answer. Instead, you will get a bunch of vague platitudes about being friendly and "taking care of our customers' needs." All very nice, but how often can you truthfully say that your service is not just good, but exceptional? Not just exceptional, but outrageously great?

In this chapter, you will discover:

✔ How to define great service

✔ How to determine what a customer is worth to you

✔ Why customers leave

✔ The ten commandments of customer service

✔ Whether or not your club's policies are customer friendly

WHAT IS YOUR REPUTATION?

How are reputations for service, good or bad, formed in the minds of the public? How much of any person's or club's reputation is true and how much is hype? In the minds of your customers and prospects, perception is reality. Your reputation is based on word of mouth and observations. It may be accurate, or it may not be.

If we see someone stepping out of a limousine in front of a ritzy hotel, we automatically assume that the person is rich, successful, and perhaps even powerful or famous. If we see that a company's stock is rising, we assume the company must be doing well; if it's falling, we assume the company must be doing poorly. If other people tell us a particular restaurant is good or bad, we are inclined to believe them. The fact that our taste may be totally different from theirs doesn't really enter into it; a good reputation is good and a bad reputation is bad. Most people won't take the time or effort to confirm either way; instead they will just accept what they hear or read as the truth right up until something happens to change their minds.

WHAT MAKES YOU THINK YOUR SERVICE IS GREAT?

The hype, the posturing, the positioning, marketing, the promotions, and the advertising must take a back seat to good old-fashioned service. As yourself these questions:

- ✔ Can you deliver the goods?
- ✔ Can you back up the position you've claimed?
- ✔ Are you who we think you are?

Everyone *says* they give good service. And everyone probably *means* to offer customers a great experience. But most have no system in place with standards, measurement, and rewards.

Great service is partly intangibles. It's people who treat you like a real person, not as an indistinguishable unit passing through their facility. It's a friendly tone of voice. It's a personal connection, not a "professionally friendly" employee. It's personal recognition.

Unfortunately, it's all too easy to come up with examples of bad service even when dealing with "quality" businesses. Here are three examples where, as a customer, I expected a big service response. Instead, I received, well...

New home

When I bought my current home, it generated a very large commission for the real estate agent who was both the listing and the selling agent. She spent a grand total of one day with my wife and me before we bought. When we moved into our new home, did we have fruit waiting in the kitchen, a bottle of Dom Perignon, or a thank-you card? Or perhaps something more creative like a refrigerator stocked with food, a certificate for a babysitter so we could go out, or a little party to introduce us to local contacts. NO! In fact, we got nothing—way to build your reputation for service, lady!

The sad thing is that while I felt the business I brought her was unappreciated, if this realtor had made a small gesture of acknowledgment, she would have received positive word of mouth and several referrals from me that would have earned her tens of thousands of dollars.

Golf club championship

A decade ago I won the club championship at my golf club in California. Did I get my picture in the club's newsletter? No! In fact, I didn't even get my name mentioned in the club's newsletter, let alone my picture! I was the most excited I had been since I was fifteen years old, but not being acknowledged was a huge letdown! Way to make your members feel special, guys! (The fact that I'm still talking about this incident years later illustrates how important it is to acknowledge and appreciate your customers.)

Foggy service

On a recent trip to Ireland, I paid nearly $300 for a round of golf on a very memorable course. There were, however, a couple of incidents that dampened my overall experience. First, I never received a response to my initial e-mail request for a tee time. Then, faced with a fog delay at 10 AM, my friend and I decided to have breakfast at the club. There were five items on the breakfast menu. I ordered a Danish and coffee, my friend a cocoa. No Danish. No problem. I ordered a scone. No scones. No problem—what do you have? The waitress left, then returned and suggested a croissant (not one of the five menu items). I gladly ordered it and was duly served a fresh croissant accompanied by one of those little individual strawberry jam pots. As I opened the jam pot, my friend and I both burst out laughing! The jam was half-eaten. By this time, soured on the service, I just dug in and didn't even bother to mention it!

After a two-hour fog delay, all of the tee times were reshuffled (fair enough). I told the starter that we were both scratch players and would like, if possible, to play with a couple of better players. He responded two minutes later by asking that we go off next, with two 68-year-old ladies from Boca Raton. To their credit, they played admirably well, but with us playing all the way back, it did not enhance our day and I doubt it did theirs! Still, all was well again when we found the bar 5 hours and 45 minutes later! (Anything longer than a three-and-a-half-hour round is generally a negative experience for me.)

We all have stories similar to these, about people and businesses from whom we thought we would get superior service, but didn't. Fortunately, there is the other end of the service spectrum.

OUTRAGEOUSLY GOOD SERVICE

Recently I had the pleasure of playing golf at the Robert Trent Jones Golf Club in Gainesville, Virginia. It's the third time I have played in a tournament there, which only goes to prove that the exceptional experiences I have had there are not a fluke but, in fact, a tradition of outrageously great service!

I find it hard to quantify just why my experiences at RTJ are so great. Like many, I am quicker to tell you when service is not good. I am also far slower to appreciate exceptional service, so I thought I would try to quantify just why the experience there is so great in the hope that it may help you in setting standards you can measure at your club (see Benchmarking in Chapter 3). How many of these can you claim for your club? What extras do you offer during your customers' golf experiences?

1   An immaculate course. From the greens that run 13 on the stimpmeter to the tees that look like greens.

2   Gorgeous setting. The setting and design along the shores of Lake Manassas with the dogwoods and azaleas in bloom is truly exceptional.

3 Comfortable clubhouse. The clubhouse was immaculate and tasteful.

4 A welcoming pro. The pro, Cary, greeted me by name although he had not seen me in 363 days. He also greeted the rest of the group by name and no doubt the majority of the 21 other four-man teams!

5 Personal attention from wait staff. The wait staff knew my drink of choice and offered it at once on the second day. (It was like being on a cruise.)

6 Great caddies. The caddie I had, Dennis, was as knowledge-able and professional as anyone on the PGA Tour. Plus, he read the greens really well.

7 Locker-room attention to detail. When we walked into the locker room they already had our names on lockers.

8 Practice-round pin sheets. We were given pin sheets even for the practice round.

9 Locker-room service. When I left my golf shoes in my locker with a missing spike, the following day my shoes had a NEW SET of spikes!

10 Outstanding food. The food was as good as that served at any of the best restaurants I have ever eaten in, anywhere in the world.

11 Outstanding rooms. The accommodations in the clubhouse were on par with the finest hotels in the world.

12 Memorable tee gift. The tee gift was memorable and something I will keep and use—unlike the dozen Titleist NSX golf balls I got for paying $1,000 to enter another club's member-guest tournament. (I was also told I could not swap the Titleists for the balls I actually play since they said "member guest" on them. Like anybody really cares!!!!!!)

13 **Well-run tournament.** The tournament was run professionally with a full printout of standings delivered to each table at lunch and dinner.

14 **Social aspects.** Camaraderie was promoted and encouraged as much as the competition itself.

15 **I played well.** Last, and by no means least, I played well. Maybe the service helped my game, but even if I hadn't played well, it would still have been an awesome experience!

While it's easy to dismiss this as a high-end club with the money to do things right, that fact is only a small part of the equation. Plus, there are lots of high-end clubs that don't do it right! Not everyone can have a world-class club in perfect condition, but the commitment to world-class service can be made even at a nine-hole public course in a bad location. It's all about vision, desire, attitude, and—most important—trying to quantify, measure, and develop a service program that elevates any course, regardless of its physical plant.

YOU NEED TO KNOW WHAT A CUSTOMER IS WORTH TO YOU!

One of the most important marketing facts to discover in running your club is: What exactly is a customer worth to you? Knowing this information not only helps determine how much money you should spend on advertising and marketing to get a customer but also how much time, money, and effort you should spend on trying to *keep* a customer. If your customers spend only a few dollars a year, then you certainly can't send them a hamper full of goodies at Christmas time. If however your customers spend thousands of dollars with you, then it might well be worth the extra goodwill!

I remember, back in the mid-Eighties, reading Carl Sewell's book *Customers for Life.* At that time he found that the average Cadillac buyer at his dealership would spend over $375,000 with him as long as he kept them happy! In my karate school, I figured out that an average student would, over the course of his training, spend about $1000. In my marketing business, my average client is worth far more than that!

- ✔ Take a look at the best 20 percent of your clients—what did they spend with you last year?

- ✔ Take a look at your bottom 20 percent—what did they spend with you?

- ✔ After throwing out the bottom 5 percent and top 5 percent that might throw off the scales, what is your average client worth to your business?

You might be surprised by how much your best clients spend with you in a year. (And you probably haven't counted the referral business they bring in.) Now, project that number over five years, ten years, or perhaps even longer.

For example, I use a local limo service at least once a month to go to the airport at a cost of $75 plus tip. This means that if I continue to use them, I will be worth well over $6,000 in business to them in the next five years and close to $30,000 over the next ten years when you take inflation into account.

As a good customer, I ought to rate the occasional upgrade from a town car to their stretch limo. I should make their Christmas card list and maybe get a small token gift once in a while. Going the extra mile and spending $25 to $50 a year on me is going to be well worth the cost and will be far cheaper than finding a new client to replace me!

The value of clients cannot, and should not, be measured only in terms of dollars spent. There are other intangible measures of a client's worth that are equally important in terms of building your business. For example, I have several clients who don't do a great deal of business with me but account for a large portion of my referrals. They are always telling others how my business has helped them. Their worth in terms of referral business adds up to far more than the dollars they spend.

Other clients are worth far more than the books show because of their marquee value or brand name. I just picked up the marketing account for a large and prestigious resort. Although the dollars involved are small, having their name on my list of clients will undoubtedly produce more business for me. Your club will encounter the same sorts of situations. Certain people or companies with whom you do business will add to other people's positive perceptions of your club. That makes those customers special!

Going through this process and figuring out just what your customers are worth, both tangibly and intangibly, on an annual basis, can go a long way to helping you focus your efforts on the customers who most deserve your attention.

CUSTOMER SERVICE IS EVERYONE'S JOB

A fact that often goes unnoticed by executives is that, despite the best advertising, media relations, and all the good intentions in the world, reputations are won and lost on the front lines. An airline is not judged by the quality of its captain or management, but by its flight attendants and its ticketing agents. I do not use a certain major airline because their ticket lady called me an idiot when I asked her to sign me up for their frequent flyer program and she found that my travel agent had already done it. Then she told me to make sure I had the second number removed when I got off the plane in Dallas. Despite my better judgment, I asked her to do it for me. She refused, saying she only had thirty minutes before the flight took off and had to deal with other passengers.

Now, you might be thinking that maybe this ticket agent was just having a really bad day, but the following week when my Delta flight was cancelled due to an equipment problem, I found myself once again standing in line with this same agent at the counter. This time, it was the person in front of me who suffered her wrath. I just smiled and never flew Delta again! A car dealership is not judged by the models it sells, but by its salespeople and customer service staff in the shop.

The point is that your staff has your success in their hands. Do you pay them minimum wage, give them no training, and yet expect great results? Or do you put your staff first so they, in turn, will put your customers first?

WHY CUSTOMERS LEAVE

It is easy to forget that the people we serve can leave at any time. If they leave with an unsolved problem, they are liable to tell a whole bunch of people about that problem. According to the best studies, here is a breakdown of why people stop doing business with any particular person or company. The greatest percentage of loss can be avoided if you train your staff well.

- ✔ 1% get injured, ill, or die.
- ✔ 2% just disappear or get lost in the shuffle.
- ✔ 4% move away from the area.
- ✔ 6% change activities because of friends.
- ✔ 9% leave because of cost.
- ✔ 10% of people just love to change.
- ✔ 68% of customers leave because of indifference to them or their child.

Let's take a moment to look at that last statistic. Almost two thirds of all lost customers leave because of perceived indifference.

THE TEN COMMANDMENTS OF CUSTOMER SERVICE

Customers these days have plenty of options, and plenty of others vying for their time and money. Make the most of your opportunities by following the ten commandments of customer service!

1 **Stay close to the wants and needs of your customers.** Ask them for honest and critical opinions on your operation. Do not argue or try to defend your position, just shut up and listen. Use surveys, telephone interviews, and idea boxes to solicit and generate ways to improve your service. Almost every innovation we have added to our consulting services over the years has been born out of a client's suggestion for improvement. (That's certainly how our SmartSites became the industry's leading web solution.)

Ask your customers questions like:

- ✔ How do you think we could improve the appearance of the clubhouse?

- ✔ How could we have a better merchandise display in the pro shop? Is there merchandise you'd like that we don't offer?

- ✔ Do our hours of operation suit your lifestyle?

- ✔ What specific improvements or additions could we make to serve you better?

Just the fact that you ask their opinions will make your customers feel more special. If you implement a customer's idea, that customer could be yours for life!

Get a consultant to help you make amazing discoveries

In addition to direct customer feedback, another invaluable tool is to get a different pair of eyes examining your business, even if from a totally unrelated sector. You are never the best person to judge your own operation. Quite simply, you can't see the forest for the trees. You need to have an outside person come in and point out obvious things that you can't see.

Solicit opinions from friends, colleagues, and peers and, if all else fails, a consultant. Invite them to ask dumb questions about your membership procedure, sales pitch, your follow up, and your service. By encouraging them to do so, you will often discover areas that could be improved. You will make amazing discoveries such as that your office smells funny, that what you think is a clean bathroom doesn't cut it when you ask a woman. You might discover that you confuse your clients with too many choices during the sign-up conference. You might find you are charging too little for your service, as is often the case when I consult with a business. Not all of this feedback will be useful, of course, but it really does pay huge dividends to have outside people look at your operation and open your eyes to what is going on around you.

2. **Existing customers are more important than ones you don't have yet.** Don't treat new customers or prospects better than old customers. It is very easy to fall into this trap and it's a surefire recipe for the destruction of your reputation and your business. For example, it's not unusual for a business, in an attempt to gain more clients, to cut prices for new customers to attract business while charging established accounts more money. All the explanations in the world, even if they are heard or read, are not going to change the perception of the older customer that he is getting a raw deal.

A great way to make sure you are doing your best is to always act like your client has just told you he is considering another club. What would you do differently to try and keep that client from leaving? Well, first of all, you would likely try to find out what was wrong But let's suppose there is nothing in particular, or at least nothing the client is willing to share with you—then what?

You should develop a system to aid in getting clients back on track. Here are some possible steps you could take:

✔ Ask everyone on staff what they know about the golfer. (They may have shared some problem with the bartender, but not the club pro.)

✔ Give him personal attention. Invite him to join a foursome of people he'd like to meet. Take time to chat about his interests (which you should have in your database).

✔ Get him involved in an event that is in the future— preferably, one that will occur after his membership expires.

✔ Invite him and his wife to dinner at the club with another couple.

✔ Ask him to chair a committee, become an ambassador, or otherwise be part of the "inner circle."

✔ Come up with your own list of other things you can do, such as giving him coupons he can give to friends for free rounds.

In short, you need to go out of your way to do anything in your power to see that he doesn't quit!

Of course, you know as well as I do that most members or golfers do not give a warning before riding off into the sunset never to be seen again. There is a solution, though: Treat each and every client as though they were going to quit each and every month, and you will soon see a dramatic improvement in your customer service and retention.

3 **Follow up on all the things you say you will do, or don't say anything.** One of the simplest ways to insure good service is to schedule a follow-up call at the very same time you resolve to fix a problem or respond to a request. Murphy's law pretty much guarantees that if you have a problem with the a client that you resolve to fix, something will also go wrong with the planned fix, adding insult to injury. The best way to ensure that such events don't permanently damage your reputation is to outline the proposed action, then immediately schedule a follow-up call to ensure that such action has taken place. When fixing problems or responding to requests, you must always have a fail-safe system to ensure that the actual requests, however simple, were carried out. In fact, nothing damages a reputation more than a few simple requests not carried to their successful conclusion. People then start to wonder: If he can't take care of such a little thing, how can he take care of the bigger problems I entrust him with?

4   **Remember and use customers' names.** Remembering someone's name is one of the sincerest compliments you can pay a person. It builds their self-esteem; it lets them know you think they are important and they have made an impression on you. The sound of a person's name, pronounced correctly, is one of the nicest sounds in the world, at least to that person.

Staff should be trained to remember and use people's names. Some people are just better at this than others. Don't put the inept ones in customer contact positions.

If you doubt the value of using names for even for a moment, think how you feel when someone sends you a letter with your name horribly misspelled. Does that start you off feeling good about the person and his abilities? Not likely. Instead, it will tend to make you shake your head, roll your eyes, and mutter under your breath. The same is true when a person continues to verbally butcher your name.

It is vital when you engage in a conversation, or are introduced to someone, to remember their name. The fastest way to lose any rapport that you are building is to forget the name and have to ask it again. It has been shown that calling someone by their name, first or last, dramatically increases the bonding and communication. Other people feel as though they know you if you call them by their names.

Some people are good with names. Almost everyone at the pinnacle of success is excellent. People like former President Harry Truman could call literally thousands of people, from senators to scullery maids, by their first names. Can you imagine the feeling of joy and satisfaction you would get by having the President of the United States call you by your first name? Can you imagine the lengths a simple attendant might go to please when the President took the trouble to remember his name? The answer is clear. If you really try to improve your retention of people's names, you will soon discover the astonishing power of this simple act.

The simple effort of correctly pronouncing a person's name is a hundred times more powerful when the name has its origins in a foreign country. Learn how to correctly say a particularly difficult Greek name, or Japanese name, and you may be the only person they have ever met who has made the effort. That makes for a powerful bonding in your relationship that will have very deep roots. The person can't help but like and respect you when you alone have gone to the trouble of learning to pronounce his or her name correctly.

Unfortunately, not everyone has the natural ability to instantly put a name to a face. To remember names or other data the first time you hear them, you must pay attention. Be really mentally alert when you are introduced to a new person. Listen to their name closely and repeat it several times in your head. Ask them to repeat it if you are unsure you heard them correctly. Ask them to pronounce it for you if it is unusual. Echo the name back to them in a way that encourages correction if necessary. "Nice to meet you, Darin..." Or you can echo the name to simply acknowledge and confirm that you have understood. Use their name as often as you can in the first few minutes you talk to them. This will help reinforce the name in your memory.

Some memory techniques suggest that you look at the face and link a facial feature with the sound of the name. This could be something like, "Roberta, for her rosy cheeks," or "Stan, for a strong jaw." The idea is to be looking at a facial feature and linking their name with that feature. This technique greatly improves your ability to retain a name.

Another technique is to link this new person to a person you know well. For example, if I meet a "Ron," I link it to my good friend Ron. I find something that is similar between the new Ron and the familiar friend Ron. In this way, your mind links the two names and individuals together, making it easier to remember the name. These types of techniques will greatly assist you in recalling and remembering the names and faces of new people. This will also help you in bonding to these people quickly, which will make meeting new people fun and rewarding.

5 **Give personal attention.** Many business relationships today come down to just that—relationships. The deeper you understand your clients' wants, needs, prejudices, and personal interests, above and beyond the actual business, the greater the chance you have of serving them for the long haul. Simple touches like birthday cards, Christmas cards, and anniversary cards go a lot further than the dollar you spend. Keep credit card numbers and sizes on file so you don't have to continually ask for them. Make mental or written notes of their favorite beverages, cigars, and foods. In fact, developing a customer profile in a database is a must for legendary service.

The profile I use has over 50 questions about my clients that over time, through various conversations, I fill in. It contains information like where they were born, where they went to school, what their parents did, what sports they like, what teams they support, which cars they drive, what religion they are, how many children they have, and so forth. Some of these things I ask point blank; others my clients tell me over time in the natural flow of conversation. All of this information is deeply valuable in building a relationship and turning conversations toward their areas of interest rather than mine.

Having taught karate for many years, one of the most interesting observations I can give you about the hundreds of hours I spent teaching private lessons is that the most important skill in teaching is, in fact, listening. (This is just as true for most golf professionals.) Over half the time I spent giving lessons was actually spent listening to my clients vent frustration, share excitement, and use me as a sounding board for their hopes, plans, and dreams. Rarely did they actually talk about karate! Find out what your golfers want to talk about. The more you know about them, the longer your relationships will last!

Remember, everyone in the world has this great big badge on their chest which reads "MAKE ME FEEL IMPORTANT." Succeed in that endeavor and you will succeed in everything. No matter what else is going on, at least smile, nod, or wave whenever someone meets your eye.

6   **Make employees—all employees—service oriented.** The best way to get all employees in a service mode is simply to tell every new employee that their number one job, regardless of position or job description, is customer service. Let them know that if they cannot answer a question or help a customer, they are to help that customer locate someone else who can, or to take that customer's name and have the appropriate person call them back later that day! Employees, like everyone else, will rise to the level of your expectations only if they are given those expectations. If you hire a graphics designer for your office and tell him that his job is graphics, on the occasions when he may be the only one in the office to answer the phone, he is not going to be very helpful. However, if he is told in no uncertain terms that he is a customer service graphics designer, he will be much more in tune to making an effort on this front. Set yourself up for service success by making **customer service everyone's job!**

7   **Be accessible.** When clients want to reach you, they want to do it now! Few things are more irritating than calling a service

provider and being shuffled to voice mail automatically, with little or no indication that the person you are looking for is in the office or traveling through Kenya on safari. If nothing else, tell your receptionist when you will be returning calls, so that the person waiting for the call can continue with his daily life. Nothing irritates me (and most other people) more than being told I will be called right back only to be hanging by the phone for two hours or more waiting for the call.

Provide real people to your web site's visitors

You are going to think I am making this up, but I assure you I am not. Recently I had a general manager call me and yell at me because I put his contact information on his web site. He told me in no uncertain terms that he did not want his members e-mailing him at all hours of the day. In fact, he didn't want them to e-mail him at all.

Don't play hide-and-seek with your customers and potential customers. Include your name, phone number, e-mail address, and street address, to show that you are a real person and a real business with real products and services to sell. A mark of the company with poor service is that it doesn't have any contact information displayed on its site, or hides it so no one can find it. (Another sign is that they don't answer their e-mail!) Show your visitors that you care by including your contact number and the times you wish to be called. Offer a feedback e-mail section to get players' opinions on your course and service. It's better they tell you there's a problem than all of their friends!

Never tell your customers about your problems or the club's; they don't care. Often, especially in situations where you spend a lot of time with a particular member, there is the temptation to cross the boundary and share personal problems with a client. In the norms of conversation they may even ask questions or probe about your personal life. In reality, they are not interested in your problems. Do not be conned into sharing them. Find out everything you can about your customers, while saying little or nothing about yourself. As the Chinese say "keep the tiger behind the bamboo!" This will only add to your sense of power and help build your reputation faster.

Be consistent in all your actions. Simple, consistent actions build reputations. It is through your simple actions that you can build your customer service. And if you combine several simple actions together you can take giant leaps over your competition as you build your reputation. After each visit to the dentist, my dentist called my house that evening to make sure I felt all right. Not only that, but when he referred me to surgery with another physician, he found out when the surgery was scheduled and called me that night to see how it had gone, even though he was not personally involved. When my child was born, he sent me a bottle of wine with his label on it. Now this is someone whom I only saw every six months, yet he acted as if he was almost part of the family. The result was simple: Even when I moved my business over fifty miles away, I still drove to his office. He had backed up his reputation with service!

Showing up is 90% of the job

As an employee of various restaurants in my youth, I built my reputation not on knowledge of fine wines or excellent service, but on the one thing that mattered most to the owners and managers— I showed up. Not once in a while, not when I felt like it, and not just when it was raining outside. I showed up, and showed up on time, every single day I was scheduled to work, without fail. In the restaurant business that simply does not happen! In getting jobs every season, my ace in the hole was the restaurant's knowledge that I would show up, and so time and time again I cut the season's job search down to just one or two calls. At nineteen I had a reputation for nothing in the world except showing up, but at nineteen, that was enough. As Woody Allen once said "Showing up is 90 percent of success."

10 **Always smile!** One of the surest ways of giving good service is to project the type of attitude you expect to get back. Pay careful attention to your body language, posture, and facial expressions. Always look as if you are having the time of your life, no matter what is going on around you! Unless you are running a mortuary, smile at all times; if nothing else, people will wonder what you are smiling about.

ARE YOU DOING YOUR BEST?

A question I often ask in my seminars is, "Are you good at what you do?" To which—surprise, surprise—most people answer with the most resounding YES of the day. Then I ask them if, in fact, they are settling for being good when they could be GREAT! Usually it get a little quiet around that time. In today's competitive climate, good is the standard—if you aren't good, you won't be around for very long. But how much more could you accomplish in building your reputation for service (and your income) if, instead of just being good, you actually were GREAT!

You must build your reputation first with your employees, then with your customers, then with your prospects.

CUSTOMER SERVICE GOALS FOR THE SUPERIOR BUSINESS

I devised the following customer service goals that, with a little amendment, you might find useful in applying to your particular club.

1. Collect information about customer preferences and habits, and use this information to personalize relationships and services.

2. Keep our present clients.

3. Keep our clients delighted, not just satisfied, with our services.

4. Help our clients improve their lives with our service so that we in turn can enjoy ours more from their compensation.

5. Ensure that our clients always speak well of our business and employees.

6. Help our present clients help us attract new customers and keep them happy as well.

7. Maintain excellent communication with our clients at all times and greet clients by name. Treat our employees well so they'll treat our customers the same way.

8. Realize that all client complaints give us a chance to improve. Act quickly and fairly to resolve all complaints.

9. Make every single employee responsive to customer service.

10. Be known as a business that has superior customer service and retention.

QUANTIFYING SUPERIOR SERVICE

Goals like the ones above are a great place to start when it comes to improving service, but what exactly is great service? Ask that question of most people and their answers will be, "I can't quite describe it, but I know it when I get it!" Great service is like good taste, it varies with the eye of the beholder. Despite this, you must specify what great service is.

A major reason that poor service happens is because in most business and organizations, great service is not *quantified*. It may be talked about, talked about, and talked about again, but rarely is it taken to the next step and measured in a host of different ways. As you no doubt already know from other areas of your business, what gets measured is what gets done.

With that thought in mind, I suggest that you sit down with your staff and identify as many areas as you can in which service is given. For example:

- ✔ Answering the phone: How many rings is acceptable?
- ✔ How often will you send follow-up cards, thank you cards, or reminders?
- ✔ How quickly will you resolve any billing problems?
- ✔ How and when will you thank people for their referrals?
- ✔ What level do you want to keep your number of monthly complaints below?
- ✔ How clean will the clubhouse be?
- ✔ How well-stocked will the pro shop be?
- ✔ What will you give players if their scheduled start time is delayed?

By specifically quantifying how you intend to measure performance, you will take a quantum jump in your ability to achieve higher levels of service performance.

Policy must back up your position

A key factor many forget is that once a reputation enhancement plan is in place, policies must allow your employees to carry out their mission without conflict. You can't tell golfers your greens are the best and then not give your employees enough budget for seed, fertilizer, and labor. You cannot build a reputation for honesty and then tell an employee to lie about you not being in the office when you don't want to take a certain phone call. If your employees don't believe your commitment to great service, you can be sure no one else will! You can't create a friendly atmosphere if signage all over the property tells you WHAT YOU CAN'T DO!

ARE YOUR CLUB RULES & POLICIES USER-FRIENDLY?

One of the biggest responses I ever had to my e-newsletter that reaches over 25,000 owners and managers weekly was the one titled "Are Club Rules & Policies Killing Golf?" While about 70 percent were in agreement with my position, a solid 30 percent where quite vocal in their dissent! Nonetheless, I feel that archaic rules and policies at many clubs are a detriment to good customer service! Now let me preface this by saying I am not against polices and rules that have a basis in logic, nor do I want guys playing without a shirt, clubs in one hand and a six-pack of Bud in the other! (Although in some places a policy like that would improve a club's income, I just don't want to play there!)

Here's a novel idea. Slay some sacred cows and let your members and guests actually enjoy themselves!

In many ways I'm a traditionalist. I play blades, would prefer the balls stop going any further, and I love the older classic courses. But I've never been much for club rules and, in fact, I think club rules hurt golf in a bigger way than anyone realizes.

For example, at North Berwick (Scotland) on a damp and foggy morning, I was asked to remove my $100 navy blue, water resistant, sleeveless sweater with an RTJ logo on it as, according to the steward, it constituted rain gear which was not allowed in the clubhouse. I had just stepped out of my car and protested that it was my only sweater, that it was dry, and that I was cold. To which came the reply, "You'll warm up in a wee minute as soon as ye get yer coffee in yea! Which, loosely translated means "I don't give a damn. Take it off if you want to come in!" I did take it off, but was cold for 15 minutes while I waited for my coffee to arrive and warm me up! To what end??? Yes, I know I was a guest and should just be delighted to be there but...instead I was cold and irritated!

At Gullane (Scotland), a monster of a course at almost 6200 yards with the fairways hard as rock after weeks of high temperatures and no rain, thus insuring that even a missed hit went 300 yards, we were forbidden to play the back tees (very typical in England and Scotland, as they consider it a privilege for the members, and, even then, only in tournaments). And so we played Gullane at 5800 yards or less with a driver and a sand wedge. If I had wanted to play pitch and putt, I could have done that on the free course at the Gullane village green! I felt cheated!

My club bans jeans (as most clubs do), a policy that costs my club about $3000 of my business because I can't be bothered to change to go to the club for lunch. (Besides I look better in a pair of $150 Armani jeans than Bob Lynch looks in his 1978 brown polyester Sears slacks!) Some clubs allow black denim jeans, but no blue jeans?! Now, I'm not asking to play in jeans, but how about you let me go in the men's bar for a burger at lunch time?

Change can happen—it just takes a Tiger to slay the beast

Okay, here's a good one: For years, almost every course on the planet, including mine, had a no-collar no-play rule! Well...that was until Tiger started wearing T-shirts to play in. Oh, but that's okay they tell me because Tiger's shirt has a mock collar? A mock collar? What the heck is a mock collar? Is that like a fake collar?

Now, does anyone really enjoy the game any less because now you can play in a T-shirt and last year you couldn't?

At most clubs, I have to wear shorts to my knees which makes it hard to walk, especially when it's dripping hot! What is wrong with tailored tennis shorts to play golf in? I've seen "Jack" play in them several times and if it's good enough for Jack, it ought to be good enough for everyone else! I'm not asking for jogging shorts—I just want to be able to walk in comfort. Besides, the people who make these stupid rules are not the ones walking in 90-degree heat and carrying golf bags!

Let's take the tenth-tee policy at most clubs. They treat teeing off like some privilege reserved for high ranking members of the Senate. If there is no one on the back nine and no one on the 9th tee, why the heck can't you play the back? And I'm not talking about first thing in the morning when the greens crew is out there. I'm talking 11 AM in this case and I'm not looking to play 18!!!

Let's take the tee-time reservation policy which, at most private clubs, is limited to seven days in advance. What if you have a guest coming from out of town and you want to make sure you can get a tee time that coincides with his flights in and out four weeks from now???

At a private club, why should that be a big deal? Isn't it member centric to take care of situations like this for the enjoyment of the member and guest? Try doing it most places and you get the old "my hands are tied story." Or they will do it but only after the director of golf, club manager, and membership secretary have discussed it! At the very least, why not have a policy where a member is allowed to make a longer-term tee-time reservation two or three times a year?

At a private club, why does the range close at 5 or 6 PM? What difference does it make (except the day the range is being cut) if I want to hit balls until dark? I really don't need any supervision. At my club, they leave all the balls out six nights a week, so it's not an issue of theft.

The only thing I hate more than stupid rules are stupid-rule signs

No Mulligans. No Practice Swings. No Coolers. First of all, such signs are an eyesore. Second, they are annoying, and, third, no one pays any attention to the danged signs anyway. If a guy cold tops his first shot, he's going to re-tee no matter what the sign says (or he can always declare it a provisional to flaunt his inferior knowledge of the rules of golf). Hand the players a rules sheet before they start, IF YOU MUST, but take all those tacky signs off the golf course.

Am I advocating anarchy? No, just some common sense. If we are to grow the golf business, we must appeal to a wider audience than we do now. We must be user friendly. The rules of golf are complicated enough without adding all kinds of meaningless signage, rules, and restrictions. Take all that money and effort and put it towards making sure members and guests have a great time at the club.

Whether you agree or disagree with any of my examples, at least consider reviewing your club's policies once a year and see if they still make sense to anyone under eighty!

SUMMARY

Backing up your reputation with the real McCoy is essential for the long-term establishment of your legendary reputation. When it comes to service, it is the frontline people and the little things that can make or break your reputation.

Understand why customers leave and what their most common complaints are, then take action to address them. Stay close to your customers and always solicit feedback on how you are doing and how you might improve. Remember that existing customers are always more valuable than customers you don't have yet.

Follow up on everything you say you will do, and check that it's been done. Make an extra effort to remember all your customers' names and give them the special attention that everyone craves. Make sure your employees are trained and that they understand that, no matter what their positions, customer service is everyone's job.

Always be accessible, or give clear instructions on when and where you can be reached. Never discuss any of your problems with customers; they don't care.

Continually question whether you are doing your best to set customer service goals and, most important of all, quantify superior service. Once you decide what you will do to create great service, back up your goals and policies by giving those who work for you the power, authority, and moral guidance to provide superior service.

Last, but not least, always be consistent in your actions and don't forget to smile!

The words of Henry David Thoreau ring just as true today in the new millennium as they did when he first spoke them, "What you do speaks so loud I cannot hear what you are saying."

Chapter Twenty

How to Develop a REAL Customer Loyalty Program

I have told you about the importance of generating leads and getting people to your club. I have stressed the importance of giving your customers good—outrageously good—service. Now, let's talk about keeping your customers loyal. Let's look at how to turn occasional golfers into loyal customers who sing your praises to others. Customer loyalty seems to be the buzzword of the moment in the increasingly competitive golf business—and it should be. Courses are rightly taking a look at their existing players and trying to figure out how to stop them from going elsewhere.

In this chapter, you will discover:

- ✔ How to identify your best customers

- ✔ How to show customers that they are special

- ✔ How to outsmart your competition, steal players, and make them loyal to your course

✔ How to turn your members and guests into evangelists
for your club

✔ How to turn a few letters and cards into GOLD

LEGENDARY LOYALTY

The problem with most clubs' attempts to start loyalty programs is that they start by offering discounts to their frequent players. Think about that. They offer their very best customers discounts for showing up! The problem with this strategy should be clear. Let's use a restaurant analogy. My favorite restaurant is the Crystal River Wine & Cheese Company. I spend over $1,000 there every single month. If the restaurant decided to start a loyalty program and give me a 10 percent discount, I'm not going to show up any more frequently than I do now. The restaurant would simply lose $1,200 a year in revenue!

I'm a loyal customer because the food is good, the atmosphere friendly, and the owner greets me by name and makes a big deal every time I walk in the door. On top of that, I know I can always get a table no matter how busy it is. In other words, I am treated like a special customer and therefore am a loyal customer.

The point is simple:

You cannot buy loyalty with discounts.

Instead let's suppose I received an occasional bottle of wine as a gift or was invited to a special wine-and-cheese tasting. In the latter case, I would probably buy a case of wine just for the invitation. You can buy play with discounts but you cannot buy loyalty! You buy loyalty with special service, small gifts, and special attention.

Think of the airline frequent-flyer programs. They are about much more than getting free flights. They're about first-class upgrades, free access to club rooms, early boarding, and other intangibles that are the real benefits since free flights take so long to earn these days. Your best customers will pay a fair price if you treat them right. Use incentives to get golfers to try your course, then convert them to loyal players with your service and extras!

Grass-roots marketing will always pay big dividends!

A best-selling marketing book explains how Hush Puppies, the famous shoe company, had all but made the decision to shut down operations in 1995 when sales of their once-popular shoes dipped below 30,000 pairs. Then a very strange thing happened. Some kids in the Village section of New York started wearing the shoes, probably because no one else was. No one knows for sure how many kids started doing this, but the book suggests fewer than 50. While their numbers were few, their influence was not! These kids were opinion leaders in the local dance-club scene of lower Manhattan. Their friends and followers started to buy Hush Puppies.

A famous New York designer noticed that the "cool kids" were wearing Hush Puppies. He featured the shoes in his fall collection. Another designer noticed the same trend and opened a Hush Puppies store in Manhattan. Suddenly a bunch of kids had done something that no amount of marketing dollars could have done— they made Hush Puppies cool again! The following years the company sold over a million pairs of shoes.

When I built a karate-school empire in the mid 1990s, I realized early on that the fractionalized world of martial arts was controlled by the opinions of fewer than 200 school owners. Each of these 200 people had an association or a network of other schools. By convincing one opinion leader to join my organization, three or four other schools would automatically follow suit. By targeting these 200 school owners (rather than the other 12,000), I was able to sign up 120 franchisees in less than 18 months.

By targeting influential opinion leaders,
the masses will soon follow.

DEVELOPING AN EFFECTIVE LOYALTY & OPINION-LEADER MARKETING PROGRAM FOR YOUR CLUB

The power of the Pareto principle

Within every business exists the phenomenon of the Pareto Principle, or the 80/20 rule. It posits that 80 percent of your business comes from 20 percent of your customers. While most understand the concept, few courses actually try to identify their opinion leaders!

Let's go back to the restaurant example. In any restaurant there are X number of customers who come in frequently and often bring friends. If the restaurant could get these "super customers" to go to the restaurant twice a month instead of once a month, it might be worth an extra $5,000 a year per super-customer to them.

The same is true of daily-fee golf clubs and of private clubs interested in member retention. A golfer might play a particular course and bring three business guests once a month. Chances are the guy is an avid player and plays six to eight times a month. If you could get him to bring guests to your course twice a month instead of once, it would be worth an extra few thousand dollars a year. That doesn't even count the potential for him to bring other "A" type players to the facility. These "A" players would in turn bring all of their guests!

While quality (whether of a restaurant's food or a golf course's greens) does play a part in customers' decisions, it plays only a minor role. Far more important is the connection customers feel to the particular business. Ask yourself:

- ✔ Does your bartender or starter remember players by name?

- ✔ Is the player acknowledged as a good customer and given an occasional free drink or golf cart?

- ✔ Does the player get a thank-you card or a Christmas card?

Scott Wyckoff, the pro at World Woods, always sends me a thank you card for taking a lesson, even though he won't take my money! In a shameless pitch for Scott (he is much too modest to have anything to do with this), if we ever opened a golf club this is the guy we would hire, and PAY HIM TWICE WHAT HE ASKS FOR.

He is worth three times what he asks for! (You too, Rudy!)

✔ How about an occasional free gift for your best customers? A sleeve of balls, a golf book, or something that doesn't cost much but makes the player feel special?

The first club in your area to offer players more than just a good golf course will slowly but surely get more of their business, and others like them! Customers' positive opinions lead other people. They do your marketing for you. Word of mouth from these opinion-leader players will do a better job than you ever can!

✔ Who are your opinion leaders?

✔ Are they tagged in your database?

✔ What have you done for them lately?

DEFINE YOUR PERFECT CUSTOMERS, YOUR OPINION LEADERS

Can you describe the qualities of a perfect customer to yourself? (See Chapter 4.) You probably immediately thought of someone at your club who's the perfect customer. That's good because the first step in finding more perfect customers is to truly understand what perfect customers should "look like."

What age are they? What kind of income do they have? What type of job do they have? Where do they live? What do they read? Where do they work? What exactly are the qualities of a perfect customer for you? (See examples on the next page.)

Do this exercise with your staff and try to come up with 25–50 people who seem to be the perfect clients. Take a look at the profiles of who the perfect client is because from now on they are the only clients you want to attract! Take the time to establish profiles of your key customers. Build the model customer, the type of customer you want to attract.

Once identified, these are the people we are going to put on our opinion leader program.

OPINION LEADER PROGRAM

Identify 25–50 opinion leaders from the people who play your course on a regular basis and are your very best clients.

These are the people who:

- ✔ Pay full green fees
- ✔ Bring guests
- ✔ Give you referrals
- ✔ Buy stuff in the pro shop
- ✔ Take lessons
- ✔ Attend special events
- ✔ Play in tournaments
- ✔ Spend money in the bar and restaurant

These are your very best customers, the type of people you need more of to maximize your club. These are your "A" clients, the top of the 20 percent from which you derive most of your income. More players like this and...well, you wouldn't need more players like this!

The idea of your opinion leader program is to design a system that makes these players feel special. By using a system, you can implement the program on a carefully planned basis and make sure that everything gets done. The players, of course, have no idea that it's a system—they just think you provide great service to them because they're special.

By making these opinion leaders feel more special and with some subtle hints, this program will turn your top 50 players into evangelists for your club.

Are you treating your clients like dogs?

Some years ago my dog, a Black lab named Winston, needed a vet. My wife took him to the nearest local animal hospital. They took care of his problem and sent him home with some tablets. A few weeks later, we moved to a new home some 30 miles away. Soon we began receiving truckloads of junk mail from realtors, insurance agents, landscape contractors, and charities. However, one piece of mail stood out—a letter addressed to Winston Wood. I thought someone must have really screwed up—imagine trying to make a cogent sales presentation to a dog! However, when I opened the envelope on Winston's behalf, I discovered that it was no mistake. The contents were indeed intended for Winston Wood. Inside was a birthday card from the animal hospital. Immediately, I felt a little guilty because I didn't even know it was his birthday. So I jumped in my car and rushed down to the store to get him a bone. My wife and I laughed and later told all our friends about the incident.

Over the next few months Winston received several additional pieces of mail, all addressed to him personally. There were Christmas cards and get-well cards after shots. Believe it or not, Winston even received a 1040 DOG form at income tax time.

Though this animal hospital was over 30 miles away, we continued making the drive whenever Winston needed a vet. Why? Because this animal hospital took the time and effort to send cards and letters to my dog. The fact is, people don't care how much you know until they know how much you care. Show them you care!

For example, do you send your members or best customers Christmas cards, birthday cards, or simple thank-you cards? Do you reward them with an occasional small gift? What would it take from you to get golfers who play 15 times a year to play 16, 17, times or even 20 times? You'd be surprised how simple that is to do, and without discounting! And with incremental growth comes exponential profits!

Opinion leader program examples

- ✔ Thank-you card (costs about 83 cents mailed)

- ✔ E-mail a golf story ("I thought you'd enjoy this...")

- ✔ A book such as *Good Bounces Bad Lies* (retails for $24.95, but your cost is just $2—$4.50 mailed)

- ✔ A sleeve of balls ($3)

- ✔ A survey (40 cents)

- ✔ A copy of a great golf article or story with a note "I thought you'd enjoy this..." (40 cents mailed)

- ✔ E-mail another golf story

- ✔ A golf audio CD (retail 14.95, your cost is $1.99–$3.49 mailed)

- ✔ A video such as "Golf's Greatest Trick Shots (retail $24.95, your cost $2)

- ✔ A $5 gift certificate to golfbooks.com (your cost is zero by sending via e-mail)

- ✔ A birthday card on the player's birthday (costs 83 cents mailed)

- ✔ Three guest tickets for free play (your cost is zero)

- ✔ Golf print of a hole from your course (your cost $1 each)

- ✔ A Christmas card (mailed 83 cents)

All of this would cost around $14.98, but let's round it up to $20. Multiply that by 50 people, and your total cost is just $1,000!

Why contact people 14 times a year? As mentioned in the Direct Mail chapter, because that number has been shown to create the optimum response. That's why catalog companies mail 14 times a year.

Now you might wish to spend a little more on your best clients or substitute some of the items for others depending on your situation.

You could also use the following as gifts:

✔ Hat

✔ Metal bag tag

✔ New-design glove

✔ Yardage book

✔ Gift certificate for a free lesson

✔ Gift certificate for free club fitting

✔ One box of the 700 dozen close-out balls you bought that are still in the bag room

✔ Lunch at the club with you

✔ A special dinner and focus group to gather input from "special customers"

SUMMARY

Not all customers are created equal. Identify your best customers using the good old 80/20 rule. Identify opinion leaders in your community as well. Target the right guys at a competing club and 20 more will follow them to yours. Find out who these people are and develop an opinion leaders program to reach them. Make your loyalty program based on gifts, service, and special touches so that your best clients don't even know it exists. They just think that you and your club are superior!

Chapter Twenty-One

Creating a Legendary Experience for Your Players

ENTERTAIN OR DIE!

Perhaps the most profound breakthrough I made in my former life in the karate business was the discovery that, unlike any of my competitors, I was not actually in the karate business. Nor was I in the self-defense business, health club business, or the more generic service business. I was in the personal development business helping people "Maximize their potential physically and mentally." That meant that our ads were different, our look and feel was different and, of course, our curriculum was different. While 21 other schools in the city of Irvine, California, battled it out for the karate business, I was the only school competing for the personal development business by using karate as the delivery method!

Too many people in the golf industry have lost sight of the business they are actually in, which for most clubs is the entertainment business. That's right, the entertainment business— NOT the service business, not the people business, and not the golf business. Golf is the vehicle by which you entertain your members or guests. Having a good course, good conditions, and a great staff are entry level items in this game. Merely adding the word "experience" to your sales literature doesn't mean much if there are no extraordinary experiences to back it up!

In this chapter, you will discover:

- ✔ Why we are living in the experience economy
- ✔ How to enhance your players' experiences
- ✔ How to adapt creative ideas from outside the golf industry
- ✔ How to change players' focus away from price

WE ARE LIVING IN AN EXPERIENCE-DRIVEN ECONOMY

Can you imagine buying a product on a regular basis where the price you pay for the exact same product varies by as much as 800 percent on any given day?

Can you imaging charging your customers 300 percent more than you do right now and getting them not only to accept it but to recommend you to all of their friends?

Can you imaging being the most expensive club in town (in your market segment) and having people lining up at your door to get in?

I hope so, because in this highly combative, oversaturated golf market your club's future success—perhaps even your club's survival—depends what I am about to share with you.

If you buy a bottle of imported beer, for example, Heineken, at a wholesale store, it will cost you about a buck. If you buy the same beer at the local hole-in-the-wall bar, it will cost you about two dollars and fifty cents. If you buy the same beer at my country club, it will cost you four dollars. And, if you buy the exact same beer at the bar of the Hotel Splendido overlooking Portofino Bay in Italy, you will pay a whopping eight dollars for the very same drink. Since the beer didn't change, why am I or anyone else willing to pay such a wide range of rates—a difference of 800 percent—for the very same green bottle filled with 12 ounces of the identical liquid? The answer, of course, is that we are all conditioned to put a premium on *the experience* rather than on the actual product itself. This is true today more than ever; consumers want an "experience." They want a taste of the good life, their own 15 minutes of fame or fantasy, and they are willing to pay highly for it.

AutoWeek magazine now lists over 50 places where, for a couple of thousand bucks, you can learn to drive like Jeff Gordon or Michael Schumaker in real race cars. Talk about an experience for the average red-blooded male! For about the same price you can pilot a MIG fighter in mock combat or float across the Serengetti in a hot air balloon at sunset searching for wildebeests.

Back a little closer to home, you can take a very average business and double your income by improving the experience. A hairdressing salon I used to visit used this strategy to almost triple their prices. One day it was a regular unisex haircut place, the next, a posh salon. The difference? Fancy tile on the floor, a new paint job, better looking fixtures, and a new name. But what really did it for me was the glass of champagne that magically appeared in my hand as soon as I walked in the door. I hardly noticed that the price of a haircut had tripled because I enjoyed the experience more than before!

PEOPLE WANT TO BE ENTERTAINED—
THEY WANT AN EXPERIENCE!

Last week, to prove a point to a course owner, I called my neighbor from my office. I said, "Allen, remember that great tournament we played in at the Robert Trent Jones Golf Club in Gainesville, Virginia? Tell my client about it."

"Okay," he said. "It's hard to know where to start since everything was so fantastic. The food was great, the entertainment was great—and, man, that magician was good!"

"The entertainment?" I asked

"You remember," he said. "That magician at the event...he was unbelievable! The best I have ever seen!"

He went on to describe some of the magician's tricks in detail for another two or three minutes. Finally, I prompted him to talk about the course. "Best course I have ever played," he said casually, but it was the magician he kept talking about (in fact, we all did!).

SO, HOW ARE YOU DOING IN THE ENTERTAINMENT GAME?

How do you entertain your customers in the golf shop?

Do you have a putting carpet set up for guests to try out a new putter right at the counter? A TV in the corner playing the instruction videos you sell?

On the range?

Do you have video equipment and computer software for analyzing your students' swings? In the winter, do you have a golf simulator where players can enjoy playing Pebble Beach while six feet of snow covers the ground outside? Do you have a selection of the latest swing aids in a barrel for members to try out? Swing aids are cheap and players love this!!!

One range has an abandoned van in the middle of the range at about 180 yards. It looks like hell, but 40 people are aiming at it and the occasional squeal of delight and loud bang confirm its entertainment value.

In the restaurant?

Is there a theme to provide topics for conversation and entertainment while you wait for your food? Themes can be simple. For example, Haggin Oaks Golf Complex in Sacramento, California, has historical pictures and stories of the club under glass at each table.

In the bar?

Do you have the latest in plasma screen TVs with picture-in-picture technology so your sports addicts can watch Tiger Woods *and* the Red Sox at the same time?

When I was in my early twenties, we used to go to a hole-in-the-wall bar in Delray Beach. It was twenty miles out of our way and had no ambience whatsoever. What they did have, or at least claimed to have, was a bottle of every beer in the world. Since, at the time, we didn't have the money to travel the world, my friends and I decided to do the next best thing and drink our way around the world! Every time we went in the barman would say, "What country will it be tonight?" We traveled from the Trappist monks' beer in Belgium to the Taj Mahal beer of India and back again.

How do you entertain them on the course?

Do you have attractive cart girls or an unusually friendly ranger who provide guests who lose a ball with another one? Staff dressed in 1920s golf attire? Plaques on the course to indicate points at which famous shots were hit? An ongoing hole-in-one-contest videotaped from above? The longest par five in the state? The toughest par three in the state? Choose a prominent feature of your course to bring out and build an experience around it. Think the 17th Green at TPC!!! That's a very good golf course but the experience is all about the

Island green. Take that away and you have a fairly typical Pete Dye golf course.

In your club's fitness center?

Recently I spent the night in a hotel that had a small but world-class fitness center. In most respects it looked just like any other gym except that several of the machines were interactive. The rowing machine had a video screen that allowed me to row against another opponent. It led me on a mad quest to keep up with the Olympic rowing team, which I did for nearly five minutes before collapsing with exhaustion. After a short rest, it was on to the stationary bike, a piece of equipment that usually bores me to tears. Not so today as my video screen allowed me to race in the Tour de France. Would the novelty wear off? Perhaps. Nonetheless, if such an experience-enhancing option were available in my area, I would be willing to pay a premium price for it. While your club's gym won't compete with a 60,000 square-foot health center, you could add a few such machines to create a better experience.

In the restrooms?

In the restrooms—sure, why not? It could be as simple as pinning the sports pages from today's newspaper to the wall of the Men's Room, or a more sophisticated approach like different-shaped wash basins. It could be as simple as just having a restroom with a running waterscape on the wall or unusual faucets. It all counts when it comes to building the experience.

In large cities many department stores actually attract customers because people know they will get clean, safe comfortable restrooms if they go to a particular store, albeit on the tenth floor! The point here is to think out of the box—don't think like a golf course owner or manager—pretend you work for Disney and enhance every area of your club's experience!

Make an audio connection

Let's say your course is a bit of a distance from town. How do you entertain your guests on their drive home? The *Great Golf Stories for Your Drive Home* audio CD series that we produced for several clients has been a huge hit. It's a great way to entertain guests long after they have left the property. It's a series of one-hour audio books with lots of great golf anecdotes. In between the stories are commercials promoting the club just as you'd hear on a radio show. These CDs get listened to, passed around, and listened to again the next time people have new golf friends in their cars. They have a great shelf life and will not be thrown away. They keep players thinking and talking about your club long after they have gone. They are, in fact, a way to promote your course, entertain, and stay connected to a guest, all in one!

CD audiobooks can complement your other promotional materials. Audiobooks tend to be kept longer and shared more frequently than most other materials.

Make a visual connection

Another way we combined promotion with entertainment was on the *18 Great Golf Tips* DVD we produced for Garland Resort. In the 45-minute DVD, Garland pro, Tom Howell, dispenses his top-caliber advice while playing different holes on the resort's four courses. This provides the viewer with quality instruction and the chance to see how beautiful the courses really are.

I was at a city-run club that served their lunches on oversize plates of different shapes and bright colors. That simple touch made me feel like I was in a fine restaurant rather than in relatively ordinary surroundings. It also made the food taste better! They would have made the experience even better had they painted the metal chairs the same colors as the plates and put something on the walls other than a lone Bud Light sign!

Make a web connection

We talk a lot about how auto responders, dynamic content, and tools like our Campaign Manger can enhance your club's web experience, but you can take it further still:

- ✔ Online golf games offer a reason for people not only to visit your site but to stay on it for hours while your ads are served to them.

- ✔ Stats programs give players a reason to not only visit your site but to track their games.

- ✔ Streaming video still has bandwidth issues, but these will no doubt be resolved and course promos, lessons, and footage from events streaming on your web site will soon be the norm at the cutting edge of the golf business.

- ✔ Virtual tours are another way to enhance a visitor's experience to your site, especially if you are in the resort or real estate business.

CHANGING THE RULES

I have visited several courses lately in what can only be described as "very tough markets." Play is down, prices are slashed, and everyone is running bigger and better coupon offers! Everyone is competing for the same dollar in the same way—by cutting prices!

While everyone agrees this race to the bottom is not a great way to do business, no one seems to have any idea of how to stop the trend. But have no fear, faithful reader, I do have the solution. Change the rules!

For example's sake, let's say you are in a market with twenty other daily-fee clubs all charging half what they did two years ago. All twenty are decent courses with 18 holes. Each one has a similar product and each one charges about the same fees. They all are trying to do the same thing—get as many people on the course as possible! There are many ways to change the rules, but the key issue is to change your customers' focus from the price they are paying to something very different—the experience. Now, I agree that there is a large percentage of seniors and others to whom price is, and always will be, a major factor, but that doesn't stop Cadillac from selling $60,000 SUVs. In other words, there are plenty of other people out there who might respond to a different offer.

My favorite golf sign

As a busy person, I hate, repeat HATE, playing golf if it takes more than three and a half hours. Yet at several courses I have been on this year, three and a half hours only gets me through about 13 holes!!!

Now, suppose that Wednesday is your slow day. Why not move the tee times back to 12-minute intervals. Add a second ranger and up the green fee ten-bucks-a-player and guarantee players will complete play in less than four hours or they get a free round of golf? Everyone will be instructed on the first tee that they will be

My favorite golf sign: I love golf, but I hate to play a course that
takes more than three and a half hours.

given a clear hole start and that if a group catches them, they must
wave them through at once (as is the custom in Britain). If you have
lost your place, the guarantee does not apply! With this offering,
you become the only course of the 20 to guarantee a round of golf in
less than four hours. Now you are instantly in a different game than
the rest of the courses. They are selling green fees; you are selling
time!

Customers are willing to pay a premium for time. Earlier in this
book I told you how I paid $10 more to ski at a resort that guaranteed
lift-line waiting times to be ten minutes or less. Judging by the
crowds there, their pricing strategy didn't hurt their business one
bit (a lower-priced ski resort was essentially next door).

As mentioned earlier, Domino's Pizza made billions selling time
(with their 30-minutes-or-less delivery guarantee), not great pizza,
simply by changing the rules. Will offering shorter play time work

in every market? No. Are there some bugs you might have to work out? Yes. Can it add thousands to your bottom line and differentiate you in a crowded market place? Yes, again!

Improve their games

Okay, your players don't care about playing fast? Then how about playing well? The standard of play I witnessed on my last daily fee outing was pitiful. Hardly anyone young or old alike kept the ball in the air for 100 yards or more and I drove all 18 holes. NGF statistics show that 84 percent of golfers surveyed said they would "Play more often, buy more equipment, eat more hot dogs, and drink more beer at the course" if just one thing happened—if THEY PLAYED BETTER! The same surveys also showed that only 13 percent of golfers took a lesson in the last 12 months! So what we have here is a GIANT market that obviously has not been satisfied.

Now, let's switch to Marketing 101. How many times have you been to McDonald's and been asked whether you want fries with that burger? Okay, every time. How many times have you been at the counter in a pro shop where the pro has invited you, suggested, or even vaguely hinted that you might want to take a lesson. I've been playing golf for 28 years now and it has never happened to me!

So back to our problem of changing the rules. How about selling a 20-lesson game-improvement package? You are guaranteed to hit the ball further and score better. Or a Wednesday and Saturday clinic package with a $1995 value for just $1595—and you get *free golf* while you are learning! (At $20 a round they would have to play 80 rounds in 10 weeks to make out on the deal! IF they play 40 rounds you made $40 a round, if they play 20 rounds, you made $80 a round! Sure the pro and the assistant have to get paid, but I am sure you can work out an equitable split. The other upside is that you end up with better players, fill a need, and build relationships! You could add free club fitting, a free video, a free book, or whatever else you can think of to add value to the package.

The whole point to this strategy is to change what people think about—from thinking about discounts to instead thinking about time, playing better, or anything else so that it is no longer an apples-to-apples comparison between your course and the one down the street.

REMODEL AND REVAMP

You don't have to redesign your holes for a PGA tournament to benefit from making changes at your club. Little upgrades in the bar, the restaurant, the clubhouse, or on the tees can increase your business and your free word-of-mouth advertising. After all, if you want people to talk about you, you have to give them something to talk about.

Some businesses like banks and insurance companies might thrive on longevity and consistency in the marketplace; however, most businesses don't. There are plenty of examples of once-solid business that no longer exist. In fact, in most businesses if you don't consistently reinvent yourself you are in big trouble.

Look outside the golf market for concepts that you could use

Take the nightclub business, for example. A "hot" club is a license to print money for two or three years. Then the bubble bursts and a new club across town suddenly becomes the "in" place. While inexperienced owners ride the tide to the very end, crashing in bankruptcy, astute club owners do just the opposite. They reap the rewards while the going is good, then close the club for several months as business starts to decline, but before it's lost completely. Then they remodel, rename, and reopen it all over again. Bars and restaurants can also benefit from this strategy, especially in a competitive market place.

Time for a new logo? A new name? A new attitude?

The interesting thing about remodeling, even if it's only a quick facelift with new carpet and a lick of paint, is that it almost always attracts new business and allows you to increase sales with existing clients. Change creates excitement, and excitement creates more sales.

Theme restaurants are now popular all over the world. My personal favorite is in West Palm Beach, Florida. It's the 391st Bomber Group restaurant located on the site of Palm Beach International Airport. As you approach the parking lot, you pass under a barrier with a sentry post and an old army jeep. The main building has been created to look like a bombed-out French farmhouse complete with shell holes in some of the walls. Out back, two huge World War II bombers sit on the tarmac at the edge of the airfield. The bathrooms are done from floor to ceiling in sandbags while they pipe in speeches from Churchill and others. The waitresses are dressed in Red Cross uniforms and the waiters are dressed as airmen. In the bar, there is a dance floor. Early in the evening, they play music from the 1940s; each hour, the music advances a decade until the current dance tunes hit around 11 PM. To top it all off, they provide headphones so you can listen to the pilots of incoming planes talk with the tower. Everything there creates the perfect illusion that you have, in fact, gone back in time. The food is great, too, but that is secondary to the actually experience of the place.

The Hard Rock Cafe, the All Star Cafe, Planet Hollywood, The Harley Cafe, The Race Rock Cafe, and hundreds of other theme restaurants all sell hamburgers for ten dollars—not because the food is special but because the places are special. The experience for the rock fan, race fan, or sports fan seeing the actual sunglasses Elvis, Jeff Gordon, or Andre Agassi wore is what counts; the food is secondary.

Let your customers experience being a king

The Five Feet Restaurant in Laguna Beach, California has some of the best food in the world but it also has a unique feature reserved for it's best customers. The restaurant itself has very high ceilings with that open industrial look. The walls are decorated with a huge mural of various individuals, each one a good customer of the restaurant. Now, if your face was immortalized on the wall of one of the best restaurants in town, where would you take your out-of-town guests for dinner? Not rocket science is it? Also what does that do for the self-esteem, ego, experience, and general dining pleasure of the customer?

Another simple example is the bartender who changes all the regular names of drinks and renames them with the initials of his favorite customers. So when Joe Peterson comes in and sits down at the bar the bartender asks, "You want a JP?" and serves him a gin and tonic with a twist of lime. When a stranger sits down at the bar and asks for a gin and tonic with lime, the bartender laughs and says "Oh, you mean a JP." You may think this is a dumb example but I've seen it done and it makes Joe's experiences that much greater. Speaking of Joe, in Sedona, Arizona, there is an Italian restaurant called Not Your Average Joe's. The walls are lined with pictures of famous athletes named "Joe" like Joe Montana, Joe Lewis, Joe Dimaggio, and so on. Once again a simple concept turned a fairly ordinary Italian restaurant into a place that I've talked about to hundreds of people, even though it was closed the day I was there!

SUMMARY

Remember, your golfers want an experience, not just to hit a little ball around a course. Maybe they want to get away from home. Maybe they want to be with friends or do business. Maybe they like being outside. It's up to you to understand what can make the golfing experience better and offer it. How can you enhance the experience you offer your customers? What can you add to offer more value? How can you use sight, sound, and smell to make your products and services more appealing? How can you increase the entertainment value of your products and services?

To succeed, your club must not only be more entertaining than any club in it's market segment, but it must also be more satisfying than the bowling alley down the street. It must be more entertaining than the baseball game on ESPN, the Strawberry Festival, Chili Cook-off, or any of the other 101 events listed in your local paper's activities section this week.

Chapter Twenty-Two

How to Dominate the Outings Market

HE WITH THE BIGGEST DATABASE OF OUTINGS PROSPECTS AND THE BEST FOLLOW-UP SYSTEM WINS!

Outings can be very profitable for your club. A wise man once said that fishing for whales made more sense than fishing for minnows. For daily fee clubs, going after group business can be a lot more rewarding than looking for 288 new players every day. For private clubs, outings can provide a welcome source of additional income.

In this chapter, you will discover how to build your outings business in five ways through:

- ✔ Repeat business
- ✔ Referral business
- ✔ Your web site
- ✔ Targeted direct mail
- ✔ Telemarketing

You'll also book outings through walk-ins and other "accidental" means. These bookings are not predictable or controllable, but will increase when you implement the systematic programs discussed here.

ENCOURAGING REPEAT BUSINESS BY STAYING IN REGULAR CONTACT

The easiest and most obvious way to increase your outing business is to sell your existing clients again.

As simple as this idea is, of the hundreds of courses I have visited, only a handful do more than send last year's outing planner for a particular event the traditional John Doe thank-you letter (and perhaps an additional postcard) some time near the start of next season.

This, of course, is not enough! Not nearly enough. You need a systematic plan to keep your club in front of outing planners regularly. Treat past clients as valued friends and do what you can to help them. Some groups like variety for their events. Even if a particular group doesn't come every year, they will come back more often if you keep in regular touch.

Follow up with calls to each of your outing contacts at least three times a year after their event at intervals of:

- ✔ 90 days
- ✔ 180 days
- ✔ 250 days

But your phone calls are only part of your new contact program. Your existing outing database of past clients should be contacted on a continuing basis throughout the year with a series of letters, postcards, and calls—and small gifts, depending on the value of the business. You cannot afford for another course to gain their attention or business. Stay in touch monthly! That's right, 12 times a year.

If you follow this step, and this step alone you will guarantee yourself more business. Just make sure the letters you send are creative!

If you contact your past clients every month, you will generate more than your share of inbound outing calls. In fact, if your database is big enough (over 400), you might well generate enough inbound calls to meet your outing goals.

If you stay in touch with past outing clients each month, the resulting increase in business will astonish you!

BUILDING OUTING REFERRAL BUSINESS

Most of the methods discussed in the Referrals chapter work for outings, so I'll be brief here. The main point is that you should be cultivating—and regularly contacting—referral sources as well as direct prospects. This means that you ask people about groups that have outings. Cultivate possible referral sources. Ask for leads from:

- ✔ Your members or regular golfers ("Does your Rotary Club hold a golf outing, or could they use a new fund raising idea?")

- ✔ People who book outings with you now ("Who else do you know who holds outings?")

- ✔ Local high school and college golf coaches

- ✔ Influential people in town (bankers, board members, politicians)

✔ Your personal contact list

✔ Golf courses in other towns (their outing clients might like variety, and you can return the favor)

✔ Local sporting goods and golf businesses

✔ Everyone else you can think of

BOOK MORE OUTINGS ON THE INTERNET

Make sure that the outing portion of your club's web page is presented in the form of a sales letter and feature the outing button prominently on your home page and elsewhere. This is much stronger than simply announcing to the world in bullet form that you are in the market to hold an event if one happens to be going! (Also see Chapter 12 on Building the Perfect Web Site.)

Having the proper sales pitch on your web site is important for several reasons:

1   **People buy for their reasons, not yours.** You need to provide them with clear benefits for booking their events with you. That means not simply listing what you offer, but providing REAL BENEFITS! Think of the outing page on your web site as an infomercial, an electronic salesperson representing your club. That means providing answers to common questions, using testimonials from happy customers, and proving point-specific benefits of why your club deserves the business rather than your competition. Include photos of attendees having a good time.

2   **It is not uncommon that the person in charge of finding a venue, for instance, a secretary, does not know that much about golf.** By providing a point-specific set of reasons for holding an event at your club, that person can either make a good decision or simply print out your well thought out sales pitch and present it to whoever actually makes the decision. This is the next best thing to having you talking directly

Give Your Players the Best that Alberta has to Offer

From the very first tee at The Links of GlenEagles in Cochrane, you know you've made the right choice for your golf tournament. On every hole there are the panoramic Rocky Mountain views as a backdrop to one of Canada's most superb golf courses. You know your players will be impressed with the velvety green fairways, the brilliant white sand bunkers and the exciting uphills and downhills.

Already at the bag drop, your guests have experienced the gracious service that they're going to enjoy all through the day. And yet to come are incredible holes that they'll remember forever, topped off by a delicious banquet in stone and timber lodge-look clubhouse. You're glad you picked GlenEagles, and you expect to return again and again.

[Click Here]{.underline} to Request a Tournament Package

At The Links of GlenEagles we have hosted hundreds of tournaments since we opened in 1997, including corporate tournaments, charity fundraisers, groups of friends and family and even a Nationwide Tour event. The reasons why tournament and outing organizers love our course so much may seem obvious, but here's a quick rundown of why you'll want to book your event with us as well.

Les Furber, one of Canada's greatest golf designers, laid out our course along a Foothills ridge resplendent with golden grasses, sparkling creeks and ponds and intriguing ravines. GlenEagles offers a grand visual experience as well as a golfing adventure. It's a round your players will talk about for months afterward.

The Links of GlenEagles is a public course, but your golfers will experience the kind of service that is usually found only in private clubs. Just a few examples: valets to handle their clubs and shine their shoes; great staffing on the course, including a starter and two marshals; wonderful clubhouse facilities.

We have beautiful dining rooms where we can serve your guests the finest Alberta beef, including sirloin, New York steak or prime rib. Chicken and ribs are also possibilities. We can do buffets or sit-down dinners; and we can provide box lunches on the course as well. We accompany our meals with lots of great side dishes.

You can play with us any day of the week and we welcome both large and small groups. Morning shotguns are now available for 60 or more participants. You can really impress your guests by booking the entire course for the afternoon for a no-hassle flat fee. You need 144 golfers for those events.

And don't forget that we're located only 10 miles west of Calgary. We're easy to reach for all your golfing guests.

[Click Here]{.underline} for the Details on Our Great Packages and What They Include.
[Click Here]{.underline} to Request an Outing
[Click Here]{.underline} for Tournament Rules
[Click Here]{.underline} for Dining Menu

The Links of GlenEagles • 100 GlenEagles Drive • Cochrane, AB, Canada, T4C 1P5 • PH: 403.932.1100 • Directions

This site is designed and maintained
by **Legendary Marketing**

A web page promoting tournament events. Note that the first link to request information appears just under the photograph so prospects don't have to hunt for it.

to a decision maker. Write good copy that covers all their questions and answers them!

3) **People want information on meetings and events when they need information on meetings and events—which in today's world is 24 hours a day, seven days a week.** I am writing this at 9:38 PM on a Friday night! I could just as easily be surfing the web looking for my next golf outing venue! Which is why it's critical to have a request form that someone can fill in and e-mail to you about their event. At one club we are averaging almost one online outing request for information a day! Every day!

4) **Your web site should be programmed to tackle the most frequelty cited problem by outing planners: lack of follow up!** When an outing planner sends a request online, an automatic e-mail should be sent at once acknowledging the request and stating that someone will reply the next day. But it doesn't have to end there!

Your web site can also be programmed to send out a follow-up letter in a week. It might say something along the lines of "By now you should have received your information kit in the mail. If not, please let me know at once. I just wanted to let you know about a special offer we have this month that gives each of your participants a $25 tee prize at no additional cost!" (If your web site can't send such follow ups, see our SmartSites!)

You could follow up the first note with another automatic e-mail a week later highlighting the benefits of having an event at your course and ask whether they need anything else to help with their decision. For that matter, it can go on and on, sending automatic e-mails until you switch it off or they ask you to stop. The great part of all this is that once you have a developed a good series and your customized letters are programmed into your site, they just work on automatic pilot!

LOOKING FOR OUT-OF-TOWN BUSINESS?

If you are in an area that gets a lot of convention traffic or out-of-town business, don't wait until the planners try to find you in your home state. Hit them in theirs. Recently one of our clients in Orlando told us that he booked two outings in one week, one from New Jersey and the other from Palm Beach. He was running banner ads on the AtlanticCityGolf.com site and they clicked through and booked an event.

Running banner ads in other targeted states is a great way to reach prospects before they ever look in your market! Of course they may also find your web site searching for outing providers in your area.

You can rent and use targeted e-mail or postal lists to drive out-of-state traffic to your web site as well. (Call your local list broker or a Legendary Marketing Outing Success Specialist for list details.)

Local convention-and-visitor bureaus and Chambers of Commerce frequently have lists of booked conventions and meetings, sometimes years in advance. Sometimes this information is available online. For example, if I go to the San Francisco Convention & Visitors Bureau web site, I can see what groups have booked for the next year.

Smaller groups than are tracked by convention bureaus and Chambers often book meeting rooms and hotel rooms at the larger hotels. Both convention bureaus and hotels frequently send out information to their inquirees that includes information about local attractions. If any of your local bureaus or hotels do that, see if they will include your golf outings sales piece (you might want to prepare a special one that identifies you as the golf outing specialst for out-of-town groups).

BUILDING A LARGE LIST OF NEW OUTING PROSPECTS

In any given market there are only so many charity events, business outings, and tournaments going on. You need to have in your database the name, address, and phone number (e-mail would be nice) of the principle decision maker of at least 80 percent of all events in your area. Armed with this information, you can dominate the outing market in your area.

How to build your prospect list

1 Keep a database of all past event contacts.

2 Watch the local paper. LOOK, REALLY LOOK, at all local golf events. Watch announcements, results, and feature articles. Look at local web sites, TV, radio, and cable. When you find an event, track down the organizer.

3 Ask every player who walks through your doors if their company or group holds outings!

4 Build a giant outing leads list. Build a list of at least 1000 people, organizations, and businesses that you know, or at least suspect, hold golf events each year. Use the Internet, local papers, Yellow Pages, Thomas Guide, Chamber of Commerce, and business, charity, and church directories. All can be found at your local library.

5 Telemarket everyone on your prospect list. Call every charity, fraternal organization, hospital, church, radio station, and car dealership in your area. Then add in fire stations, bars, and any other organization, company, or person you think might hold a golf event.

✔ Ask if they ever hold golf tournaments? If yes;

✔ Ask who is in charge?

✔ Get the name, address, and phone number of the person in charge. Try for the e-mail. (The best

way to do this is to offer them something, like our
booklet on "How to Run a Successful Outing."

✔ Ask when they hold their outing.

✔ Ask how many players typically play in their
outing.

✔ Ask where they held their outing last year and
whether or not they have booked it this year.

✔ Get the person's permission to send them
information on your tournament packages.

✔ Ask the person if they know anyone else who holds
golf outings. (You will be astonished by how many
referrals you will get by tacking on that simple
question.)

✔ Enter all the data, especially any extra info you
can glean that might help you sell this prospect,
into the Customer Relationship Manager part of
your website.

(Legendary Marketing can do all this for you.)

During the telemarketing effort to build your prospect list, you
will uncover a number of hot leads that are ready to book an outing
now! It's quite common to uncover a dozen or more really hot leads
during the telemarketing effort.

Some real examples of leads from telemarketing

✔ John at the Post Office would like Eagle Sticks to contact
him about outing options. They used to hold their outings
at the country club, and most recently at Crystal Springs,
with about 100 golfers attending. They haven't held an
outing for two or three years but are currently discussing
it and will be holding a meeting Wednesday to make

some decisions. In the past they've held their outings in October, on Columbus Day.

✔ Donna from the Bar Association would like someone to contact her with outing options and information for their outing. Last year their outing was held at Bent Tree in August and 110 golfers attended. The outing is always held on the third Monday in August.

✔ Sonya at the Car Center has not yet planned this year's outing and would like Eagle Sticks to contact her. Last year the outing was held at another local club in August and 144 people attended.

Other benefits from proactive telemarketing

While the main goal of the telemarketing campaign is to build a database of outing leads, there are several other benefits that go along with the proactive nature of the campaign. You will uncover lots of informal groups such as firemen or police officers that might travel from course to course under everybody's radar but are great sources of incremental business.

You will find groups or organizations that ask you for offers or coupons that they can give out to their group. You will also be calling several thousand people who will be hearing the name of your club. This has a trickle-down effect in driving incremental play just based on top-of-the-mind awareness and suggestion.

The way we do it

For our clients, we put together an automatic follow-up campaign designed with one thing in mind—to make your life easy! That is to say, every letter, every postcard, and every promotional item is focused on getting the prospect to call you, before you have to call them!

MARKETING TO YOUR TARGET MARKET

The best way to target groups is to market your tournament packages through a combination of e-mail, direct mail letters, postcards, and promotional items. You can always end with a phone call or two thrown in for good measure towards the end of the campaign if they still haven't called. Your competitors might take one of these actions, hitting a typical prospect just once, or perhaps twice, a year.

You are going to do all these things and keep doing them all year, to ALL your prospects!

Not a single month will go by during the season when you do not send your 400+ prospects a call to action—a reminder that your course is the best choice for their business!

If you plan your campaign in advance and systemize it as described, this is not nearly as complicated or as difficult as it may seem. When you look at the potential returns versus the actual cost of marketing you will be hard pressed to spend your dollars in a better fashion for any reason. (Legendary Marketing can do all this for you, too, of course!)

NOW IT'S TIME FOR SOME THUNDERBOLT MARKETING

Thunderbolt Marketing is a strategy that Legendary Marketing designed to hit prospects in multiple ways. We send about eight letters in a short period of time—a strategy designed to make a big impression. The technique works not only because of its frequency and repetition but also because of its creativity and ability to connect with and stimulate prospects on different levels, and even with different senses.

Gathering your weapons

There are many different ways to contact your prospects and hit them from different angles. Here are some suggestions for items you might want to consider as part of your Thunderbolt campaign. Remember the more different and creative ways you find to get your message in the hands of outing planners, the more effective your campaign will be!

We typically look to see what a club has on hand in the way of promotional items and first use simple items like scorecards, yardage books, and so forth.

Postcards

Postcards are cheap to print, cheap to mail, easy to produce, and, most important, effective in keeping your message in front of your prospective clients. Rather than using one design, get four done at once (it's cheaper that way). I like to run my cards in a theme so that each card stands on its own merits but also fits into an ongoing series that will highlight the specific benefits of holding an event at your club. One might talk about catering, others about the great range, or the staff's experience, or the course.

Sales letters

Everyone uses letters to get appointments or interest but the Thunderbolt letters must stand out from the ordinary. They must challenge, entertain, inform, and interest the reader. It cannot be the typical John Doe outings letter that basically says;

> Hi, I'm Bob, call me if you ever are thinking of a golf tournament! [See Chapter 11 on Legendary Direct Mail.]

Your sales letters must have at the very least:

Postcards are a low-cost way to reach prospects. Notice the different headlines: the first is time sensitive; the second highlights features and benefits; and the third motivates the prospect to turn over the card to read the rest of the message.

✔ Great captivating headlines

✔ Interesting, benefit-laden copy

✔ Testimonials to back up your claims

✔ A demand for action

✔ A reason for acting now

✔ A P.S. that sums up the entire offer

These letters will work even better if you build them around a simple promo item. Enclose a tee, a plastic bag tag, a score card, or the like and not only will you insure that your letters get opened but you will find your response rate increases dramatically.

Booklets

Booklets have always been a particularly successful approach for me. They position you or your course as an expert. They have great credibility since they shouldn't actually make a sales pitch. Rather they should lead the reader to believe that you are the answer to the specific problem that the booklet addresses. They are cost effective to produce and can be distributed in a variety of ways to add value (to see an example, go to www.LegendaryVault.com for a pdf download of a booklet).

Brochures

Brochures are common sales pieces and one component of an overall Thunderbolt plan. However, rather than just sending them on their own, they should be used in conjunction with a letter and personalized to your client. Pages should be folded, highlighted, key-point-circled, and referred to in the letter. Make the brochure an interactive tool, not just a hunk of sales hype. Tell the prospect in your letter what you want them to do with the material. It also goes without saying that the brochure itsself must be a sales piece that focuses 100 percent on selling outings.

DVD attack

Video scares a lot of people because they think it's very expensive and complicated, yet with today's technology you would be amazed at the results you can achieve for as little as $10,000 (the DVD should last you several years). A five-minute infomercial is optimum. CDs and DVDs also make for easy mailing. See LegendaryVault.com for sample DVDs.

Specialty products

Specialty products are also ideal for the purpose of Thunderbolt marketing and come in all shapes and sizes. There are thousands of products that are available, from the sublime to the ridiculous. I suggest using ones that are neither. Instead aim for a product that is (a) out of the ordinary (which rules out calendars, note pads, and magnets) and (b) has longevity. While our goal is to elicit an instant response from each part of our Thunderbolt campaign, we know that not everyone will be won over during our initial strikes. That's why we want our clients to keep and cherish the items we send them so they will remember us when we return for the second campaign with reinforcements.

One particular product that I like for this is a poster. I have used several different types, from a blueprint of the perfect golf swing to a full-color poster of a famous golf hole. I have used cards that clap when you open them and others that actually talk to the prospect for 15 seconds. Be creative!

First wave

Once you have decided on the eight ways you will approach your key prospects, and have all the components in place, it's time to start your campaign.

KEY POINT—Before you read any further: Remember, you are not sending a random pitch to a worthless list of businesses in your community taken from the Chamber book! This is a pre-qualified

Special Events Are Our Specialty

Red carpet treatment is what you will experience when you arrive at Sierra Lakes Golf Club; lasting memories is what you will take with you.

Ideally located at the foot of the San Bernadino Mountains in the city of Fontana, Sierra Lakes is the Inland Empire's number one choice for golf outings and tournaments both large and small. Each year, we host hundreds of groups of all kinds: corporate outings, fund-raisers for charitable and non-profit organizations, get-togethers for small businesses or groups of friends.

We welcome the opportunity to dazzle your guests with our highly acclaimed golf course, spectacular mountain views, elegant yet inviting clubhouse, exceptional cuisine, friendly service and attention to detail.

"Sierra Lakes is perfect for golf outings. The course is challenging but fair for all types of golfers, always in great shape, and the exquisite ball rooms provide an atmosphere which will make your banquet something to remember," says Tournament Director Ben Smith.

"We also have a country club style setting with a beautiful clubhouse that makes people feel right at home. After the tournament is over, people want to stay and gather in the lounge or on the patio. Your event will not be one where people turn in their cards and take off."

Whether you have a 160-player shotgun start or small group of 16 with a few afternoon tee times, the professional staff at Sierra Lakes will do everything to make your day a resounding success!

While We Do the Work, You & Your Group Will Enjoy:

World-Class Golf In a Magnificent Setting

Designed by renowned architect Ted Robinson, Sierra Lakes Golf Club is rated 4.5 out of a possible 5 by Golf Magazine and it's easy to see why. This knock-your-socks-off beauty of a layout features palm trees, fescue grasses, and spectacular views of the San Bernadino Mountains. On hole after hole, you stand on the tee and feel as if you can reach out and touch those imposing mountains just beyond the green. Several lakes and plenty of sand come into play, offering fun and excitement for players of all abilities

A Spacious Clubhouse At Your Disposal

Relax and unwind in our lovely 20,000 square foot clubhouse overlooking the 9th green and a sparkling lake. You won't feel the least bit crowded -- our banquet facilities can hold up to 400 people. And our friendly, attentive service will make you and your guests feel right at home.

Wonderful Food

Leave it to the Food and Beverage pros at Sierra Lakes to come up with delicious possibilities for your golfing guests. Would you like our top-of-the-line carved beef and chicken forestiere buffet, the Mexican buffet or an olde-fashioned chicken and beef barbecue? Or perhaps a simple deli buffet with all the trimmings? We offer these mouthwatering choices and more. Bon appétit!

A Fully Stocked Golf Shop

Before the tournament begins, browse our golf shop to pick up a hat, gloves or balls.

We also carry many fine brands of men's and women's apparel, including Ashworth, Gear for Sport and Callaway. If you'd like, we can suggest prizes from our merchandize -- or perhaps gift certificates will do. Special pricing is available for group volume purchasing.

An Ideal Location

Resting at the base of the San Bernadino Mountains in Fontana (also known as California's Inland Empire), Sierra Lakes has the virtue of easy access combined with the tranquility of the desert. It's a quick drive from cities like San Bernadino, Riverside, and Pomona, and just about an hour-and-a-half from Los Angeles and Palm Springs.

All You Need to do is Relax & Enjoy a Great Round of Golf

From start to finish, we can assist in handling every detail for you, ensuring an event that shines with perfection. We'll help determine the format that suits you and develop a complete schedule of activities. A variety of formats, pricing and starting options are available.

On the day of the event, we'll set up a registration area with rules sheets for all players, an alphabetical contestant list and pairing sheet. Scorecards with players names and handicaps are prepared in advance, and carts with signs designating pairings will be lined up to ensure a smooth start. We can even set up contests such as long-drive and putting competitions.

To Book Your Outing, or for More Information on Sierra Lakes Golf Club, Call Ben Smith, Tournament Director, at 909-350-2500, ext. 14.

Please Hurry -- Our Schedule Fills Up Fast! email us at tournaments@sierralakes.com

A brochure promoting special events. Benefits and features are in the heads and subheads. Notice the call to action just under the phone number.

targeted list of REAL people who book golf outings! They are going to book an outing this year and you are going to MAKE sure that you are first and foremost on their mind each and every month!

Depending on where your club is located, you are going to want to do one of two things. If your season is seven months or longer I would mail every month. If your season is six months or shorter, you can either cut back on a few mailings or double up in the early part of the year when people in your state are most likely to book their events, sending out letters twice a month in late winter or early spring.

I like to start the Thunderbolt with some basic reconnaissance like a postcard. This gets your proposition in front of them via first class mail in the cheapest possible way and also allows you to receive free address corrections before mailing the more expensive pieces. While you often hear it said that it takes seven times to create a good impression, I don't believe it. I have often had good response with one hit, but your chances of a positive response do increase proportionately with each subsequent mailing provided you keep the information interesting.

After a postcard, mail your outings brochure along with a tightly written and benefit-oriented cover letter.

The second wave

In the second wave you should start to use your big guns. I like the idea of allowing the collateral information to build in intensity so that the very best information hits in contacts four to seven, which is when we have found response is typically at its highest point. Send them the audio CDs and videos in these waves. Write your cover letters so that each package builds on the previous package and highlights one to three specific benefits of doing business with you. Always refer to how the video, audio, or other collateral material backs up your point!

The third wave

The third wave starts in the eighth mailing and should be your mop-up phase. By this point you should have had the majority of your response and now you are just cleaning up the last few stragglers. At this point you can go back to postcards or use some of your specialty items with additional sales letters. End your campaign with a final appeal to try your club and the best sweetener you can possibly give.

Then it's time to sit back and enjoy the business you have already generated, which may well be more than enough, or to jump on the phone and squeeze a few more clients out of your campaign.

No more cold calls

If you follow the ideas and strategy I have just given you, Thunderbolt marketing will work for you. Even if you didn't get the response you had hoped for by mail, you can now follow up by phone. Everyone hates cold calling, but once you have Thunderbolt-mailed that prospect (one or more times), it's hardly a cold call any more. You've sent him more mail than he gets from his mother, his brother, and his best friend combined! A common response you'll get to your call is that they enjoyed your series and meant to talk with you.

When you call, you can immediately, with confidence and integrity, tell the secretary that Mr. X is expecting your call. You can do this for two reasons. First, in one of the last letters you should tell the prospect to expect a call. Second, the response I usually get from people who have resisted the temptation to call me is something along the lines of "I wondered when you were gong to call me."

Rather than being annoyed by a continual bombardment of mailing pieces, I have found just the opposite response from most people. I have even had e-mail and letters from business owners who told me that due to various other commitments and obligations they could not take advantage of my offers but they praised the high quality of the material and wished me every success. The majority of people respect the traits of persistence and tenacity, especially if backed up with quality. These traits are so rarely found that you will find people are positively disposed towards anyone who displays them.

Following up by phone can increase your Thunderbolt success significantly and you should certainly take the extra effort to do it, but the real beauty of Thunderbolt marketing remains in the in-bound response it generates. (Legendary Marketing even offers an appointment-setting service for outings and memberships on a cost-per-lead basis.)

SUMMARY

Fish for whales not minnows! Outings are big income generators and should be give special marketing attention at most clubs. Build a database of quality outing leads and follow up relentlessly with a carefully thought out Thunderbolt marketing campaign!

If you follow the plan I have outlined, you will get more inbound leads than you have ever had before and, with proper pricing and follow up, can easily add six figures to your club's income! This outcome, of course, still depends on your staff's sales ability. (See the chapters on Sales, Promotions, and Pricing.)

AFTERWORD

I sincerely hope you have enjoyed and profited from *The Golf Marketing Bible*. I have tried hard to pack as many Legendary ideas and strategies as possible into one book. These strategies are current. They have been tried and tested in the tough conditions of the last five years and they will work for you!

Even the best ideas only work when they're applied. That part is up to you. Start with some bite-sized steps. While instant results are possible, it generally takes two years to get everything you need in place. And it only works cumulatively if you are committed to a real marketing system, either mine or one you devise yourself. (See bonus chapter.)

You must have a plan, a calendar, and a central point like our SmartSites where you can manage all of your marketing information. Your online and offline strategies should be seamless and your staff must be trained in how to handle the leads you generate.

I'm sure this book has taken your thinking in many different directions and I'm sure it has stimulated you to come up with many ideas of your own. If you have any questions or would like to share your ideas please don't hesitate to call one of my Legendary Staff at

800-827-1663. And, if your travels find you in Florida, please stop by for a round with me at Black Diamond Ranch.

All the best,

Andrew Wood
Marketing Legend
Andrew@LegendaryMarketing.com

P.S. Knowledge is power; be sure to pass this book along to others in your organization.

The Golf Marketing System that Never Fails

In this bonus chapter I'm going to share with you lots more exciting ideas. I'm going to give you specific examples and case histories and I'm also going to tell you in detail about our Legendary Marketing, Golf Marketing Success System. This is the only proven marketing system in the golf industry that guarantees you results or your money back! *(One reason this chapter is a bonus—not counted in your 400 pages—is that it is a bit of a sales pitch for us. My theory is that when you realize how much work some of these steps are, you'll want to hire us to do them for you!)*

I'll prove to you why something you have suspected for years is almost certainly true: Your current marketing is just not working the way it should! In fact, it may not be working at all!

MY LIFE IN GOLF

First, here's a little background about me so you know where I'm coming from. I have worked in just about every job at the club level.

I have worked construction building courses. I've worked on the green's crew, in the restaurant, in the bar, in the pro shop, in the cart barn, and at the lesson tee. I've also worked at all types of operations: resorts, private clubs, and daily-fee operations. I've won a few local amateur events and got to the final qualifying stage of the 1984 British Open. But, in another place, in another time, I started my career in the golf business as a bag boy.

Well-intentioned, but untrained

I thought of myself as a good bag boy. I never once showed up for work late in over four years. I never called in sick and I never took a golf ball, tee, or dime from a member's bag (or anywhere else, for that matter).

One day, months after I had started the job, the head pro came to me and said, "Andrew, Mr. Thompson said that his clubs were not cleaned last time they were put in the bag room." "Okay," I said "I'll make sure I clean them." As I cleaned them, I was thinking to myself that not only were his clubs not cleaned last time...they weren't cleaned the time before that, the time before that, or, for that matter, ever! It had no more occurred to me to clean the clubs before I put them away than it had occurred to me that I could fly with fairy dust!

No one had told me to clean the clubs, so I simply took them off the cart and put them away. No one had trained me to be a bag boy and no one had shown me a system of how to greet people, take care of their clubs, and how to make the golfers happy. I wasn't working in a *system*.

I made some people happy but in ways I can only cringe about in retrospect. For instance, we had an Italian member who used to ham up his New York connections. When I took his clubs out of his big black Caddy, they used to disappear, if you know what I mean. He'd come out of the pro shop and ask where his clubs were? I'd shrug like I had no clue and he'd laugh, palm me a couple of bucks, and tell me to go see if I could find them. I'd go get the clubs from where I had conveniently put them out of view.

There were other variations, like when I made him an offer he couldn't refuse or when I'd pass him a hand-scrawled ransom note of what he should do if he ever wanted to see his clubs again. He'd give me a couple of bucks and I'd hand them over. Hardly the consistent country club experience we were trying to project but, hey, I had been given no system, no training, and no role model to follow, so I improvised as best I could.

Too busy fighting alligators to drain the swamp?

At most clubs, a lack of training and systems results in improvisation to some degree at every phase of the operation, but I'm just going to focus on the most important aspect, the marketing. Marketing is the lifeblood of your business—the one aspect you cannot afford to leave to amateurs or to chance!!!

But that's exactly what most clubs do!!!!

Over the last ten years I have been constantly amazed by the inability of clubs, including some of my own great clients, to get things done in a consistently predictable manner. I am talking about things that are as critical to their long-term success as cutting the greens every morning. But every time I start to talk to them about the incredible solutions I have that will solve their marketing problems, something happens!

For example, I was going to meet with a club manager about his marketing problems. I got to the club and there were ambulances all over the place. One of the green crew had come around a blind corner on the cart path and T-boned a guest and his wife, sending a 65-year old-woman *flying through the air with the greatest of ease* straight into a Palmetto bush!

Not surprisingly, our meeting was a bit delayed and unfocused. Halfway through the conversation on how to turn his club around, he asks me if I know a good lawyer.

I go back to the office and call one of my best clients to discuss this week's e-blast to drive play at his club. He's out on the course dealing with a broken water pump and it's been 98 degrees all month! He doesn't get back with me for another week.

Undeterred, I call another GM to talk about increasing his outing business. He's busy talking to the police as his third employee in six months is being lead away in handcuffs for stealing green-fee money from the till.

I plunge ahead with my calls. The next call is to an owner who wants to know where he can hire another person to do membership marketing for him. The last one quit to go work in a law firm—less stress!

It's the afternoon now and I have a manager/head pro in my office who works for a large management company. He is here to participate in training on how to use his SmartSite effectively. He spends a full five minutes with my training specialist before he comes back to my office and says, "You know, Andrew, I'm really not very interested in this stuff and I've got my clubs in the trunk. How about we go play Black Diamond?" I oblige; at least on the course he has to listen to me tell him what he *should* be doing.

Considering the above example, is it any wonder that:

- ✔ Most clubs don't grow.

- ✔ Most clubs don't have any success with their marketing programs.

- ✔ More and more clubs mindlessly discount and erode their market because they have no clue how to do anything else.

The FACT is that most clubs don't have a chance because they DON'T have a sales and marketing system in place. I mean a step-by-step, connect-the-dots, do-A-then-B-then-C type of marketing plan, not just a budget or an Excel spreadsheet. Those that do (I have never seen one, so clue me in if you know of one) likely don't have the time or the people in place to implement them effectively.

Although I have never been to a golf club that doesn't have great service (just ask 'em!), most golf operations today are, in fact, woefully understaffed. Even where they are not, staff is often asked to perform tasks for which they have no experience, no training, and often no interest.

- ✔ The young girl with the AA degree becomes marketing director because she happens to have a rudimentary knowledge of Microsoft Publisher and did a flyer for last month's dinner dance.

- ✔ The golf professional gets pushed to the Chamber of Commerce to sell memberships because ownership feels it's better than doing nothing! Which it is...but only just.

- ✔ The woman in accounting or reception ends up stuffing and mailing letters because there is no one else to do it!

Even those with the very best intentions are caught in the vicious cycle of doing the same things over and over again and getting the same less than stellar results. Which not coincidently is Einstein's definition of insanity mentioned in the introduction.

CHANGING IS HARD

I had just finished speaking for eight hours at a PGA seminar when one of my very best clients came up and grabbed me by the arm. "Andrew!" he said in a harsh whisper, "You've just told every one of my competitors exactly what they need to do to put me out of business!"

"Wally," I said (names have been changed to protect the guilty), "I've been telling you how to do this every week for the last five years and your people still don't do it! What makes you think anyone in this room is any different?"

He laughed because *he knew I was right.* Even with the best intentions in the world no one in that room was going to change what they were doing more than the traditional 10 percent shift!

They can't—they don't have the people, they don't have the systems, and they don't have the time!

SYSTEMS WORK!

Let me give you an example of a system that we use to dominate the outing market or boost membership in any area of the country. In fact, this system has been so successful for our partner clubs that it's more like a secret weapon. It's good old-fashioned telemarketing. We call people and ask them if they run outings (or would consider membership in a club).

This effort generates 4000+ calls and brings in at least 400 leads in six to eight weeks and has brought in as many as 795. I know of nothing that works faster or is more cost effective. It costs less than $10,000 for 400 leads. At one club, they booked six outings worth over $50,000 in six weeks. Another sold $70,000 worth of memberships in two weeks. Used in conjunction with direct mail, we sold over 250 memberships at $18,000 a pop in a single year at one club and over 100 memberships at five more. But you do the math...if your membership fee is $10,000, you get your money back with the sale of just one membership. If it's $2500, you get it back in four. Either way you have a lifetime of dues to look forward to. If you get 10 or more, it's a home run.

Can you run a system, or follow up?

How easy is it to develop and implement this type of system yourself? Honestly, it's not easy, but I'm going to share our entire process with you in detail so you can decide for yourself if you have the time, the talent, and the training to put this powerful weapon to work in your club.

To hire one person who does a professional job of telemarketing, we have to interview 40 people. We do this every month, every single month, by running weekly ads and holding seminars once a week to outline the opportunity and requirements to potential employees.

Once we hire a person, we have a 40-page, step-by-step training manual on how to do the job astonishingly well. It tells how to build a database of highly probable prospects from scratch. It details what to say on the call, what questions to ask, what offer to make, and how to record the data. New hires study it, read it, and are tested on its content.

Next they shadow one of our top performers for a week just to see how a professional does the job. Then, under close supervision, with the help of carefully crafted scripts, they go to work making as many as 200 calls a day!

(*Sales Pitch*: Of course, you might decide it's easier to outsource it to Legendary Marketing and not have to worry about anything except following up on 400 leads!!! And we have just recently added a service to actually set appointments at clubs! What's more, we do it on a cost-per-lead basis!!!)

Now, you might say as most people do, just give me the leads, the leads, the leads, all I need are the leads...my staff will close them!

And close some of them they will, but what percentage? How many memberships will they sell out of 100 leads? One in thirty? One in twenty, one in ten? Or perhaps, heaven forbid, none at all!

Then I ask the same question again. If I provide your club with the name, address, telephone number, date of the event, and number of players in the group for 100 potential outings in your market, how many will you close? Most clubs don't know the answer to that question. When they guess, they are usually wrong by as much as 80 percent because most people hate rejection and most hate to sell! Oh, they will take orders like the world's best waiters, but when objections are raised, questions are asked, facts are challenged, they will fold quicker than a Laura Davis lawn chair. (In other words, your staff doesn't sell many outings when they have to do the work!)

HOW DO YOU SELL?

Let me share with you a second system and a prime example of how your club is leaving, conservatively, $200,000 or more in income on the table each and every year by simply not having a MEMBERSHIP or OUTING SALES SYSTEM in place.

While I was on the road last month, I took a membership tour (unannounced) at three clubs. I could just have easily been inquiring about holding an outing or buying real estate. The results would have been about the same.

At the first club, an attractive young girl pointed me around the club. By that I mean her presentation consisted of pointing at things like the 18th green, the menu, and the locker room and telling me, "That's the 18th"…"That's the menu"…"That's the locker room." I could have given myself the tour.

She asked nothing about me, which is a shame because talking about oneself is one of everyone's favorite subjects—and especially mine! She did not ask how often I played. Nor did she think to ask if I was a member of a club, whether my family played, or if I even had a family. Had she asked me almost any question, she would have found that my primary residence was over 1300 miles from the club, hardly making me an ideal prospect! She just skipped the whole greeting, rapport-building, and qualifying steps of the sales process and went right into the presentation (such that it was).

Having made her presentation and failing to answer even rudimentary questions about the course like what type of grass was on the greens, she asked if I had any more questions. I didn't, so the presentation ended. Never at any point did she ask me if I wanted to join! Never did she float any trial closes to take my temperature and see just how interested I was in joining...and you can rest assured that I won't get a follow up letter or phone call. If, heaven forbid, I am wrong and I do, I can almost guarantee it will be a John Doe letter saying nothing of consequence.

At the other two clubs, a middle-aged woman, back in the work force after 15 years, and a middle-aged man, formerly an assistant golf professional, tried their best. The golf pro certainly knew a lot about the course and even knew what the slope rating was, but there was still a lack of process. The greeting was lame, the rapport-building weak, and the qualifying nonexistent. Neither actually handed me a membership application or asked me to join. Not really all that surprising since studies show that 63 percent of all sales presentations end without the salesperson actually asking for the sale.

But think of the wasted time!

Think of the wasted money!

Think of the incredible waste of opportunity!

Train, train, train

I don't fault any of the three individuals for their abyssmal performances. This is the exact type of situation that I opened this chapter with when I told you about my start as a bag boy and not having been given any training or direction. Things haven't changed at all.

Trust me when I tell you this: I know how hard it is to find great salespeople, but you don't have to. Imagine if all you did was provide some basic but specific sales training to help your people sell memberships, outings, banquets, rooms, or real estate—take your pick!

Imagine that you could provide them with some simple scripts to help them greet, build rapport with, and qualify prospects—and close more sales. Imagine that you could improve their sales ratio from 1 out of 30 to 1 out of 10. That's a two-hundred percent increase and, the truth is, with a little training and direction, you can do much, much better.

How do you take average people and turn them into great salespeople? You do it with a system. You provide a step-by-step method that they can follow and you provide them coaching on exactly what to do to improve their performance.

(*Sales Pitch:* Guess what, we have all sorts of proprietary, advanced material that we use for our clients. Manuals 16–22 of the Legendary Marketing, Golf Marketing Success System cover all aspects of selling memberships, outings, banquets, and real estate. There are structured presentations, the perfect answers to over 60 objections and stalls, proven closing techniques, role playing, and tests so you can actually measure if your staff is making any progress. We also provide tele-seminars, week-long membership and outing sales courses at our office, and even on-site training.)

There is nothing you can do in the name of marketing that will increase your income faster than training your frontline staff how to sell! NOTHING!

Having said that, most clubs have faith in their staff's ability to sell, so I challenge you to a simple test of Selling 101. Call us and we will arrange an online test so you can see exactly how your staff really rate.

(Sales Pitch: Now imagine for a moment that not only do you have a highly trained outing or membership specialist on your team making proactive outbound phone calls to uncover leads, but you also have a database specialist, a list specialist, a world class copywriter, an e-blast specialist, a web specialist, an ad specialist, a direct marketing specialist, and a dedicated account manager to pull all your marketing together on your staff.)

Think about that for a moment a dream team of marketing professionals at your disposal implementing world class marketing for your club, on time every time with predictable, measurable results!

How the heck are you ever going to do all that in house?

You don't have enough time, you don't have enough people, you don't have the knowledge—heck, you don't have enough life left to do all these things.

SYSTEMS, SYSTEMS, SYSTEMS

(Sort of Sales Pitch: Now let's take a look at how this concept of systemization works in another area of marketing to predictably drive players to your door. Done right, direct mail is far and away the most effective way to market golf. [See the Direct Mail chapter.] We have SOLD MILLIONS OF DOLLARS in memberships using direct mail, generated millions in real estate sales and millions in outing sales. Yet when I first talk with them most clubs tell me they have tried direct mail and it doesn't work!)

As discussed in that chapter, the problem is not that direct mail doesn't work but that it's very rarely done right In fact, in most cases, the direct mail campaigns I see from clubs don't just do a few things wrong, they do the EXACT OPPOSITE of what works!

Every direct mail campaign Legendary Marketing produces is checked through a 76-point formula derived from the knowledge of the world's best direct marketing minds.

For example, it's a proven fact that indenting the first line of each paragraph improves readership of a letter. Yet I have just gone back and forward with a manager who keeps taking out the indents because he doesn't like the way it looks. I tell him I don't care how it looks, I want it to work for him and to make it work, you make it easier to read.

I win that battle and move to the next. He doesn't like the way the sentences hang at the end of the page so you have to go to the next page to read them. This is an old direct marketing trick to make the reader do exactly that! Nobody likes to be left hanging mid-sentence, so readers automatically turn to the next page to finish the sentence.

He wants the lead page of the accompanying brochure to be in reverse type (white ink on a black background) because he thinks it looks classy. Classy looking maybe, but it's a proven fact that it is 33 percent harder for the human eye to read reverse type. Why make your direct mail harder to read? It makes NO SENSE!

Without going into all 76 rules for improving response from your direct mail campaign, the point is simple. If you want MAXIMUM response from your direct-mail campaign you should comply will ALL 76 rules. For each rule you break, there is a corresponding penalty to pay in terms of readership and response. In plain English, every rule you break costs you money!

We check all creative work against our system so we are sure we are wringing every last gasp of response out of every single e-blast, sales letter, print ad, or sales script! Then it must be tested and measured to make sure the response is good enough before going out with additional campaigns. That's a system that insures MAXIMUM returns, and insures that your overall marketing becomes increasingly more predictable and more effective over time.

The above is the science of advertising, not merely my opinion.

PROVEN RESULTS

If you were to read the writings of the world's great advertising minds, including Bob Stone, David Ogilvy, Dan Kennedy, Jay Abraham, and Claude Hopkins to name but a few, you would discover the very same laws. Few, even in the marketing field know of or follow these laws mainly because most in the industry want to waste your time and money talking about brand, image, and awareness—all for the most part very intangible, which is exactly why most advertising agencies and design companies do it!

The last thing an ad agency wants to do is have YOU hold them accountable for generating a certain number of leads. Then they would have to perform. Then they would have to test, then they would have to develop and follow systems because all the creativity in the world will not outperform a well thought out marketing system.

(*Definitely a Sales Pitch:* Each component in the Legendary Marketing, Golf Marketing Success System, from the web site surveys to direct mail and telemarketing to print ads has been tested. Each process from benchmarking to budgeting is structured to provide you with extraordinary results. Each key facet of marketing from Lead Generation to Loyalty has been broken down to its key elements and structured in a step-by-step format and orchestrated into a blueprint for success.)

But even that is not enough at most clubs because most clubs have neither the time nor the employees to implement even the most rudimentary follow up. So to make sure it's done on time every time exactly as planned, we can do it for you!

That's right—we can update your web site; send all your e-blasts; write, fold, stuff, and mail your follow-up campaigns; sort your data; survey your customers for feedback; and implement your loyalty programs. That way it gets done, on time, every time, with astonishing results!

By now I am sure that you agree systems are great but what about creativity and innovation—isn't that an important part of marketing?

Yes, it is, and we have a system for that as well!

ONLY SOME EXPERIENCE COUNTS!

Most people in their forties, like me, claim to have 20 years experience. When I hear this in interviews I always ask, do you really have twenty years of unique experience, making you exponentially smarter than the year before or did you just experience more or less the same year twenty times?

Their blank expressions usually say it all.

Ask your web provider, designer, or ad agency what the last ten marketing books they read are and 95 percent of them won't be able to answer because they haven't read ten books combined since they left college!

I spend an average of $700 a month on books, tapes, seminars, and information about sales and marketing trends, techniques, and tactics. I have done this for well over a decade. I am blessed by being a fast reader and have read up to 200 nonfiction books in a single year. But I don't tell you this to impress you. I tell you this because I am doing this for you so that you don't have to! You can be safe in the knowledge that Legendary Marketing is fanatically committed to continued improvement or as the Japanese refer to it, Kaizen.

You cannot outlearn my staff! It's part of the Legendary Marketing culture—either learn or leave. And with our learning comes constant innovation. EVERY single member of my staff is required to read 20 minutes a day in our library—a library packed full of books on sales, service, and marketing!

Together with our intimate knowledge of the golf business, this culture provides us with an astonishing advantage in adapting techniques that are successful outside the golf industry and producing stunning results for our clients in it. Think about it:

**If all you do is what all your competitors are
doing, how can you outsmart them?**

You can't—you have to be smarter, faster, and flawless in your follow up! This is why you need a system; it's just too hard without one!

Having built a nationwide franchise from scratch, I have a unique entrepreneurial understanding of just how detailed and step-by-step a system must be to bring extraordinary performance and results from ordinary people. For as Abraham Lincoln observed, "God must have loved the common man for he made so many of them!" But...an ordinary employee armed with a step-by-step system can perform at extraordinary levels. Consider McDonald's. They took the spotty-faced teens, the old, and the handicapped and built one of the world's most successful companies—not on the backs of their superstar staff but on the backs of great systems.

HOW WE WORK WITH YOU

Now, you may or may not agree that the previous information truly makes Legendary Marketing a unique business partner for your club, but this one you cannot question:

> I will write a custom, written guarantee based on your
> club's unique goals and objectives that states that we
> will dramatically improve your club's marketing
> performance or I will give every dime you spend with
> us back. If I cannot deliver results for you I don't want
> your money!

That means that we are selective in finding new partners; we don't work with every club. Not every club is a good fit for our program and we are not a good solution for every club. That said, if what I have said here makes sense to you I do invite you to take the next step.

Give us a call; let's get to know one another a little bit more. One of my marketing specialists will send you a complimentary copy of our first two system manuals. They are more detailed versions of the first two chapters of this book. The first, *The Legendary Point of View,* will introduce our underlying business philosophy so you can decide if it make sense to you.

The other manual covers our benchmarking procedure so you can give us an in-depth snapshot of your club and its goals for the future. If you agree with our philosophy and if we are sure we can help you based on your benchmarking data, we can take the next step. You have nothing to lose and a great deal to gain from taking this step.

Should we both decide to move forward and form a partnership, we will ask you to do two things.

The first request is that you let us know exactly who else you do NOT want us to work with. This will often be your immediate competitors—knowing the power of the Legendary Golf Marketing Success System we can certainly understand why you don't want them to get the same advantage you do.

The second is for you to tell us who else you think would like to work with us; all new partners are required to provide two high-quality prospects who would make good additional partners for Legendary Marketing. It's only fair since we're cut off from working with your competitors! And at this stage of our business we feel that working with like-minded individuals makes a lot more sense than chasing around looking for the right fit with dozens of different clubs.

Once we have agreed to work together we will start working through the additional 30 manuals in the Golf Marketing Success System—but don't worry, after the first few we will be doing all the work for you. (Again, these are more complex versions of some of the chapters in this book plus extra proprietary material.)

Manuals 3–6 focus on defining your unique selling proposition, defining your different market segments, laying out a plan for tracking and measuring your results, and developing a realistic budget for accomplishing your goals. Let us show you how to BANISH the word DISCOUNT from your language by clearly defining your advantage in the marketplace.

I talked with an owner in Texas recently who was proud that he was still generating 55,000 rounds a year while his competitors were stuck at 40,000. The only problem was that, when pressed, he admitted that although he was filling up his course he was still losing money! Discounting yourself into bankruptcy is not a marketing strategy that has much of a future!!!!

You have to differentiate or you will die.

Our marketing specialists will give you the tools and ideas to make your club stand out in your market, no matter how tough your market is!

Manuals 7–12 focus entirely on lead generation and building a database of PRIME customers in your market. There we will visit over 50 proven promotions, e-blasts, direct mail, print ads, online strategies, and how to build a referral machine.

E-mail is generally the first thing we do because it's fast and cheap. Since we own over 3 million e-mails of golfers we can generate traffic in any major market in the country instantly.

Direct mail is second because it is by far the most effective form of marketing as you know that 100 percent of the people you mail to play golf. You can also know how much they make, what car they drive, what credit cards they own, and about 100 other facts that will help you decide if they are casual golfers or if they are golfers who would be interested in your club.

Telemarketing has already been addressed and is really a secret weapon few clubs ever use.

Referrals are, of course, your most cost effective way to generate more business, but they don't happen by accident in sufficient numbers—you need a system.

In later months, once we have increased your traffic substantially and trained your staff how to sell, we will show you how to implement an astonishing loyalty system that does not involve discounting. This will get players back to your course again and again spending more money while you reduce your marketing costs.

Your entire campaign will be managed and run through an amazing web site we will do for you. Your SmartSite is not only the world's most advanced golf-specific web tool but it's the command and control center for all your marketing efforts.

From your SmartSite you will be able to segment all your data and set up an entire year's worth of e-campaigns that are triggered by people's responses to your questions. You can track all your outing banquet, and memberships leads. You can see what stage of the sales process they are at and print mailing labels for postal follow up. Your SmartSite also works seamlessly with a growing number of POS systems so you can effortlessly upload data from your counter into the world's most power golf marketing tool. In fact, the SmartSite is a compete customer relationship manager.

Our SmartSites really do accomplish things that no other web sites in ANY industry can do. However, the problem is that even the best web sites are not effective if they are not updated and used—updated with content and results; updated with new promotions for capturing data; updated with pictures of members and guests. While our staff have done a great job of training people onsite at the clubs to do this themselves, they simply don't have time, so here's what we do. E-mail us your information, news, and tournament results, or call us by phone or send a courier pigeon, and we will update and manage your site for you!

That's right—you do nothing but provide the information. We do the rest!! ALL of your online marketing without the headaches or cost of hiring someone onsite to do it!

In other modules we will consult with you on pricing, packaging, PR, customer service, experiential marketing, and specific programs for membership, banquet, outing, and real estate sales.

Nothing has been missed.

Nothing has been forgotten. (If you come up with something we're missing, we'll develop a custom module for you and add it to the system! Since we do that for other clubs too, we're always evolving. This is the same for the web sites. When we develop a new feature, your site is automatically updated.)

Every single aspect of driving maximum response from your golf marketing has been carefully documented, orchestrated in a step-by-step manner, and measured.

For the very first time you will know exactly what response you derived from every single ad, every single e-mail, every single campaign.

Your database of prime customers will grow astonishingly quickly.

Your increased communication with your customers via your SmartSite Campaign Manager and direct mail will substantially increase their participation at your club for incremental growth in every area!

Best of all, the marketing specialists at Legendary Marketing will do all the calls, all the ads, all the mailings, all the updating to your web site, and all the e-mail blasts. In fact, we do everything so you can focus on what you do best—serving your customers!

Call now as we can only take a limited number of partner clubs in each state. There is absolutely no obligation, and you have nothing to lose and a great deal to gain. Only one club in your area can be the market leader, let it be you!

The number to call is
800-827-1663 (USA)
352-527-3553 (International)
or visit us online at
LegendaryMarketing.com

INDEX